THE ONLY FILM IN TOWN

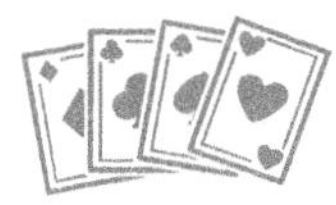

THE ONLY FILM IN TOWN

How a Little Film With a Big Heart Was Made in Rural Nova Scotia

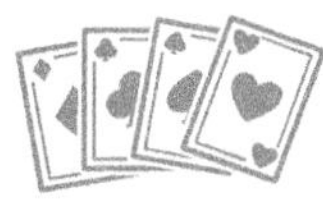

STUART CRESSWELL

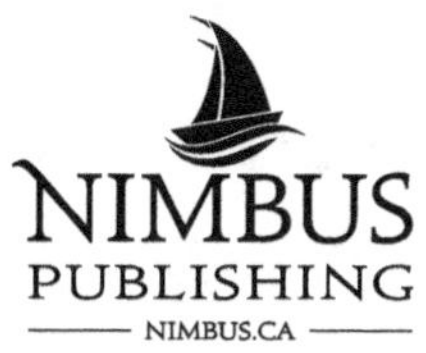

NIMBUS
PUBLISHING
NIMBUS.CA

Nimbus Publishing Limited
3660 Strawberry Hill Street, Halifax, NS, B3K 5A9
(902) 455-4286 nimbus.ca

NB1314

Cover & interior design: John van der Woude, JVDW Designs

Library and Archives Canada Cataloguing in Publication
Cresswell, Stuart, 1962-, author
The only film in town : how a little film with a big heart
was made in rural Nova Scotia / Stuart Cresswell.
Issued in print and electronic formats.
ISBN 978-1-77108-637-0 (softcover).—ISBN 978-1-77108-638-7
(HTML)

1. Only game in town (Motion picture : 2016). 2. Motion picture—Production and direction—Nova Scotia—Tatamagouche. 3. Motion pictures—Production and direction. 4. Cresswell, Stuart, 1962-. I. Title.

PN1997.O4645C74 2018 791.43'72 C2017-907985-9
C2017-907986-7

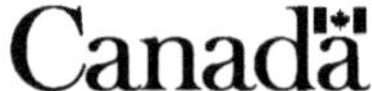

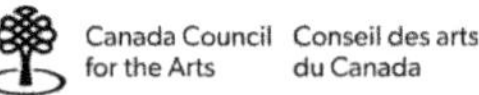

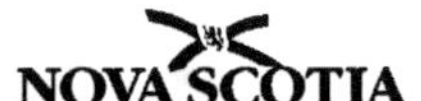

Nimbus Publishing acknowledges the financial support for its publishing activities from the Government of Canada through the Canada Book Fund (CBF) and the Canada Council for the Arts, and from the Province of Nova Scotia. We are pleased to work in partnership with the Province of Nova Scotia to develop and promote our creative industries for the benefit of all Nova Scotians.

To Aubrey Roy Cresswell and Edna Maud Cresswell and Andrew—the archetypes of perseverance.

TABLE OF CONTENTS

PART FOUR: POST-PRODUCTION

FOREWORD

The hardest thing for an actor to be is not working. For me it has been many years of filling the spaces between work in film and live theatre and never saying no to opportunity. The last few years have been busy for me. Nonetheless, to be compelled by professional commitment to turn down a chance to work with artistically committed people and an exciting new script was rankling. Such was the case with *The Only Game in Town.*

The script? Got halfway in and my mind exploded. Some off-the-wall funny brilliance. It's a wonderful script.

It is so coincidental—synchronistic really—that I played solitaire competitively for the entire duration of the Vietnam War. Our battalion had the finest players from the world over and we had a special squad: The Ruby Rumpholes. We squared off with the Viet Cong Congas in Pyongyang at high-stakes Solomono. Things were almost to the Double Gee when we were ordered out. I guess the world just wasn't ready for us.

I'm proud of myself for promoting talent—young and old—yet prouder still of the people who make something for no other reason than the joy of doing it.

The doing makes us better at it.

Keep on.

—The late John Dunsworth (Actor, director,
best known as Mr. Lahey, *Trailer Park Boys*)

INTRODUCTION

This is a book about the making of a film. Not film in general, but one in particular.

Making a film has been done before, of course. It's quite commonplace nowadays. You can make a film on your phone. There are many festivals around the world for people to screen films made in that way. Why should anyone care about the making of a low-budget film in Nova Scotia?

The fact that a book is being written about the making of a particular film typically means one of two things: either the film was a spectacular and perhaps surprising success, or it was a spectacular failure. The documentary *Lost in La Mancha* about the making of Terry Gilliam's film, *The Man Who Killed Don Quixote,* is about a production that went badly wrong. The timing of this book and film also coincided with the release of the book and film *The Disaster Artist*—again about the making of a truly bad film.

So we might surmise that the film that is the subject of this book—*The Only Game in Town*—is some kind of tragic failure. Well, it may yet be a box-office flop and a financial failure—although with a very small budget of $250,000 it won't hit the record books as one of the worst in cinematic history—but unlike *The Man Who Killed Don Quixote*, at least *The Only Game in Town* will see the light of day. Just don't ask me when.

As I write this introduction, I am painfully aware that this film remains in post-production, although there is hope that it will soon be complete. It may, of course, go on to be a massive worldwide hit, in which case there is another reason for a book such as this. But right now we'll stick with what we know.

It is March 2018 now. The film began shooting in December 2014. Many of the young cast had been attending workshops and character-building sessions since February 2014. The journey has been a long one.

Films can take forever. Hollywood has lots of stories of films that were carried around by the director for a decade or so. All the same, it's clear to most people that films normally have set periods of various stages of production. Development, which can take months and years (and yes, for our film a decade is about right); then, when people get hired to work on it and it becomes a serious proposition, we move to pre-production; and then, when the actors turn up and the cameras roll, we move to what is called "principal photography."

It's most often the case, for economies of labour and overhead and just the ease of working in such a way, that principal photography happens in one or more solid blocks, perhaps moving from one location to another with small gaps in between. However, that isn't a rule—and like many films, especially ultra-low-budget ones such as ours—the shooting schedule can be whatever is needed to make it work for cast and crew and locations.

I want you to be aware of that, because one of the many ongoing battles our film has is around the definition of "principal photography." (In fact, you can see an "official" definition, the one supposedly used by the Nova Scotia government on the next page.) Our period of principal photography lasted from December 2014 to May 2017, when we reshot a few scenes. On each day during that extended period that we were actually shooting, we were engaged in principal photography. As I write this, I am preparing for a battle with the Nova Scotia Department of Finance, which has decided that our film—because of the often fragmented nature of our principal photography—doesn't meet its own definition of principal photography.

That may sound like a rather philosophical discussion for us to have over a cup of coffee, but for us it has a bearing on whether or not our film falls into the category of the pre-2015 system of Film Production Tax Credit or not. And that decision carries with it a not insignificant amount of money, which makes up around 30 percent of the planned financial structure for the film.

What makes all this particularly irksome is that the main reason our film got delayed and ended up with principal photography failing the government's criteria was because the newly elected provincial government, under Liberal Premier Stephen McNeil, finally gave in to the Department of Finance, which had spent many years chipping away at the film tax credit. In fact, the Department of Finance had been openly hostile to the process, and saw the opportunity presented by a new government to scrap the tax credit system. I have no doubt that the Department of Finance was actively putting its side of the argument to government consultant Laurel Broten as she compiled the report that effectively became the blueprint for the provincial government's policy change.

The changes were put into effect while we were in production—bad news for us. As you will see, it left us with few options.

That filmmakers have to argue with "bean-counters" and non-industry people about such things as the definition of "principal photography" is a statement about the way the industry is seen in Nova Scotia, and perhaps other parts of Canada too.

And that, dear reader, is why this book has been written about this film in particular. For a period of almost two years, a low-budget comedy feature film that should have been the career launching point for so much young talent, has had to bear the brunt of a series of challenges and setbacks and bitter battles with people and organizations you would think would have bigger things to occupy their time than making life hard for filmmakers.

When the Liberal government announced in November 2014 that there would be no changes to the way the film industry was supported in the province, filmmakers around Nova Scotia finalized their plans. With our own prep already done throughout 2014, we started shooting.

When the government then went back on its word just a few months later, in March 2015, we were caught between a rock and hard place. I don't know about you, but I cannot afford to throw away $25,000, and at that point, that money—10 percent of our budget—was already spent. The government then announced that productions that had already started were eligible for the pre-2015 system, so we felt safe to continue.

There's the principal photography definition that I'm ready to argue about. Productions that had started principal photography before July 1, 2015, were considered to be under the old system of tax credits. Productions that hadn't started slammed on the brakes and revisited finance plans and applied for the new incentive fund being offered by Nova Scotia Business Inc. (NSBI). They could do that because they hadn't started. Our film was *not* eligible for the new fund...because we had already started production.

Here is the relevant section from a "clarification" issued by the Finance and Treasury Board on May 5, 2015:

> *Productions that commence principal photography before July 1, 2015 will receive the tax credit based on current rules.*

> ***Principal photography*** *is a well-recognized term in the screen-based industry and generally means the phase of film production in which the movie is filmed, with actors on set and cameras rolling.*
>
> *The Department of Finance & Treasury Board will use the following Canadian Audio-Visual Certification Office (CAVCO) definition to determine when principal photography begins:*
>
> > *"The phase of film production during which the movie is actually shot, as distinct from pre-production and post-production. Principal photography begins with the first day of shooting of significant scenes which involve the main photography unit, e.g., in drama, scenes with actors rather than simple establishing shots."*

I'm clear on that. I was from the start. The actors being on set is the way I have always identified principal photography.

That period of 2015—March through to August—was a surreal time in Nova Scotia. I am reminded of the great British horse race The Grand National and the year that the start of the race fell into slapstick. When the starter signalled a false start, only a few of the horses continued, believing the race to be on; Esha Ness, a fifty-to-one outsider, went on to win the race that never happened. That's what it felt like for me as we stumbled on with our film while all around us, productions had failed to start, service companies closed down and left the province, and major TV franchises simply shut themselves indoors and waited.

The filmmaking landscape was barren and quiet in Nova Scotia, apart from a small film about a boy with Asperger's and a knack for the game of solitaire, being shot entirely on the North Shore by a British ex-pat (that's me) who now calls that region home. We were, it seemed, the only film in town. It's at that point you begin to look around and wonder if everyone knows something you don't. We were the film world's Esha Ness. Where had all the other horses gone?

Perhaps that's why we took so much flak from all sides that summer. There were no other targets, and it was too easy for the focus of attention to fall on us.

The story of what happened and how—somehow—we kept going (and more importantly, *why* I kept going) is contained in these pages. I have tried to recreate the anger I felt at times, when faced with the prospect of another battle with a faceless bureaucrat. That's another connection to Terry Gilliam and his struggle to make the Don Quixote film. Gilliam's work invariably centres on the battles of the individual versus society and rampant bureaucracy. (His cult classic *Brazil* is one of my favourite films.)

In truth, the anger has subsided over the last year and been replaced with the dogged focus of an exhausted marathon runner. Nothing else matters now, only getting the film finished.

Here in these pages you will hopefully come to understand how this film came through some difficult times and, more importantly, how I was trapped by my own history into pushing on with the film when reason suggested otherwise.

Right now, I'm just hoping that the book doesn't come out before the film....

—Stuart Cresswell

THE ONLY GAME IN TOWN

"Why did you want to make this film?"

That's the trouble with these film festival panel sessions; someone in the audience is always ready to ask the really difficult questions.

I had recently completed the production phase of my first feature film, *The Only Game in Town,* and found myself sitting on a discussion panel at a film festival in Nova Scotia with my head still reeling from the events of the previous twelve months.

To many people, "why did you want to make this film?" seems like an obvious question to ask. It's the sort of question that immediately suggests that the question-asker has an appreciation for the artistry of filmmaking—the inner passion and creative drive that forces people to abandon all common sense and embark on some compulsive act of creation. The film (any film) is seen as a statement of some high ideals and the filmmaker's attempt to scream out to the world.

Well let's get one thing straight. I don't subscribe to the artistic analysis of films as though we're examining a piece of literature or masterpiece of classic art. It's all "The Emperor's New Clothes"–type claptrap to me. Sure there are some films that have a message, make us question a world view, and documentaries certainly are usually the result of someone driven to use the medium to speak their heart's words. Nor do I deny the "artistry" involved in the skills and techniques of making films. We carry art and artistry around with us, and we invoke it to enhance the things that we craft. (My college drama teacher, Jim Edwards, always asked us: "Do you love yourself in art? Or do you love art in yourself?")

But the question "why did you want to make this film?"— though it may be intended to lead to some discussion about lofty goals and a chance for everyone to compare notes on the deeper meanings that are invisible to all but the enlightened—is a poor question to ask particularly in my case. My "creative" involvement in this film extended into all aspects. Ask a writer why he wanted to write the script and you will get a different answer to when you ask the producer why he wanted to produce the film. I know, because I was writer, producer, and then director. My compulsion to make the project mixed my underlying need to be "creative" ("artistic," if you want to go there) and the very different world of business.

You see, that simple question suggests something else that most people don't consider. It makes the assumption that someone is drifting around, existing in the world most people inhabit, until *WHAM!*, the artistic big bang occurs and they suddenly have a purpose in their lives and go off to conceive and then give birth to some ninety minutes of audiovisual splendour.

It speaks to me of amateur and part-time "creators." I don't intend to be disparaging to such—we've all been through it, and it's a necessity for most. The problem I have is that in a world where every taxi driver is a budding scriptwriter, every waitress an actress in between roles, every teacher a stage director on weekends, and every insurance salesman a prolific portrait painter by night, the public assumes that creative people—particularly people working in the film and TV industry—do what they do as a sideline, a hobby, or a way to earn some extra vacation money.

In my view, the 2015 events in Nova Scotia were a direct result of that shared public perception of the careers of those of us in the film and TV industry, a perception that had been carefully nurtured to the point that we were not taken seriously, and that meant it was perfectly acceptable to destroy our industry because we all had other jobs anyway.

So while the audience in attendance for the festival panel politely indulged my stuttering and vague answer to the question, you, dear reader, shall have the privilege of my honest answer.

I'm a full-time producer. I earn my money by producing film and TV projects. If I don't produce any projects, I don't earn any money. Now, it will become clear that because I wore three different hats for this film, the answer will be a little different for each role. I wrote the script because I couldn't shake the idea for the story and its characters out of my head; after almost ten years carrying them around with me I thought I should commit them to paper. I produced the film because that's my job. I directed it because...well, you'll see why later. But in essence, I don't see the making of this film to be any more about art than it is about earning a living.

Or how about the "art" that sits within the "heart"? This film is full of that. It's full of characters you fall in love with. It's full of young people passionate about the creative process and even building careers—ironically at a time when the government doesn't value those careers. The film is about little people, life's losers, who don't give in and who strive to "do the right thing."

"Heart" isn't why I wanted to make the film, but it's why we all kept going.

So why did I want to make this film? There is no single answer. Please see the list below (and feel free to add to it; I'm certain there are more valid and acceptable reasons).

- Needed to earn money
- Wanted to show off the beauty of North Shore Nova Scotia to the world
- Wanted to promote young talent from our region
- Wanted to boost rural businesses
- Wanted to use it as a stepping stone for my own career
- Wanted to entertain people
- Wanted to make people laugh
- Wanted to see if young people in Canada today are any different than young people were in the UK forty years ago when I was a young person (and you know there is no difference—young people have to go through the same pain of first love today, just as my friends and I did.)
- Wanted to give life to this group of characters I seemed to know so well
- Wanted to share what I thought was a nice story that might lift people and make them feel good
- Wanted to share a creative process with new people to see what "magic" might happen
- Wanted to complete a quality feature film that I would be proud to put out into the world
- Wanted to explore how first love might be for a teen with Asperger's (it was painful enough for me and I don't have it!)
- Etc., etc., etc.

Let us not forget inertia.

Projects such as this can trundle along for years. For as long as the writer (or creative team) continues to fiddle with the text and hide it in the desk drawer, the project is safe, protected from the critical glare of the public, unsullied by prying eyes. But once someone—a new team member perhaps or the writer who has put on a different hat—starts to push the project out into the world, one of two things will happen:

a. The script fails to ignite any great interest. A script needs to be read, by other people, not family and not people who are going to be polite about it, but by people who don't need to fawn all over it. This can be achieved by entering it into contests, paying for a script consultant, discussing it with potential directors and funders. Chances are it will fail here and be kicked back into the bottom drawer, and the writer will shut himself off from the world to lick his wounds.
b. People like it. As the writer, you now move on to do table reads. You approach a director. You enter contests. You hire a script consultant. You take the criticism and make improvements. It doesn't go away. People laugh in the right places. You then push it further and further until it becomes an entity in itself. You spend what seems like an eternity pushing treacle up a hill, and then it has its own momentum. *You* don't want to make the film. It wants to make itself!

It becomes an unnatural thing to stop the film once it reaches this point. Trust me, I know.

Here's another reason why I "wanted to make this film." Because two decades earlier I stood on the verge of shooting a feature comedy, *In the Air at Whitby,* that looked set to go big. And I stopped myself, stopped the film. I believed at the time it was only a temporary halt. I found out then that often an aborted film can never be resuscitated. That moment never comes back.

My friend Colin Vearncombe, the singer and recording artist known for his international hit single "Wonderful Life," had always had a soft spot for that film. He often asked me if I would ever try to produce it again.

"You should," he would say. For that film, he had written a song, "Famous," which appeared on a later album of his, too good a song to sit around waiting for a film producer to get his act together.

Another of his songs, "This is Life"—which, you will see, has some relevance to our film and to this book—has a line perhaps more fitting for a producer who abandons a film on the eve of shooting: "Does your courage seem to fail you as you take your chosen path?"

Yes it does. It can do. It did in 1996. Perhaps the biggest reason I made *The Only Game in Town* in 2015, and why I pushed on when everything stacked up against us, when it would have been right and acceptable to quit, was because I didn't follow through with *In the Air at Whitby* in 1996.

And there is another reason. Perhaps this is the answer that the panel audience wanted to hear. It would be their sort of thing. I would have said it something like this: "And you know, deep down, I had to make this film because I need to lay some demons to rest in my own life. My brother is severely mentally and physically disabled. Exploring the impacts such things have on family—even on a lesser scale, even in cameo during a comedy—is important to me. Family dynamics affect us most in our lives. A story about a family where a mother loves a child who can never display reciprocal affection is all too real for me."

One of the young actors commented very early on in the project that the mothers in the film get a raw deal. I never intended it to be that way, but sometimes a writer puts a character in a certain position and the die is cast and that character's life is mapped out. The two mothers in the film—Cormack's mum, Cathy, and Odette's mum—both have a difficult time.

Cathy is the loving mother of a boy who has never been able to relate properly to her and resists her demonstrations of affection. She copes, most of the time, but sometimes the fact that it's not possible for her to have a serious conversation with her son when they're together in the same room is just too much for her. Odette's mother, played to perfection by the fantastic Colleen MacIsaac, is struggling through life since her husband had a stroke and is left bedridden.

I don't know why both mothers get such a rough ride in the story. Well, perhaps I do. My own mother had a pretty rough ride caring for my brother for forty years. But there was no intention from the outset to bring the mothers' struggles to centre stage as transpired with later rewrites of the script. Even then, the tough emotional scenes fly by when you read the script. But when they're acted out and you watch them on screen, it's hard not to be moved. I'll take no credit here. Colleen MacIsaac and Fiona Kirkpatrick Parsons did the hard work.

Their scenes were planned as twists and turns, diversions and tools to give our young main characters something to play off, to grow. I always think it's good to throw in some dark even in the funniest of comedies.

Shows such as *Only Fools and Horses* and *Frasier* were fully able to be the funniest sitcom around and then, when you least expect it, have you in tears. But the mother scenes in our film, and especially the major tear-jerker with Colleen MacIsaac and Jessie Craig (Odette), left everyone on set utterly shell-shocked. There's always some kind of rumpus going on the moment the director calls "cut," but on the day we filmed Colleen and Jessie in Gina White's kitchen in Truro, you could have heard a pin drop.

So why did I want to make this film?

That's exactly the sort of question that will take me a whole book to answer.

What is the Film About?

The Only Game in Town is a comedy feature film. It tells the story of Cormack Vertue, a teenager who sits on the lower end of the Asperger Syndrome spectrum, which affects the way he relates to most people. He has what is possibly a savant skill for the card game solitaire—he always manages to get the cards to complete their full sequence. Always.

This is, of course, a completely useless skill, except that in the school he attends, there is a solitaire team. It turns out that all over the world, schools and community groups and private clubs play solitaire—a game for one person, as the name suggests—competitively. There are tournaments and national championships, and teams take it very seriously. Cormack's skill at the game suddenly elevates him to a person of real interest, instead of the outsider he has always been.

The story takes place in a sort of "Anytown," Nova Scotia, called Midlothian, a fictional small town by the sea. I wanted to give the place the sort of name that could easily have come from the many Scottish settlers to the province. I am surprised there isn't a Midlothian in Nova Scotia. There is one in Virginia, but the original Midlothian is the historic county in Scotland that contains everyone's favourite Scottish city, Edinburgh.

For a while, Cormack believes he has found the love of his life in Odette, the girlfriend of the school hockey star. So the film is about young people, first love, growing up, and at the heart of it all is family and friendship.

Cormack is a conglomeration of various people I've known over the years. He's not a fantasy character or a two-dimensional figure, but in writing him and then depicting him on screen, there is a major problem: it's difficult to get emotion out of him.

WIN A YEARS SUPPLY OF BEER!

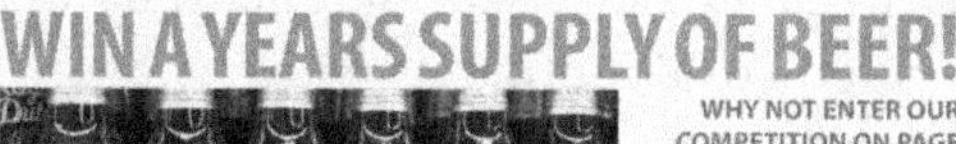

WHY NOT ENTER OUR COMPETITION ON PAGE 12 FOR A CHANCE TO WIN A CRATE OF BEER EACH MONTH FOR 12 MONTHS

STYLE

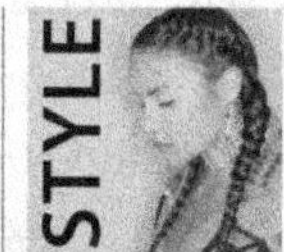

MIDLOTHIAN ECHO

MIDLOTHIAN ECHO

Friday 23rd July 2017 MIDLOTHIAN ECHO *Issue 29876*

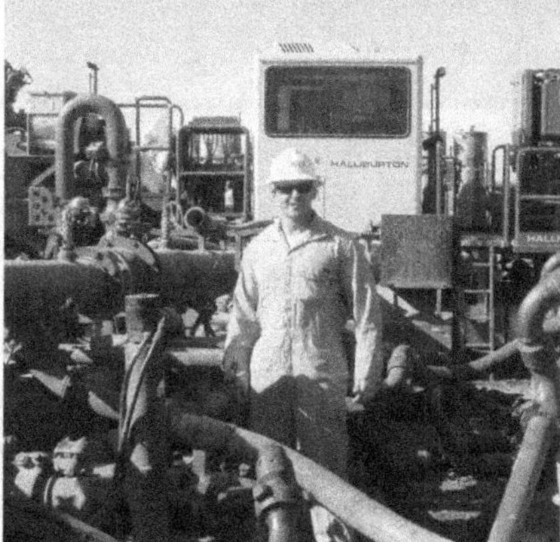

Nova Scotia Govt thinks fracking is renewable energy!

Climate change committee confusion over fracking idiocy.

By Walter Mitty

Whilst the rest of the world is looking to tackle climate change and has moved into the 21st Century, policy makers in Nova Scotia are paving the way to turn much of Nova Scotia's landscape into Shale Gas wells in a controversial energy plan that seems to confuse shale gas with a sustainable resource.
The leaked policy paper casts doubt on the intelligence of these morons and begs the question how on earth did they get elected?

Continued on page 3

Film industry in Nova Scotia savaged by a Liberal U-Turn

By Stuart Cresswell

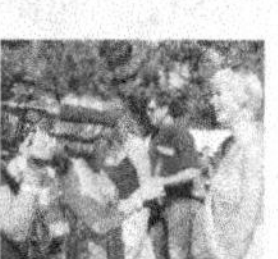

The Nova Scotia Liberal government today went back on an election promise and subsequent announcement of no changes to the film industry tax credit system, and scrapped the valuable incentive. Businesses have closed and talent has left the Province.
"You can't trust these people!" said one film maker. Protests outside the Legislature building will take place this week..

Dude, where's my glacier?

By Gaia Plotter

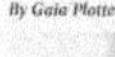

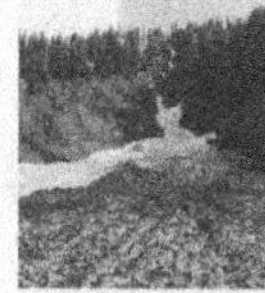

The Nova Scotia coastline could look very different in the near future due to the effects of global warming and retreating glaciers. Canadian glaciers have been melting at an alarming rate in recent years, dumping tons of fresh water into the oceans, raising sea levels. Many Canadians are worried that the film 'The Day After Tomorrow' may come true sooner than anticipated. Other are more worried about being evacuated into America and having to swear allegiance to Donald Trump.

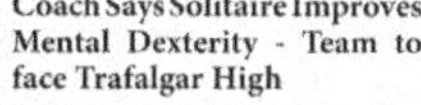

10 THINGS TO DO IN NS BEFORE YOU DIE

OUR OWN BUCKET LIST GUIDE TO NOVA SCOTIA
PAGES 10-11

WEEKEND SPECIAL

A ROAD-KILL RECIPE BOOKLET FOR EVERY OCCASION IN NS
PULL OUT SECTION

LOOK AFTER YOUR LOGS IN WINTER

HOW TO KEEP YOUR LOGS HEALTHY DURING THE WINTER MONTHS
PAGE 22

Coach Says Solitaire Improves Mental Dexterity - Team to face Trafalgar High

By Jack O'Harts

Midlothian Education Centre Solitaire Coach Alex Crowley believes his new team could challenge Provincial Champs Trafalgar High, when they play this week. Competitive Solitaire has seen an increase in participants in recent years, but Crowley doesn't think it's just because there are more fat kids who can't play regular sport.
"It's primarily because young people today are looking for something they can do in their rooms when no one is watching them, that solitaire is on the increase."
Asked if he thought the his team had a chance against Trafalgar, Crowley insisted that his team had shown spirit in training, and stamina levels had increased. "We're short on kit, most of the squad will only have handkerchiefs to wave, but we have a few Aces up our sleeves."
There may be an illegal move there coach!

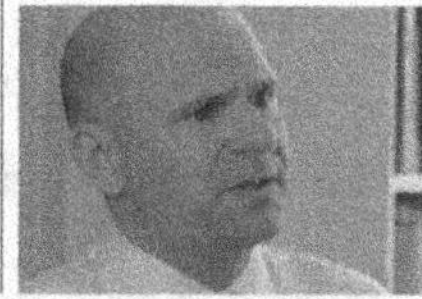

A satirical Midlothian newspaper produced for the film by graphic artist Conrad McEwan. In one story, a coach explains the benefits of playing solitaire.

Well of course it is. That's the whole problem. That's what his mother battles with. We have a character who cannot make eye contact, his face is largely blank, and he responds in ways we don't connect with.

I remember as we shot some scenes at Tatamagouche Elementary School way back in December 2014, Ash King, the camera guy, turned to me and quietly said: "Can he do more with his face? He's just blank!" He was talking about Jesse Hemmings's portrayal of Cormack, thinking him to be not a very good actor. Truth was, Jesse was spot-on with his portrayal, but it did raise the issue for us about how this will translate on screen.

I got caught out by someone just like him many years ago. I was walking to a meeting at a local school when I passed a group of boys. One of them hurled a load of abuse at me, and I marched him into the principal's office to complain, only to learn that the boy had Asperger Syndrome. From that experience, and my own sharp learning curve, came the scene in the film where the teacher Alex Crowley takes a mouthful of abuse from Cormack and mistakes the signs of Asperger's for the normal teenage indifference to authority figures.

Cormack has elements of other people in there too—even myself. There are similarities between Asperger's and OCD (obsessive-compulsive disorder), reflected in the snippets of Cormack's character, that come from me. I'm not saying I have OCD, but anyone who watches me line up placemats, cutlery, and condiments on the table during a meal will know what I mean. If things have a place or sequence or order, then that is how they are supposed to be placed. CDs and records are stored alphabetically by artist and album title. Things of different sizes have to be placed small to big or big to small. Edges and angles must associate with other edges and angles.

And the jar of buttons at Cormack's Gran's house came right out of my childhood. My dad had three older sisters who essentially brought him up—his mother died when he was three, and he was barely a teenager when his father died. On Sunday morning visits to my Auntie Joan in Whitwick—a former mining town in northwest Leicestershire—I would be given a massive jar of buttons to put in order, while the adults went into the front room to discuss the latest developments concerning my brother. Imagine giving a child a jar of buttons to occupy their time nowadays! Well that's what I was given for recreation in the late '60s. I have a jar of buttons we used as the prop in the film that I can't wait to test out on my two-year-old grandson, Henry...although his mother might have something to say about that. I imagined Cormack enjoying the challenge of arranging the contents of a jar of buttons while his Gran played solitaire and baked cakes.

All in all, I like Cormack because I like his vulnerability. In fact, despite his condition, he leaves himself open to be vulnerable. He's never "loved" before, but when he suddenly realizes he is in love, he falls hook, line, and sinker. He has no mechanism to cope with it, and the order that he needs in his life soon vanishes in love, obsession, and conflict.

I have been particularly pleased that two people, each with connections to and first-hand knowledge of children such as Cormack, commented that the character was fully believable, with even some of the more comic demonstrations of his condition coming across as being very real. The scene where Cormack hoped to speak to Odette, but just stands there in close proximity as Odette and her boyfriend Alastair are locked in a passionate kiss, was described as "very accurate."

The hardest part of portraying this on screen, of course, is that much of the engagement the audience should feel with the main character cannot be there. Getting the right balance between portraying Cormack as honestly as possible and allowing the audience to connect to him was one of the hardest things we had to do.

While checking facts for this book I was pleased to read this: "Nonverbal skills in individuals with AD [Asperger's Disorder] are also impaired. For example, individuals may not express a full range of facial expressions. At times it may appear as though the child is looking through you and he evidences poor eye contact. Failure to develop social relations is another characteristic of this disorder. Some believe that the insufficient conversational and nonverbal skills lead to poor social relationships." (From the International OCD Foundation.)

So yes, I think I wrote Cormack correctly; and more importantly, Jesse Hemmings played Cormack accurately. I hope people get it. I know it's a difficult subject to handle, especially in a comedy where most pages of script have a couple of gags or more, but the last thing I want to hear from an audience afterwards is: "So in that scene, why did he…?" Just go with it, people! Not everything makes sense to everyone all the time.

The film is also about friendship. The only people whom Cormack is able to connect with are his three misfit friends, Rob, Joe, and Chris. And they are misfits, with their own quirks and personality traits that put them way down the social pecking order.

I may not be the first to notice this, but teenage boys do tend to be superficial. Long conversations about feelings or opening up about what's troubling them are things that don't tend to happen. As a youth worker many years ago, I learned that you have to engage boys in some kind of task, and while doing that you might get little snippets of the way they feel. By and large, a group of teenage boys will talk about things in very superficial terms, hiding behind attempts at humour and bravado. It's because of that, and his long relationship with Rob, Joe, and Chris, that Cormack is able to blend in with them almost seamlessly. His Asperger's is not evident to them in the shallows of teenage male recreation.

The Only Game in Town is also a subversion of the sports movie genre. We take competitive solitaire and the rivalry contained in it, add the dramatic momentum that exists in a sports movie, and make something that isn't competitive very much so.

Among the standard elements of such films is the disgraced former-player-turned-coach who uses the skills of his protegé to regain his reputation.

Teacher/solitaire coach Alex Crowley is named after Aleister Crowley, the occultist whom the British press once dubbed "the wickedest man in the world." Our teacher is nowhere near the level of despicability of the original Crowley, whose mesmerizing stare filled me with dread as a youngster. The part of Alex Crowley grew through each rewrite of the script until he was second only to Cormack in scenes and lines. And that's because of the sports movie element. Through Crowley we learn that competitive solitaire is a real thing, that it has history and traditions, and that people take it seriously.

PULLED A MAGDA

Alex Crowley copied Magda Goebbels illegal solitaire move

The solitaire move made infamous by Magda Goebbels, wife of Nazi Party Propagandist Joseph Goebbels, was used again by our very own Alex Crowley. It is alleged that Alex used the move on several occassions on his rise to fame as a solitaire legend throughout Canada. He has denied the accusation of course, but experts have examined footage of some of his competitions more thooughly in light of the revelation and declared that he has in fact used the illegal Magda move on at least 25 occassions. Some have called for Alex to be exiled from Canada, while some of suggested he meet the same fate as Magda Goebbels herself.

"Pulling a Magda," or to "pull a Magda" is a phrase invented as part of the back story of competitive solitaire. It involves changing the sequence of cards in your hand so that you can get to the one you need to continue the game. It came about because the second most despicable act of Magda Goebbels's life was to cheat at solitaire in 1944. The wife of Joseph Goebbels, she was also a strong supporter of Adolf Hitler.

So there it is. What the film is about in a nutshell. Almost. And for anyone embarking on their own film project, I wonder if you despise the twenty-five-word pitch as much as I do. Let's try: a comedy about a troubled teen with Asperger's and a savant skill for solitaire who becomes obsessed with the girlfriend of the school sport's hero.

What do you think? Would you watch the film based on that pitch? It's bound to lack several key elements. First love might be implied in that pitch, but what about friendship? What about the sports satire and the menace of Crowley?

It all goes to show the really hard job filmmakers have in trying to sell complex stories with a few words in a program guide.

PART ONE

THE WRITER'S TALE

THE MAKING OF A WRITER

I'm a writer. There I said it. If I could do one thing for the rest of my life, it would be to earn a living solely by writing. I would spend all day at it, every day. Since the 1980s I have earned money from writing—not enough to buy the rest of my time, but enough to make me feel like a writer.

"There are no writers, just rewriters."

That's true too. I am the world's best at writing 50,000+ words and then locking them away, never to see a publisher or a producer. I revisit them, in much the way you would visit an aunt after you've moved away, perhaps once in a decade.

It's nice to reread after all that time. You feel proud, remind yourself that the idea was sound, the essential story was a good one. *How clever I am!* So perceptive to have written this all those years ago.

Then the self-critic takes over and away you go again, rewriting a paragraph here, a chapter there, only to click save and close the file and hide it away for another time.

Few things I have ever written stand up to my own scrutiny in later years. I don't know if that's a writer thing or a Stuart thing. Virgos are perfectionists, ultra-critical, and more so of themselves. For me those traits are very true.

Imagine having the luxury of never having to release any of your work until you were completely happy with it. All the creative people I know battle with having to balance their desire for perfection and the publisher/distributor/record company's need to stick to a deadline. To prove the point, I just added this paragraph three hours before the final deadline for the manuscript. Even after it became clear that other people—professionals, mind, not those people who simply knew me—really liked *In the Air at Whitby* (the first feature film script that I had optioned), it still comes as a surprise when my work gets a good reaction. (It's at this point that someone is going to raise their head off the pillow and ask: "So why did you want to write this book?")

I hope it will become clear why I needed to write this book. It's a story in itself, and while it's a story about making a film, it's a story just the same, with characters and drama and twists. Maybe someday, someone (most certainly not me) will make a film about this book....

But before we get to the film, we need to see who the writer is, and as this is "The Writer's Tale," we need to see what made the writer.

I Used to Lie

I'm not sure when it was that I discovered that I loved telling stories. I know I used to lie a lot, in the same way Walter Mitty or Billy Liar used to lie. "Embellish the truth" is perhaps a better way of putting it. I never meant harm by lying, and if I look back I can honestly say (!) that lies were not designed to enable me to profit at someone else's expense. They would be things like telling the folks I was a jockey at the local Donkey Derby and I almost won a race. It was clear that it would be so easy to disprove such a claim, but it never occurred to me that telling a tall tale such as that could have a downside.

It's entirely possible that the storyteller in me came out of a desire to see more in the world than life seemed to offer in a 1960s council estate in Shepshed, Leicestershire, England. Not that I ever had a downer on my childhood. Quite the opposite, I loved it.

We were poor. All of us. No one had more than anyone else so there was no envy. School was a five-minute walk away and the school was full of kids from the same village and everyone knew everyone else. Whenever I made a new friend at school, my mum, Edna, would be able to give me the family history of that new friend.

Our council house was on an estate built in the 1950s to house workers for the umpteen hosiery factories in the village. The village was growing, but it still nestled in farmland and meadows and large woods and parkland. Although home was a council house, it was a semi-detached, with a very large garden by today's standards in the UK. At the back of the garden was a large grassy paddock with horses. Across the road was one of several communal greens, with huge oak trees and thick grass that was good for the estate children to play on. A short walk down the road there was a park with a walled paddling pool, swings, slides, flower beds, a bandstand, and more grassy areas.

We had space to play in, to explore and to grow. Out of school we could walk miles through fields and old rail tracks, fish in broad streams, make up games, and learn about the places we shouldn't go and the kids we needed to avoid.

We could play football for hours on end. In the summer we might decide to play cricket instead. We built tree houses and "scrumped" apples from private trees. I feel blessed because I'm sure mine was the last generation where children could have such experiences. Where we were allowed to play.

It's true that I often found myself with plenty of unsupervised time. Before I started school, my younger brother Andrew became ill as a result of the whooping cough vaccine. He became mentally and physically disabled, and from that point, really, my parents were needed elsewhere. My two older sisters were old enough to have their formative years under their belts by the time Andrew's condition began to really affect home life.

How my parents coped—and they coped for over forty years—is a testament to human resilience. My dad, Roy, was eighty-three when finally he and Mum accepted that Andrew could be better looked after by professionals and they moved him into a residential care facility. My dad died a year later. I think if I have inherited anything from them, it is a stubborn persistence and the ability to keep going far beyond the point when all signs say stop.

My dad worked all his life in the same hosiery factory. When the George Braunds factory burned to the ground in 1965, a month after my brother was born, it meant my dad, with three children and a newborn baby, was without income for a year (there was no welfare for such things then). He must have been at his wits' end. I can remember watching from an upstairs window as he peddled his bike down the road toward the factory on the night of the fire, the sky red with flames.

This isn't the place for too much of my parents' story, but it's a good story too, and I think it deserves to be told in full some day.

In short, from the age of five, I would come home from school to a frequently empty house, as my parents would often have to race to the hospital in Leicester with my brother. I learned to fend for myself. I wasn't always brilliant at this. One cold morning I got up and got myself ready for school, putting my socks in front of the fire to warm them up. That morning I went to school with scorch holes burned into my socks and the smell of flaming fibres in my nostrils.

Another time the only thing I could find to eat or drink before I ran off to play football with my friends was a bottle of Warninks Advocaat. For those who don't know, it's a Dutch drink, essentially eggnog and brandy. I'm not sure how much I drank, but I wasn't very good at football that night. (My mum's working-class pride would have her horrified that people now know her son went out of the house drunk at the age of ten, so please keep this to yourself.)

School and lessons really meant little to me. If it hadn't been for the friends that I shared school with, I would have abandoned it as a bad idea from the start. In fact, one morning when I was five, I decided that I should indeed abandon it and sneaked off home, expecting the house to be empty, only to have my mum drag me back to school by the ear.

It would be impossible for me to write anything, and certainly impossible to have written *The Only Game in Town,* without the kind of childhood I had. Those experiences have coloured the way I see things. I missed having a brother to be best pals with. It was given to me very briefly then snatched away.

Life wasn't normal, in that I could visit my friends' houses, and their families made me feel welcome, but this was not the case in our house. We essentially lived in one room, and there would always be a tension if anyone came to the house. Confronted by any new situation, my brother Andrew could explode into a violent fit. The whooping cough vaccine also made him severely autistic, and he demonstrated traits that by themselves would have been bad enough.

This isn't the place for such discourse, but if anyone asks why I am totally against the modern-day drive for mandatory vaccinations, I hope they can see that with my life experience I can have no other opinion.

When I was given the writing task of "fleshing out" Odette's character for *The Only Game in Town*, it was clear we needed to see something of her backstory. We needed to understand why this attractive and popular girl was prepared to invest some of her time in Cormack. The backstory I gave her was right out my own teenage experiences. Despite her love for Alastair, there is just no way that she can allow him to visit her home and see the way her family has been forced to live, to see what her mother has been reduced to.

It's a complex situation. It requires Odette to be outwardly the "golden girl" and yet be carrying around the shame of her home life and the guilt for being ashamed of her own life. (Jessie Craig portrays both elements superbly.)

My dad took the brunt of the worst of Andrew's fits. Even as a frail old man, he was still determined to take Andrew to Mencap gatherings or push him around town in his wheelchair. When they came home, Dad would have deep scratches on his arm where Andrew had grabbed him as a result of a sudden change in my brother's demeanour.

All aspects of Andrew's life became my dad's. He volunteered with the local Mencap charities, embarked on numerous fundraising activities, and even dug the foundations for Glebe House in Loughborough when they wanted new facilities to care for those with learning difficulties and autism.

Mencap is a UK charity for people with a learning disability. It provides support for families and caregivers, and my dad was actively involved in the Charnwood region. I'm not sure how many thousands of pounds he raised for them, but he was inspiring. I became a regular sponsored walker myself on their behalf and even did a fundraising parachute jump.

Through his working life, my dad worked shifts at a hosiery factory. Fifty years of service to the same factory—that too colours my views of life. But Dad's shift patterns meant that I was mostly unable to have friends home to play. More than anyone, he would need his sleep to recuperate.

I am struck now, thinking of it, that every play I've written, every film script, despite all the advice about keeping numbers low, have huge speaking casts. This may have something to do with finally having the opportunity to "play" with a lot of friends. I'm a solitary person who loves company.

Confronted with daily nightmare scenarios as a child, I would daydream, disappear into different places in my head, have adventures, create stories. Almost before I could write, I was imagining all kinds of scenarios and using that imagination to tell stories.

On the days that Dad worked, my friends would come around to my house and we'd play outside. It could never be inside the house, but we had a good-sized yard (except for the few years we were really poor and Dad turned the whole lawn into a vegetable garden). We would play soldiers or it might be the Wild West and "cowboys and Indians" or even Robin Hood, if one of us had been given a bow-and-arrow set for Christmas, but more often than not it was the Second World War. Cricket stumps made good Sten guns, and my dad's gooseberry bushes made great cover for an ambush.

Perhaps here a note about the Second World War and why it was a significant source of inspiration for me growing up. The mid-sixties was of course only twenty years since the end of the war against the world's worst baddies. Our parents were the generation that had lived through it. In Britain, many essential items were still rationed into the fifties. In inner cities you could still see piles of rubble from the Blitz.

War and Football

The proximity of the Second World War even played a part in the outcome of the 1966 World Cup Final between England and West Germany. England's footballing legend Jack Charlton explained why he never had any doubt about England's third and crucial goal, where Geoff Hurst's thunder strike hit the underside of the crossbar and bounced down over the line (or not over if you're reading this and happen to be German). The uncertainty and controversy that followed had two entire nations biting their nails. But the coolest character on the pitch seemed to be Jack Charlton himself. Afterwards, "Big Jack" summed it up when he shared what he thought when he saw the referee and West German players confront the Russian linesman for a final decision. "As soon as I saw them go to the Russian linesman I knew he would give [England] the goal. He was Russian and we were only twenty years since the war; he would have known people that suffered at the hands of the Germans. He was going to give the goal."

The Second World War gave us the ultimate "baddies" for any dramatic scenario. We're still a long way from showing Nazis in any kind of sympathetic light, so it's an easy set-up for a writer, filmmaker, or game designer. In short, when I was growing up, the Second World War was still very close and a rich source of heavy drama.

Still, I don't think I'll ever write or produce a Second World War feature. The closest I ever will get is *The Trumpeteer*, a short film made in the early 2000s for BBC. There were Nazis and the French resistance and guns, but it was on a small scale and all over inside fifteen minutes.

In *The Only Game in Town*, however, there was another opportunity to go back to the Second World War. The scenes of Magda Goebbels playing patience ("or solitaire as they call in it the new world," as Magda says in the script) also gave me an opportunity to pay tribute to the classic British comedy series *'Allo, 'Allo!* More than that, it gave me the chance to play around with the start of the film. I found myself, deep into post-production, building the opening sequence of a Second World War air raid on Berlin, with bombs dropping, sirens sounding, and flak guns flakking.

I thoroughly enjoyed the task, even panning bombs from left to right for stereo effects. It was crucial that even the dropping of whistling bombs be done for comic effect. I can't wait to see this scene in the cinema.

Here's the thing. My soldier games were not some random "bang, you're dead!" free-for-all, with endless arguments over who shot who first. On the rare times my friends would come around to play, they would find themselves in an organized production, with backstory and precise plot and action. I would direct them in where to stand, what to say, who to shoot.

I didn't have friends—I had life-sized puppets!

I realize now that I was effectively the game master in an elaborate role-playing game—a film director without a camera. At the time, this was play, the way I entertained my friends on long summer days.

I was also capable of occupying my own time without ever being bored. I had all sorts of model soldiers, scenery, and so on. I played with them the same way I played with my friends. The toy soldiers had lives, stories, emotions. Battles were simply the backdrops against which personal drama was played out.

Imagine my horror when I would go to a friend's house to play with model soldiers and their battles were decided by throwing balls or pebbles at the lines of soldiers we had spent three hours positioning! This wasn't playing with soldiers; it was skittles!

When I reached ten years old, it was up to the big school, with a uniform and a mile-long walk to the edge-of-town establishment. I still hated it, but they did have big open playing fields and bigger play areas ideal for football. Even though school didn't start until nine o'clock, my friends and I would arrive at eight to play football for an hour before prison started.

I don't know when exactly, but I began to love the act of writing. Even today if I'm down in the dumps, a new pen and some clean virgin writing paper is all the therapy I need. School did provide some opportunity to indulge the need to write, but all too often other classes got in the way. Still, teachers would dish out new exercise books if yours was full, or lost, or stolen, or forgotten. So every day I needed a new book because mine had was full, or got lost, or stolen, or forgotten. I had found an endless supply of empty books in which to write. And write I did.

What's more unusual is what I did with that writing. Yes, it's still here at home in a drawer, but I mean what I did with it before that, while writing

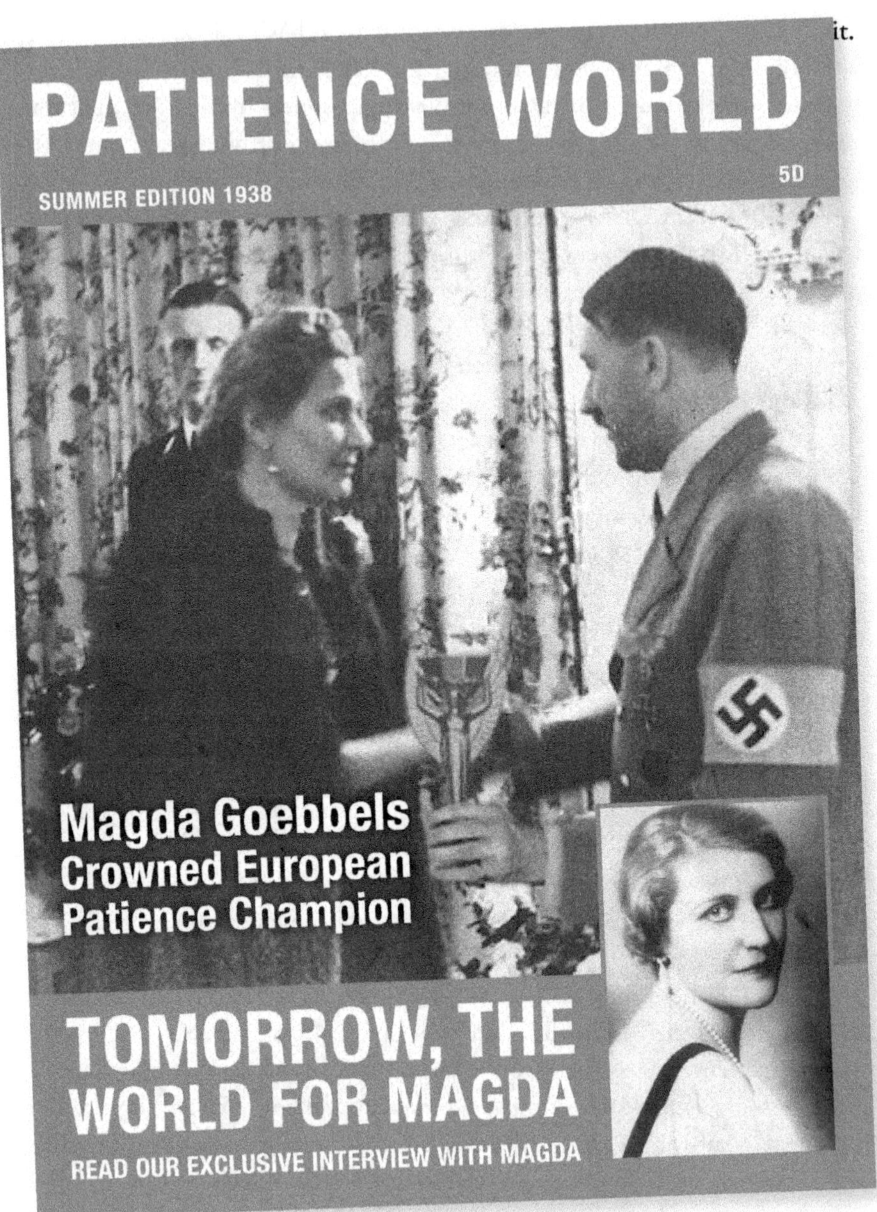

Another fake magazine cover. This purports to be from pre-World War Two Europe, and shows European patience champion Magda Goebbels receiving a trophy from Adolf Hitler. This magazine appears on the table in the Magda Goebbels scene, which also shows Magda drinking from a mug with the motto: Magda, Keep Calm and Invade Poland.

Somewhere during my first year at high school, as a ten-year-old, I thought I would write a Second World War drama. Yes there were battles and people got killed, but the characters in the story were all based on my footballing school friends. Morley, Dawson, Oliver, Strafford, Bowley, Cope, Hewitt, and others, all there as the inspiration for grown-ups in a world of terrible danger and sadness.

And every morning, my football friends arrived at school at eight o'clock, and before a ball was kicked, they wanted me to read the latest chapters of the book. I would stand in the centre of a huddle of ten-year-old boys as they listened attentively to the unfolding drama.

I was a storyteller. I still am. I will tell my story because that's what I do. Regardless of the size of the audience or even whether they are really interested. If I'm sitting on the ball you have to wait for the story to finish before you can play with it!

But listen they did. For almost two years that story grew, thanks to the never-ending supply of school exercise books and the most eager audience anyone could hope for. If I spoiled your mornings, boys, I'm sorry, but thank you for giving me the encouragement to keep writing.

Most of what I learned at school has long since been forgotten, which suggests it was pointless: working in base 3 or 7, technical drawing, French, undoing the bra of the girl in front with a deft movement of the fingers, falling off a chair for comic effect, applied mathematics....

Yes, I was the class clown. Yes, I understand that also makes me an annoying nuisance, both to teachers and to other students. I was that irk that others wish would shut up and grow up. For me, making people laugh was a defence tactic; it helped me avoid being beaten up by the tough kids. It got me through the drudgery of incarceration at school. It removed me from the realities of my home life.

There were many occasions, growing up, that my mum required my help. I could go to school later in the day if I first walked to the local shop to buy food, papers, cigarettes. The early years of my brother's life were, in a word, horrific. I would witness my parents trying to combat his violent fits and convulsions, their fear and their sheer despair at their lonely struggle, and in all honesty, such things left a deep mark on me. Although there was little I could do to help, leaving one or both of them alone to cope with it all filled me with dread, for heaven knows what I could come home to. But there are no excuses; every one of us has tough times, if you fall down it's your own fault. I wasn't going to use my parents and my brother as an excuse for me cutting class.

My mum, along with her sisters, also spent years caring for her mother who was on her deathbed for what seemed like most of my childhood. My mum's life was nothing more than caring for another person every waking hour. When my grandma died there was no reason for my mum to leave the house anymore—she could do all the caring she needed to do there; she didn't leave.

So I'm sorry if you were in my applied mathematics class and your life was ruined because you can't remember how to do differential equations, or your French holiday was ruined because you missed the bit about the pen of your aunt; but for me, making a big show of falling off my chair at a completely inopportune moment helped take my mind off a few things.

I was lucky to have a few decent teachers. Some seemed to enjoy my writing, although not always the style, which was similar, in fact, to the physical comedy routine of falling off my chair. It's all about the…timing.

"The story is excellent, though the random bursts of humour throughout are not always well-timed!"

Bless my English teacher, Mr. Davis. I was doing random bursts of humour long before *Family Guy*. But I will forgive him, because he would send many of my stories off to the local papers where they would be published. My audience was growing. (Whether they liked it or not!)

I was spurred on by these successes. After more exercise books full of novels, and huge sheets of pink paper full of what I called "rhythmic prose," I fell by accident into drama classes at the age of sixteen. I had found another way of expressing myself, and I took great pride in being the best character actor I could. It wasn't always easy; too many times I'd be cast as the foppish, handsome lead when I really wanted to be the scene-stealing villain. Still, I began to see how I could create stories using real people, just as I had done when I was small.

I also began to write sketches and quickly thereafter full plays. I wrote and published a satirical student comic that got me suspended from college, an incident that caused an almost irreconcilable rift between me and my by now exhausted and world-beaten parents. Yet still, I was caught between the long solitary slog of the writer and the immediate impact of live performance. Theatre provided the best opportunity to satisfy both needs and force my world view on others.

At sixteen, though, it was clear that I had identified what it was that I wanted to do. Writing was something I would always do. Whether it earned money or not, I would write whenever I could, and when I'd retired from "work," I could still write. But through theatre I had learned that the director is able to take the story and share it with audiences. So I wanted to be a director. A film director!

"So how does one become a film director?" I asked the careers officer. He rummaged in his drawer and gave me several brochures from local banks that were hiring at the time. If you are reading this and you are sixteen, please, go and work in a bank. You will earn decent money, pay off your mortgage early, and have nice holidays every year, a new car here and there, and a level sort of life. I know, because I didn't choose that road.

It was about this time that a BBC TV crew visited the house across the road. I poked my nose in where it wasn't wanted and quizzed the crew about becoming a director. (Things took a turn for the worse when I began suggesting where they should set up the cameras to get good shots of the oak trees on the green.) It turned out that if you wanted to be a film director, the first thing you had to do was go to university.

I don't know whether any youngsters my age from my council estate ever went to university. I can think of none of my contemporaries who did. Many left school at sixteen, the first chance they got. Staying on beyond sixteen to do the two extra years' schooling to get to sixth form and earn A-level qualifications wasn't necessary; there were jobs of all kinds, and university was really for people who wanted to be teachers. Consequently, there was no expectation that council house kids would want to go to university; besides, the cost was well beyond the means of council house families.

I was already causing my family financial woe by daring to stay on into the sixth form. I was expected to get a job at sixteen and add something to the family funds, but it felt to me that I needed more time to figure out if the dream of working in film and TV was achievable without going to university.

Sixth form gave me the chance to search out a new route. Nonetheless, it still equated to school. If it had not been for drama classes, I would have struggled to drag myself there at all. Out of all the subjects offered in sixth form, only drama provided the level of learning and discovery I felt I needed.

With any idea of university abandoned, I had to find a different way into directing. And theatre was it.

3

STAGE FRIGHT AND THEATRE

I used my time in theatre class to learn all I could about performing and directing and staging. I directed as often as possible, even simple sketches and short plays, until things started to happen. On leaving sixth form I got work in a theatre-in-education company and began to write stage plays.

Theatre-in-education companies were in abundance in my part of the world during the early eighties. Essentially, small touring bands of actors would be invited to schools to perform plays that had heavy elements of social awareness or issue-based storylines that were supposed to inspire new thinking in their young audiences. They were a world away from the glamorous stage musicals that were so popular in Shepshed and required very little in terms of staging or props or costume. As an actor, you would be essentially vulnerable on stage with nothing to hide behind, and indeed you were often within breathing distance of the audience.

During my drama studies, we had worked a lot on the style of theatre developed by Jerzy Grotowski, who gave the world the "poor theatre," and my slide into theatre in education was made easier because of that training.

In the evenings I performed in more "standard" theatre settings and in a range of plays. I preferred comedy. But there was one major problem with my performing life.

As an actor, I was petrified before I went on stage. The thought of waiting in the wings for my cue and then entering and saying my first line filled me with dread. Once on stage I could handle it. I learned to feed off the audience. I could sense the anticipation for the big gag and the applause. Having developed acting skills for two years, I often found myself with a lead role. We did a lot of Shakespeare in those days. I played Prospero—the aged sorcerer from *The Tempest*—at the young age of nineteen.

I played Rosencrantz in a wonderful production of Tom Stoppard's *Rosencrantz and Guildenstern are Dead* that toured little villages around the East Midlands. The part of Guildenstern was played by my drama class partner and long-time best friend, Phil Marriott. From the writings of Tom Stoppard I learned much about constructing a play (or script) from a number of sources. But I discovered that I could not go on with the acting game. The stage fright was crippling me, and I would often get rather ill. Putting myself through the emotional and physical stress night after night took me to the point of burnout. I would arrive at the theatre hours early, if possible, and try to go through routines to prepare myself for my first entrance. I would try to eat, keep down what I'd eaten, time bathroom trips and arrival in makeup, but the more I made of it the worse it got.

Eventually I had to face facts that the theatre wasn't earning me enough to live on, so I worked bar and then found myself a genuine full-time job in a hosiery factory. I think all sons must walk in their father's footsteps for a while; it's a humbling experience.

Theatre became something "on the side," though I was paid to write and direct at various levels of theatre for around fourteen years. I found my greatest opportunities for writing and directing came with the Shepshed Youth Theatre. I began to write stage plays for large casts of young people—surely the best start for someone destined to write a film with a cast of forty plus.

I remember fondly the young people I was lucky enough to work with back then. And there's something else about the work I did with community theatre that has stayed with me. I gave opportunities to perform on stage as part of decent theatre productions to young people who struggled with learning difficulties. One mother, her face beaming, thanked me for giving her the chance to see her daughter on the stage. Unfortunately, some of the actors in the troop didn't like the involvement of "non-actors" in speaking roles; they told me it detracted from the quality of the overall performance.

One thing is for certain: it would have been easier to not include them. But I have never been one for taking the easy route. Giving opportunities to *all* young people to perform in quality productions is in my blood. (I remained true to those beliefs during the entire process of *The Only Game in Town.* And when the crunch came in the summer of 2015 and I had to choose between delaying the film and going with the young people who had shown faith in me for more than a year, it was an easy choice to make.)

My community theatre groups always varied the types of plays we did, but I found the best responses, from cast and audience, were from comedy. I was honing my skill as a comedy writer. I was also picking up other people's plays and directing them.

If you ever get a chance to see *The Mask of Moriarty*—a superb spoof of Sherlock Holmes stories by the late Hugh Leonard—you should. I've directed it many times with different casts, and it works every time. I'd love to do it as a film one day. It's the sort of humour that inspires my thinking when writing my own stuff.

One of the favourite pieces I ever wrote for theatre, again with a large cast of loveable characters, was *A Passage to Gretna Green.* It was then, in 1986, that I began to realize I could make people laugh—a lot. It was like the falling off the chair routine, but on a much larger scale.

Not everything I wrote worked, but overall everything helped me to develop a style and to test the water with directing.

I got married. Bought a house. Had children. My job in the factory became a management job. But in the evenings I would write: books, plays, film scripts. But something else was happening. By around 1993, although still working in theatre, it began to annoy me that I had very little to show for more than a decade's work in theatre. Months of writing, planning, producing, and directing would culminate in a few weeks of stressful performances to a few hundred people. I had embarked on the theatre journey to train me for film, and with film, the audience would be larger and the record a permanent one. I had to find a way to get back on track.

I felt that I still lacked all of the necessary skills to switch from theatre writing to screen, so took myself off to Leicester University to do a part-time master's program in screenwriting. Funny how I enjoyed school now.

I was lucky enough to write a comedy film script—the aforementioned *In the Air at Whitby*—which was optioned by a decent producer and very nearly got made. I made some useful contacts as a result and made some great friends in the industry that are still my go-to guys to this day.

Yet I still needed more skills, and so I began to direct live TV at a local cable station and found myself involved in a number of low-budget films and TV projects in one role or another.

Still I was writing, still I was looking to direct. Looking for anything that would push my career forward, broaden my network, develop missing skills.

I wrote a sci-fi comic called *Cyborg Warriors*—forty-eight pages in full gory colour—and for this I was lucky enough to work with some great artists. One of them, Conrad McEwan, remains one of my best friends and chips in with some great artwork when needed on one project or another. He designed the Midlothian school crest and the really funny newspapers used in *The Only Game in Town*. *Cyborg Warriors* makes a cameo appearance in the film too; in the scene where Cormack is spying on Odette and Alastair, he sits in the huge Adirondack chair in the middle of River John and peeps at them from behind a copy of the *Cyborg Warriors* comic.

I dabbled in low-budget videos—a little bit of acting, but only as a means to get on set and learn as much as I could about all of the processes; then helping to make the project happen; and then, finally, directing some short films.

A new TV station opened up some eighty miles from where I lived, and I was lucky enough to get a job there and help them launch a 24-hour broadcast schedule. Time was limited for my own projects, so I directed where I could, but I began to work more as a producer, and short films, commercials, and promos became my daily grind. I was actually doing what I had always wanted, and it had only taken me twenty-five years. Who needs university? Apart from the part-time MA in screenwriting I had done it the long way. It's funny, working long hours in the TV business was pretty close to the goal I'd set myself at sixteen. But I missed writing. Perhaps I missed being creative. Possibly I missed calling the shots. I was living my dream but I just itched to have time to write some of my own words again.

The desire to "buy back" more of my time to write was a major factor in moving to Nova Scotia. It seemed like a good idea, despite potentially ruining the lives of our teenage sons. That and the underlying guilt and sadness that only migrants really know, when your family and friends watch you leave and wonder, *Why?*

Finally, life seemed to come full circle. Moving to Nova Scotia meant I had reached the point where I could spend more of my time writing and not starve.

So that is the back story of "the writer." He's a stupid but sensitive kind of chap, and words are the tools he uses to try to express himself and share with others the way he sees the world.

Now, at last, you get to read about the writing of this particular film. I started at eight o'clock in the morning, had a forty-five-minute lunch break, and it was all finished by suppertime.

Well of course not. But wouldn't it be funny if it was? Wouldn't it be good if it really happened like that?

Sometimes, you know, it does. Only a few nights ago, I woke for no reason and found myself unable to get back to sleep but never fully awake. For the next two hours I ran through a complete film in my head. I saw everything, heard all the dialogue, met the characters. It will be one of the easiest scripts for me to write, and I can't wait to make a start.

But for *The Only Game in Town*, as usual for me, there is no quick and simple answer to how this script came to be. To find the start of the idea we have to go back to 2005 and the bar of The Leicester Haymarket Theatre during the intermission in a performance of *To Kill a Mockingbird*. For that is where the concept was born and the characters burst into my head.

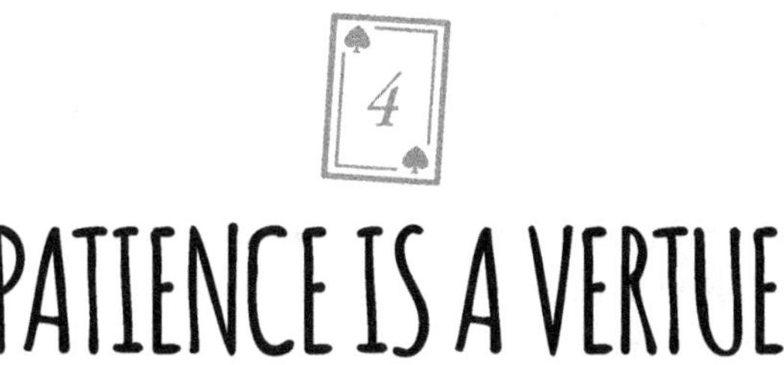

PATIENCE IS A VERTUE

Only recently I have been doing some IT housekeeping on some old drives. It should have surprised me, but didn't, that I found some early scripts and outlines for *The Only Game in Town* that were more than a decade old.

Back then it was called *Patience is a Vertue,* a play on the old saying that my mum would fire at me when I stamped my foot and demanded instant gratification of some sort. "Patience is a virtue," she would say. I wasn't about to argue with her that actually Pope Gregory didn't cite patience as one of the seven holy virtues, although come to think of it, I probably did argue with her. The inability to know when to keep my trap shut is another of my character flaws. "Your mouth will get you hung!" was another saying that Mum would fire at me. Now that would make a great title for my next film!

So the original title was for a story about a young boy whose surname is Vertue and who is good at solitaire, but in England we call solitaire "patience." See? Even now it's too contrived. It needed a snappier title. And as any Andy Williams fan will tell you, "solitaire's the only game in town." So that became my working title after about five years.

But a film is more than a title. How on earth did I come up with the story?

Well, the story was inspired by *To Kill a Mockingbird.* My elder son, Oliver, and I were at a performance of the classic play at Leicester's Haymarket

Theatre. It was early winter 2004 and other than the familiar setting of Leicester's popular theatre, I don't really remember anything about the play or the performance.

That may be due to the conversation with Oliver during intermission, which centred around younger son Charley and his relationship with the very close friends he'd had since starting school almost a decade earlier. There was a closeness, a bond between them that ran so deep (and still does), and yet they seemed to survive by avoiding any deep conversations. We also contemplated Charley's effortless ability at sport, all sport, and an apparent gift for any and all games of chance.

Our conversation moved quickly to how such things might appear in a film. The idea of competitive solitaire and a sports movie treatment of the subject made us chuckle over our intermission tea and cookies (though we called them biscuits).

But I spent the entire second act of *Mockingbird* running through a story of my own in my head. That's how it works sometimes. From a small kernel of something funny or absurd or exciting or dramatic, there sometimes grows an idea that just won't go away. Like a snowball rolling down a hill, some ideas just keep getting bigger.

If there are no other demands on your time, the evolution of such snowballs can happen quickly. But at that time, as with most of us outside the top 2 percent in the creative world, I had to juggle work, children, partner, parents, mowing the lawn, decorating the house, fixing the car, taking the dog for a walk, and all else. In fact, looking back it amazes me just how much I had written in my life up to 2004. I must have neglected one or more of those essential things. Racked with guilt, I'm guessing it would have been my wife, Josephine, and sadly my parents. There is never enough time.

Moving to Nova Scotia was essentially an ambitious plan to change the work-life balance, to buy me more time to write. ("How's that working out for ya?" I hear the reader ask with a smug tone.)

Aside from the first twelve months, I'm busier now than I've ever been. (For one thing, our lawn is ten times the size of the one in England, so I spend even more time mowing it!) I have boxes and drawers and folders and computer drives full of half-written stories, whole series of sitcoms, film outlines, and first drafts. Ideas come easily. (Wait! I've just had another one!) But that's the way it is. The idea isn't the difficult thing.

And that's just it. Certain ideas stay with you, keep you awake, get you out of bed to feverishly pound away on the laptop at some unearthly hour (kind of like I'm doing now…yawn!). If I knew what made a good idea, I'd stop having all the bad ones.

Or maybe that's it. Having ideas, any idea, keeps your imagination in good shape so you can have the really good ideas. Sports people use muscle-memory exercises to push the limits of their technique in the quest for better performance. The brain is the writer's muscle. Theories abound of the brain as a muscle that can be trained to improve the performance of many cognitive functions—maths, languages, memory.

There are many things a writer needs to do when an idea comes. The first one sounds simple, and many writers do this, inspired by stories of great films that were the result of a few lines scribbled on a matchbox and shown to a studio executive: you take that kernel of the idea, the first thing that came into your head, and you throw it out there.

I've worked on both sides of that situation. I've been the writer who thinks the idea I had that morning was the best idea anyone's ever had and will make millions but only if I act now and push it in someone's face. And I have also been the producer attacked by people with wild hair and in need of a good night's sleep, who claim to be writers because they have three lines of scribble and a photo of a horse.

Writer, beware! You had the idea, and quite possibly so did millions of others. Or something very similar. We live in a connected world, where a sort of collective consciousness exists to allow most of us to see the same patterns and to create the same sense of order out of the chaos. Three lines of scribble do not a genius make. I guess Brad Pitt could scribble three lines down and it could well be a movie next year, but I doubt Brad Pitt is reading this trying to figure out how to write a movie. So for you, my reader, if the three lines of scribble are going to be thrust into a producer's face, you'd better have the ninety-page first draft in the satchel at your side.

Because, of course, there is that very real possibility that while the producer is frowning at you as you get all excited about your idea, he could always go home and have a very similar idea, but slightly altered and benefiting from his inside knowledge. It's not always intentional of course, and these days writers are always asked to sign submission waivers that give producers a get-out clause if they get six ideas that are very similar. But I've had it done to me, in a big way, and it's very hard to prove an idea has been stolen—and the legal fees to try to do so are very high.

So, in short, I'm not a fan of having an idea and then immediately spitting it out. We could equate it to the process of eating fast food: cut out the middleman and put it straight in the toilet.

For the more sensitive of you, and those of you actually reading this in a fast food establishment, we should equate the process of writing to that of having a baby. The fun part is the idea, that three minutes of passion and elation as you conceive, but then this idea needs time to gestate. You need time to roll over and more importantly get over yourself in thinking you're the best and no one will ever match that performance and won't the wife be impressed when she finds out what you've done.

The idea needs to be left for nine months—seems about the right length of time. It may grow. And for me this is the only true option for a writer with an idea. Tend it, nurture it, question it, argue with it. *The Only Game in Town* was effectively a ten-year journey from idea to principal photography. A lot had happened in between. Essential stuff.

Take time to make that idea "your" idea. Flesh it out and invest it with your time and energy. When it's more than a collection of words, and before you send it out into the world, protect it by registering it with an agency (I use The Script Vault), but never, ever, ever consider it the final draft of the script.

Above all, a scriptwriter needs to hear the characters speak his or her words. This is invaluable and I fully recommend it. Some script software have tools that read out the dialogue—they are very robotic and I'm not sure if they provide anything meaningful to the writer. There are some script contests that have as a prize a reading of the script by actors—very useful. It's so useful, regardless of whether you enter such a festival or not, you should try and get some actors to read the script aloud.

Getting good honest, relevant feedback is crucial, and sticking to a rewrite plan is a good task. Another mechanism I like is to trim out all the dialogue, tell the story by using visual elements only—almost as a silent movie. Put the dialogue back in a little at a time and see how that works.

Take your time in finding a producer. Do your homework and don't send out a mass email. Producers aren't always looking for scripts, but if your script is hot they will thank you for it.

Why do some ideas stay the course?

The Only Game in Town didn't grab me or later readers because it was about a kid who never failed to get out (i.e., have the cards in their complete sequence) at solitaire. It was because the kid and his friends and their relationship to each other and to others around them reminds us of people we know. People like people. Fill your story or film with characters you care about—that's when the idea stays with you. Because you as the writer cannot bear to go through the day without seeing them and hearing them speak.

Testing the Waters

There comes a point when you have to be brave. Authors need to have their work published, so they approach agents and publishers. Screenwriters, technically, should be approaching producers. If you're hot enough as a screenwriter to have an agent, you're likely to be asked to write scripts, and your "spec" scripts will get a decent read wherever you send them.

Starting out, you'll have to hustle. And this is where the lines between writer and producer often blur. They did for me way back in my theatre-in-education days, and I never hold it against a writer who "adds value" to their script by connecting some actor or director to the project. However, some writers have been too enthusiastic about this and submit a screenplay with cast suggestions and budgets and in some cases even an Oscar application form.

That takes you very much into the realm of the producer, in which case, why are you sending your script to another producer? Be clear about the relationship you want to have with the person you send your script to. Be aware that a producer may need to have enough elbow room in your project to get it made. That can mean, in practical terms, ignoring your cast list and even (heaven forbid!) bringing in another writer for rewrites.

Whatever your intentions when sending out your complete script, you are taking a brave step, and one you can never take back. So again, make sure baby can walk before you throw him in front of a speeding train.

For me, the next step was obvious. Coming from England (as I do) where writers who are also producers who are also directors is frowned upon, I have a natural aversion for such a creative team structure. This is not so unusual here in Canada, and in fact, in recent years, it has become more common to see the big three roles of writer, producer, and director taken by the same individual. Still, making a film is about a creative team and the spark that can ignite new ideas and observations.

I was also very conscious that I had produced and directed countless documentaries and shorts over the years, including one with a budget bigger than *The Only Game in Town*, but I had never produced or directed a full-length scripted feature. I was going to need some help, and I wanted to share the journey.

The first person I thought of was Cory Bowles. I had first met him at a script-development workshop a few years earlier without realizing his pedigree at the time. I found him to be a likable chap, and we seemed to be on the same wavelength on many things. Only later did I realize he had such a track record through such things as his work as an actor on *Trailer Park Boys* and his own film *Righteous,* which he wrote, directed, and starred in.

So there was the initial "Hi, Cory! Remember me?" Followed by, "Here, take a look at this. What do you think? Do you want to direct this?" I sent him the one-sheet, a detailed outline, and I sat back nervously and waited.

I was surprised to receive a very quick and very positive response. We talked on the phone for an hour and both agreed we could do a good job of this film. We were also on the same page regarding our approach: this film needed some really good young people.

It's important to talk about the setting too. I was tentatively looking for external approval from Cory. Call it lack of self-confidence if you like, or it could equally have been a lack of confidence in my new surroundings, but I wanted to know for sure that, as a producer, I was picking up the right film. I had first got the idea for *The Only Game in Town* in the UK; would it work in Nova Scotia? Talking to Cory helped. It helped a lot.

In my heart I knew the film could be set and filmed not only in Nova Scotia, but right here on the North Shore. I have a strong sense of community. In my life I have only lived in two communities: Shepshed, England; and Welsford on the outskirts of River John, Nova Scotia. There are similarities between them: rural surroundings; decent, hard-working people; and a richer past than the present—more industry, for starters. They both have suffered from vanishing town centres and an abandoned railway; they both have families that have been connected to the community for generations. And, I will say this—both have been seemingly abandoned and forgotten by the powers that be. Both places rely on the time and efforts of residents to make things happen. There's a good case for twinning Shepshed and River John, don't you think?

In my time in Shepshed I was happy to involve myself in community events. I edited the town newspaper for a couple of years. Raised several thousand pounds over the years for local charities and groups. Gave time whenever I could. I try to do the same here in River John, and I had every intention of making this film within our communities from the start. I was just creating an opportunity for someone to argue against it. As producer, I would have to justify the decision at some point, if only to myself.

And the truth is, I couldn't give a toss about watching films set in cities. They don't resonate with me. Rural people, rural communities just *are* quirky, full of characters. Humans behave differently when they live rurally. I wanted to show that and how that's true here.

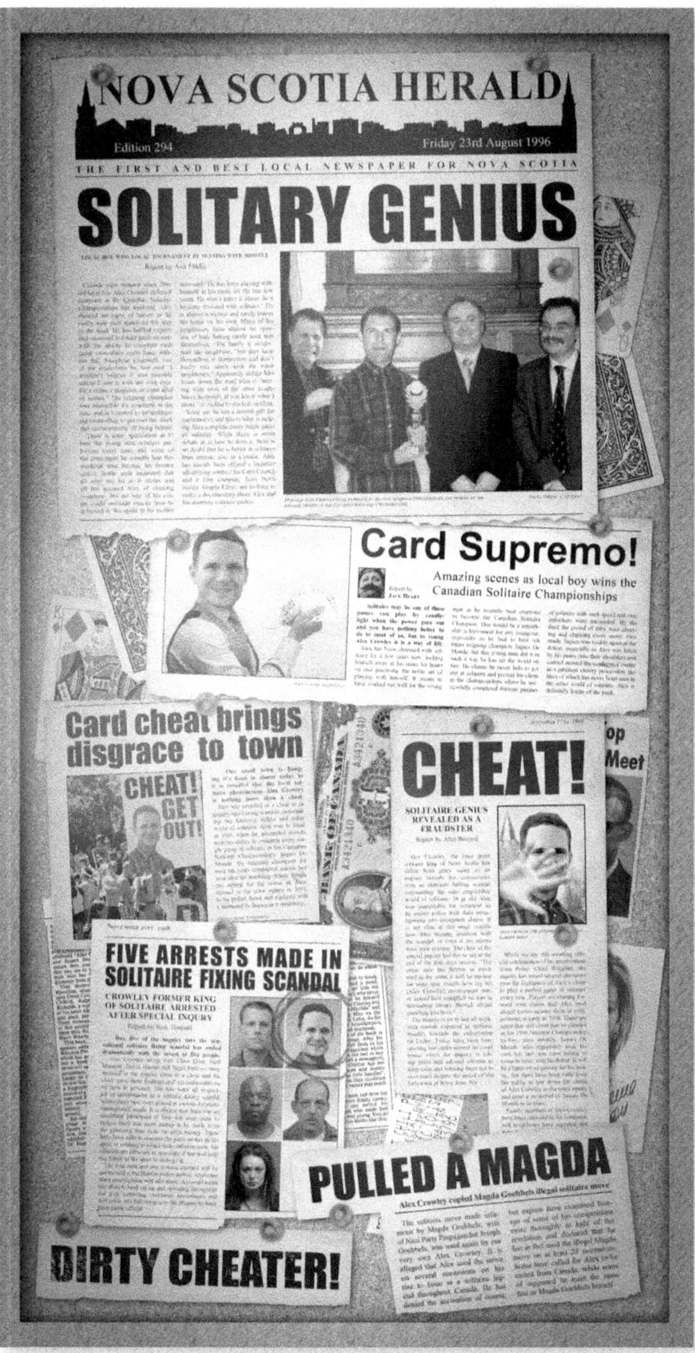

Crowley's memory board of newspaper clippings from his early career. All the clippings were posted on a a corkboard.

So if Cory had suggested filming it on the South Shore, I may have had a serious problem. But that was another reason for turning to Cory. His connections to Truro—known as the "hub of Nova Scotia," given its central location—were equally as strong as to Halifax. Why shouldn't he favour filming on the North Shore? Truro is mainland Nova Scotia's second-largest population centre, and many of its inhabitants spend summer weekends by the beaches along the North Shore, being at most an hour's drive away.

But that's all "producer thought." I was still in writer mode, really, and that's what I felt I needed. Another set of eyes looking over the script. It's strange that even with the knowledge that I could write well enough to have audiences love the stage plays I'd done and the short films and comedies I'd written, doubts still existed and I needed to know if I could pull this off.

We all need a parachute. Cory Bowles was mine.

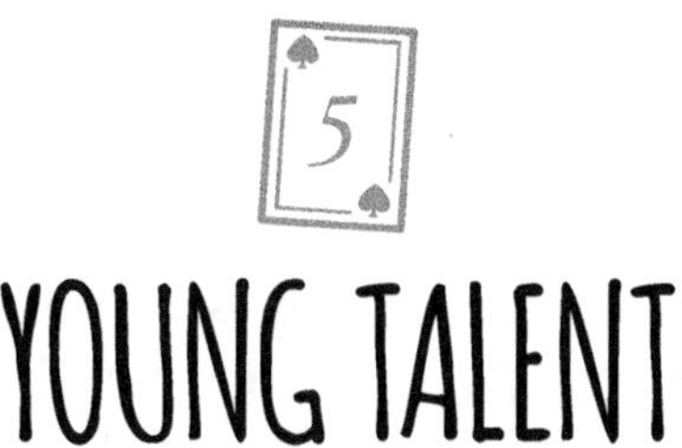

YOUNG TALENT

I had always said I would only do the film if there were young people around who were strong enough to do the characters. I met with Cory to suggest that we offer workshops along the North Shore of Nova Scotia, to see what talent there was.

Cory invited me to the set of *The Moblees*, a CBC kids' show that he was working on. Being on set reminded me of my days working at studios in Leicester, Nottingham, and Peterborough (England, not Ontario). For many years I'd written a weekly column in the *Leicester Mercury*, which at the time was the largest circulation regional daily paper in the UK. That led to a brief spell as a correspondent for the BBC and a few trips to the studios in Leicester or Nottingham. That was the last time, until *The Moblees*, that I had set foot in a genuine studio environment.

We chatted during his lunch break, and he signed director papers and the like. Then I grabbed a few bits of him speaking to camera about his vision for the film. We were right there on the same page. He thought the workshops were a great idea.

I started by speaking with Brian Holmes, principal of the nearby Tatamagouche Elementary School, who gave us permission to run the first of our workshops in the school. Then we contacted the local press—the *Pictou Advocate*, *New Glasgow News*, *Truro Daily News*, *The Tatamagouche Light*—and began announcing one workshop after another. I contacted Amanda Gillis, who ran a youth theatre in New Glasgow, and she hosted a couple of workshop sessions. This was easy. Not only was I calling on my own ancient experience of running a youth theatre, but here was a group of young people already conversant with youth theatre–type exercises and improvised scenes.

The numbers attending the workshops were starting to increase. We went on CBC Radio (the interview was at some ungodly hour in the morning) and we even made the Halifax newspapers.

Very soon, I was increasing the intensity (and frequency) of the workshops, pushing the young people until I could begin to see real characters emerge.

Some exercises would be fun. Games like Sit, Stand, Lie, where three actors act out a scenario where one of them must be either sitting, standing, or lying down at all times. Other scenarios included a mysterious hole appearing in the street. Sometimes I gave out scripts of sitcoms and got them to act them out. This was another chance for me to gauge the way my transatlantic humour was received. We acted scenes from *The IT Crowd*, *Red Dwarf*, *The Vicar of Dibley*, and others. I am pleased to say that not only did the young people deliver the sketches perfectly, they—and the adults who watched it all—found them hilarious.

I needn't have worried about the potential young talent in the area. As the workshops progressed, starting in the cold of late winter and moving through summer 2014, sometimes as many as eighty young people would show up to do improvisation, exercises, and little scenes from the first draft script.

I was looking for signs the young people had the ability to concentrate. I watched for groups of friends and how they might work together. I looked for interesting mannerisms and quirks that could be used, or would need to be avoided.

It felt rough for me though. Cory and I had decided at the start to do workshops rather than put the pressure on the young people in a single audition. Young people, especially those new to this, might buckle under audition stress, or even not bother to turn up. The idea was that a workshop would allow them to show their talent in a more relaxed way. But in reality, in my head, I found myself treating each workshop essentially as an audition, wanting to see that rare spark that would bring a character to life, create a star of the future.

At the end of each session I gave each person some time in front of the camera and asked them some general questions. Most had real fun with this and some characters shone through—more as entertainers perhaps than actors. What I needed was actors.

The video clips could be reviewed by me and Cory as we progressed through the year. I looked for interplay between the young people and how different groups worked together. The four main characters—Cormack and his friends Rob, Joe, and Chris—needed to look as though they had been friends for years and, more importantly, that no one else would ever befriend them.

Satisfied that the talent pool I'd hoped for was there, I was able to prepare a second draft of the script and dare to plan aspects of the production. These workshops and screen tests essentially became the casting sessions for the film. By the end of the summer of 2014 the parts for nearly all the young people had been filled—no auditions, they just "became" those characters.

Stef Hemmings, Actors' Mother and Film Extra

Two of my actual kids (Jesse Hemmings and Kasey DeVries) and one whom we half claim as ours (Aldo Orsi) had roles in *The Only Game in Town*. It was a joy for me to watch as they went through the process from audition workshops, to script reads, and finally, to production. Working on *TOGIT* gave them a great real-world introduction to film and the many hours and retakes and waiting...and waiting that it takes to get to the ninety or so minutes of the final cut. And yet, the very long, very hot days of filming never dampened their enthusiasm. Without Stuart at the helm, this first foray into a full-length feature could, potentially, have turned any of them away from such a career path. Instead, they came away with a great sense of accomplishment and increased confidence in themselves and their abilities.

Among those who stood out in the early workshops were Graci Young, Hanna Conrod, and Brennan Marks. All three were products of Amanda Gillis's youth theatre in New Glasgow. Working out where they were best suited though, was a major concern.

Brennan was a live wire, a real cheeky comedian. That didn't quite work for the four main boys, and I didn't see him as one of Cormack's arch rivals—the boys of MacDonald's gang. Hanna was superb. For a long time I was sharing script readings for the part of Odette between Hanna and Jessie Craig. Both were perfect, both brought something different to the role.

Graci too had talent in spades. I was simply struggling for meaningful parts for young females. Determined to try to keep young people involved—and to honour my pledge to give screen time to everyone that had been part of the workshops—I revisited the script. I would add characters into scenes and share lines out that were originally given to a single character. I wrote some scenes simply to put a particular young person in the film. The part of Emma was written especially for Graci.

Emma essentially began as a foil for Odette's character, someone we could get hints about Odette from, the fact that she was popular at school, had a close clique of girlfriends. It's typical of *The Only Game in Town* that the minor characters—and there are so many—have such interesting stories of their own that I should want to explore those characters further. There isn't really the time in the film to do that, so that is why I'm interested in pursuing a sitcom version (but more on that later).

Emma was a great little invention—a loyal friend who stabbed Odette in the back at the first chance to steal Alastair away.

Ultimately, Brennan, Hanna, and Graci chose not to appear in the film. I hate losing young people. I'm a little like some sort of sheepdog, running around keeping them all together. To all the "sheep" I lost along the way, thank you for the energy and excitement you gave in the early days, and I hope you found new opportunities your talent deserves.

Other aspects of the film were moving along parallel to the script rewrites and casting workshops. With most of the scenes taking place in or around a school, I asked Brian Holmes if we could actually do some filming at Tatamagouche Elementary. Brian is another British ex-pat. His daughter Grace had been in a short film of mine, *Broken*, and Brian had featured in a documentary I'd made called *Nova Brits*, about some of the many recent British migrants to our part of the North Shore of Nova Scotia. He had also acted in local stage productions. He was on board fully, not only giving us workshop space and promoting the sessions around the school, but also giving a sense of security and credibility to children and parents. Brian is also a decent actor in his own right and came on board as Mr. Alex Crowley, the chief villain and school solitaire coach. It also meant that we could use Tatamagouche Elementary as our main location.

In September 2014, Cory Bowles appeared on Global News talking about *The Only Game in Town*. People began to sit up and take notice. The press began to take an interest in what we were doing. I appeared on CBC Radio a few times and was invited to speak at film festivals. For me, the thought that we could really do some good for our region became increasingly important.

Things were slotting into place. But I need you to read the last few paragraphs again. We had a cast of young people, most still at school; we had a school principal acting as a school principal; and we had a school offered as a school location. Yes, we would need to schedule around school hours and term times and commitments to education and exam periods and so on, but by September 2014 we had all the key elements required for front-of-camera in place and were waiting for the green light.

Remember this, because there is a follow-on from this in the producer section.

Completing Script an Achievement

Now you have already noted that I am a cynical old git, who clings stubbornly to a particular set of values and whose views on the creative process are perhaps not in tune with your average artistic soul. That's fine.

I've come to learn that, contrary to what I once believed, I'm not alone in my views.

I recently met the talented and visionary director Tony Palmer. Like me, he loves his music in film (I hope you get that impression when you see *The Only Game in Town*), and he must have interviewed for various film projects some of the most creative people of the twentieth century. He doesn't like to the use term *art* when referring to film and will quote several ancient tribes who didn't believe in art, you just "do the best job you can do."

I have written countless short film scripts. I would expect no more adulation than a cup of tea and the warm feeling inside that comes from completing a piece of craft. I have heard that the mark of a good film writer is a good short film: it shows an understanding of the elements needed in a full-length script. If you can't master the short, you can't master the long form.

I disagree. Mostly. A short film needs to be simple and not have subplots and obviously not too many characters. A short film doesn't need the standard structure of a full feature—a beginning, a middle, and an end. A short film can be a slice, a piece of a story, left open to the viewer's own interpretation. Audiences are far more sophisticated nowadays. Music videos and even TV commercials can operate on many levels for audiences who are aware of subtle clues and inferences in the visuals—clichés, if you want.

In short, anyone and his dog can write a short film script. No more than fifteen pages, a couple of characters. Really, you can knock one off in an afternoon. The process, of course, still has some value, and that would be based on the goals the writer sets himself (or herself). Even more valuable is the process of producing a short film. Yet still, the scale of the task stands no comparison to a feature. One is a good hike with a rucksack and a picnic, the other is Scott's doomed expedition to the South Pole.

Again, apologies if I seem dismissive of what to many is a great achievement. I have done enough short films to know the work that goes into them. If I never did anything else, I could (and should) be really happy with the short form content I've been involved with. But there is no comparison from a short film to a feature.

So when someone tells me they have written the third draft of a feature screenplay, then I am instantly impressed. That in itself is an achievement to be proud of. And so it was with a certain amount of inner peace that I completed the second draft of *The Only Game in Town*.

Inspired by the workshop sessions, I had written a ninety-page script that I thought was the best thing since sliced bread.

I was quick to heap praise on myself. The outline and treatment had a certain flow about them, and the act structure and timings had been laid down in my head. Not only did the script match the pacing of the treatment, but, using the formula of one page of script equals one minute on screen, I could clearly see the script structure worked perfectly and would make a film of one hundred minutes in length. A job well done!

For the first time in my life I decided to enter the script into a number of contests outside Canada to see if anyone in the industry could see its potential, but more importantly, to alleviate my concerns about my writer's "voice." I've been writing since day one; thankfully I've evolved over the years, but there is always the fear that other people just might not get it, and like some random voice in the wilderness I'll write words that none will read. There's also the cultural issue: I'm a Brit living in Nova Scotia—does anyone this side of the Atlantic grasp the subtleties of a writer brought up on *Fawlty Towers*, *Dad's Army*, and *Chariots of Fire*? I love Nova Scotia, but I cannot hide from forty years of British culture. British culture tainted by a lifetime of Stuart-isms.

So when the script's latest draft—my sense of humour, the settings, and even the game of solitaire—began to get good feedback from readers around the world, people who don't know me, such praise told me that the story would travel. Not everyone will like it. But there are many people who will.

At this point I turned to another of the good guys in the film industry. Craig Cameron is a Nova Scotia producer and film-industry professional I have wanted to work with for a number of years, and having a decent script that seemed to read well, and a director in Cory Bowles who also believed in the undertaking, I felt I had the project that could entice Craig to join in. He did and the three of us met to discuss the film, the next steps, the budget, the market.

Craig gave me a piece of advice, though, that sent the anxious writer in me running for cover: "You need to get a good script consultant to read it." To me that sounded like handing in your essay to a teacher with a red pen. For the first time in the process I felt as though I were about to be judged. Up to now, everyone had been easily persuaded by the merits of the script and the planned film. In this world of reputation and the emperor's new clothes, I was about to allow a skinny little boy to see through the fabric of my work and tell the world I was actually running around naked.

Believe me, I would never live that down.

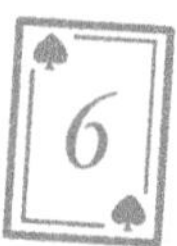

NOT EVERY SCRIPT IS BRILLIANT

All films start with a screenplay, the story. The signs were that I had a good one. Yet still the nagging nails of doubt scratched the back of my neck. I had always been dismissive of filmmakers in the modern age, the video age, where the costs of making a low-budget feature were such that anyone could buy a camera and "be a filmmaker" who exploited the access to the equipment to make their own film without ever needing to answer the really difficult questions about their project.

And this potentially could be me. I was producing this film, from my own script, and it worried me. Yes, having Cory direct it meant there would be a different voice. And yes, being honest with myself, if someone else had come to me with this script, I would have demanded I produce it. But still, could I be falling into the trap of self-delusion?

Why is a script consultant important? Well, I was lucky enough to sit alongside Bill Niven, one of Canada's top and most respected producers (another one I'd love to get an opportunity to work with!), at a film festival, where he reiterated a point he'd made some months before: "It has to start with the screenplay—a good story well told. You also need the magic that the director, actors, and crew bring to it. But I ask myself all the time why Canada has not ever had a real worldwide breakout film. An industry friend of mine in LA said to me, 'No one ever gives your writers up there the hard notes.'"

What does that mean? Well, not every script is brilliant. Not every script will be brilliant one day. Some may improve, but you can't turn a bad script into a brilliant one unless, as a writer, you are prepared to have your work scrutinized to the minute detail.

In Canada, the bulk of the film industry is funded by government agencies, or allocations of public money that are administered through broadcaster arrangements. I'm not criticizing the work they do, but there is no difference for the funders in funding a film that gets made and flops or not funding a film that could have made millions. Their role is to get films made and to get Canadian films seen around the world.

That is not the same as elsewhere. Seeing as Bill's friend lives in LA, let's look at what happens in Tinseltown. If a studio executive finances a film that loses money and gets trashed, he'll likely lose his job. But if he turns down a film that then gets picked up by the studio over the road and goes on to win awards and make massive profits, he will also likely lose his job.

The point is, our LA exec really has to know the qualities of the script he's reading. He has to know what that potential is. He has to read it, and by reading it I mean read it as if he were the average Joe in the audience, but then give you feedback as if he knows what makes a great project.

The "hard notes" are the ones that are hard for the writer to read. Craig Cameron was asking me to go into the lion's den where I would be savaged and my work ripped to the bone.

Growing up in England, I was very aware of a strong filmmaking tradition in Canada. We were treated to good films, superb animation, and even a TV series that my whole family would watch on a Sunday tea time: *The Forest Rangers*. This program quite possibly planted the seeds of immigration without me knowing it. It's strange because Canadians I've spoken to since have never heard of it. I can even hum the theme tune.

In more recent years of course, there is *Due South*, which we all thought was a great piece of TV. It was some good feedback from actor/writer/director Paul Gross (*Due South*'s star and executive producer) on one of my scripts that planted later seeds of immigration to Canada.

One of my favourite films of all times is the Canadian film *The Last Winter*. I saw this in the UK and it cemented my opinion of Canadian films as having a high standard.

Imagine then, having given up everything and moved my family to Nova Scotia, and then establishing my own film and TV business in 2008, what it felt like to be surrounded by so many films with a common theme. Where was the gentle, understated humour? Where were the stories I had come to expect? It concerned me enough that the original plan to make scripted features was put on hold as we tried to see where we would fit in. That's why we shifted to documentaries and took some time to better understand what the industry here was about.

Everywhere, it seemed, were films about drugs or stoners. Or even when they weren't about them, there would be a casual reference to them. I sat in the audience at the Atlantic Film Festival with one of the investors in my company who had come from the UK to get a feel for how his investment was doing. We were treated to Atlantic Canada's top film, *Growing Op*. This was released shortly after *A Bug and a Bag of Weed*.

I could very well be wrong, and I have met the filmmakers behind both of those films and I like them a lot, but I have to question whether such films can expect to travel around the rest of the world where a cultural obsession with recreational drugs doesn't exist. It's clear such Canadian films as this had never reached audiences in the UK, or I would have had some idea before we came over.

As I write, Ashley MacKenzie's first feature, *Werewolf*, has rightly won her many accolades. It's a story about a couple who are addicted to methadone. I'm prepared to be hauled over hot coals for this, but I think there are far more and better stories to be told by Canadian filmmakers and that Canadian audiences deserve more variety.

The Only Game in Town takes place in our time. Yet I was adamant that the characters would not live their lives with cellphones stuck to their ears. That might make it seem odd as a contemporary setting for a teen romance film, but the reality is that even today there are many parts of rural Nova Scotia where a cellphone signal is a thing of fancy.

In the main though, I just wanted to show that playing such things as competitive solitaire and sorting through a jar of buttons might actually be reasonable ways of passing some empty minutes.

I was actually surprised that we ended up with three scenes in the film where modern technology was being used: Cormack playing PC solitaire in his bedroom; Crowley discovering through social media that Cormack belongs to his lost love, Cathy; and Rob, Joe, Chris, and Cormack actually playing a video game while they discuss dating strategies. I'm not sure I truly like any of these scenes and wish I could have written better ways to move the plot and characters along. I am pleased we managed to maintain the illusion that Midlothian and the characters operate in their own "world" by having Chris reliant for his calculations on a slide rule.

I have heard early criticisms about *The Only Game in Town,* that to many the film is "unrealistic." That because it creates its own "reality," it's "strange." In response, I say this: Nothing we point a camera at and then show to others is real. Even the most dedicated documentarian is not going to show us more than reality as they saw it through the lens. All filmmakers create the reality they need for their story.

The world of *Trainspotting* and all its gritty, urban realism is not real to me. The world of a stoner movie is not real to me. It's taken for granted we can show a world where drugs play an important role in people's lives. Yet to me, such a film has no relevance to my world and my experiences. To most, a film set in urban Scotland must show a world of drugs and violence to be considered "true" or "realistic," and yet in *Gregory's Girl* the hero attended a school in urban Scotland in the eighties devoid of gangs and any sense of aggression.

My point is that the notion that all stories must have a basis in a particular lexicon of "realities" is an imposition of a cultural framework; we are being told what our "social norms" are. That we only believe some stories to be "real" is at least a hindrance to creativity and at worst an attempt at social engineering through the media.

Some years later I was back in the cinema during the Atlantic Film Festival to see a film by another Canadian director, Deepa Mehta. *Midnight's Children* was a work of pure beauty and brilliance and remains one of my all-time favourite films. Canada has a rich history of quality films and a culturally diverse talent pool able to tell a wide range of stories. It was unfortunate for me that we arrived at a time when that wasn't being reflected in films.

But I was wary of getting a script consultant from Canada not only because of the "off-centre" way I'd built the world my characters inhabit and the British versus Canadian culture thing, but also because not long after moving to Nova Scotia, a professional script reader asked that I send him the script that almost got made in the UK: *In the Air at Whitby.*

The script for *In the Air at Whitby* is funny. There are no two ways around it. Everyone thinks so, and I hope one day someone will make it. But the Canadian script consultant believed it to be a "fantasy." That is what he called it. It's set in the world of amateur theatre in the UK. But he had never experienced it, so to him, the setting and the story and the characters were unreal to the point that he thought he was dealing with a fantasy comedy.

The story is full of characters that really existed and centres on events that really happened. Yes, folks, apparently even when I'm living in the real world, I'm in a fantasy! So I figured there was no hope whatsoever that my new script would be understood by anyone in Canada.

I would have to choose a script consultant carefully. So I thought about the type of comedy that pushed the boundaries of "real" settings and situations. I thought of things like the British sitcoms *The IT Crowd* and *Father Ted*, and that led me instantly to the great Irish writer and director Graham Linehan. In reaching out to him I was immediately pointed to the script consultant he uses, Andrew Ellard, based in London, England, and connected with him with some unease.

Now anyone who has ever required major surgery will tell you that when faced with something scary and terrible, the most important thing is to deal with a professional who knows his job completely. That's how it felt working with Andrew. He instantly put me at ease, gave me a lollipop to suck on, and took possession of my script.

December 2014 had been a strange month. I know this really is the writer's story, but writers often get rewrites during production, and this was going to be no exception. The need to get some scenes done so we could guarantee using some of the young people before they became too embroiled in their important final months of study, and to film in some settings that it appeared we could never get locations for, meant that we had two shoot days during December.

Everything seemed relaxed and I had filled myself with writing confidence, believing that Andrew would be able to do nothing to improve my script, which was all well and good as we scheduled the next weekend of filming for January.

On December 24, I received an email from Andrew that said, "Hi, Stuart. Apologies that this is coming in so close to Christmas. I'd recommend ignoring it until you've made the most of the festivities—even good notes aren't ones you want when you're having fun!"

Christmas Eve. Bah! Humbug!

So come on, what would you have done? That's right! So the night before Christmas, all through the house, everyone was making merry except Stuart who was reading twenty pages of hard notes. That's one page of notes for every five pages of script.

And yes, it did ruin my Christmas. And New Year. Why had he been so cruel?

So I left it alone and pretended I hadn't ignored his advice to leave it until after Christmas. I packed it away, tried to focus on festivities and fun, and then came back to it in the new year as Andrew had suggested.

I sat with the notes open, scribbling solutions and changes on the pages of my script. And you know what? It all made sense. Andrew hadn't savaged my work, he had saved it.

The rewrite fleshed out some of the supporting characters, corrected some of the plot issues, made it easier for the audience to follow. I will always be indebted to Andrew, who gave the right amount of criticism and encouragement. But most of all, he knew exactly the questions that I as the writer needed to have asked. In finding the answers to those questions, I would be improving the work greatly.

No Writers, Only Rewriters

My problem, and one I imagine I share with most writers, is that I could rewrite forever. At least once the film gets made, there is a natural place to stop.

Launching in to the work spawned by Andrew's notes of genius, it was clear these rewrites felt different. There was purpose to them. Everything felt different. I wasn't rewriting because of the usual habit of perpetual tinkering that usually takes hold. These were rewrites with purpose.

No one loves a big head, but I am convinced that if I had sent the script to contests at this point, I may well have a few trophies in the cabinet. I fell in love with my script all over again. Trust me, if it was awful, I would say so. Here, now, in the middle of winter and in the middle of a spell of shooting several scenes that we needed to get in the can, there was a script that had come to life.

I had geared much of the writing to the young cast members and had determined to stay loyal to those young people who had thrown themselves into the project from the start, giving me so much inspiration. Several scenes existed just because I wanted those young people to have their day in front of the camera. That was how it was going to be. The plan was to spend an afternoon shooting this scene there, a morning here, until we could bring in the adult cast and "knock off" the rest of the film in a week. However, due to rewrites, the January shoot days were cancelled.

To say I was pleased with the revised script is an understatement. I have written nothing else since *In the Air at Whitby* in 1996 that seemed so easy to write and was so full of funny, charming characters that you just want to see more of. Some scenes, on the page, stood out for laughs. Tommy, the deaf, dumb, and blind solitaire champ had me in stitches. And not just me. Andrew's notes are a great way to see how he reacted when reading it.

You can see where he reads page 48 and doesn't like it, doesn't get what's happening, and then, when the pay-off happens on page 50 it all changes:

- Page 48: So we go from a fairly natural, human, real-world chat between Cormack and his mates about his condition, then to the '80s teen movie bully-and-hot-girl set-up, and then to a deaf-dumb-blind gaming prodigy named Tommy—a real *Dodgeball* kinda gag. I really hope it's clear that each of these forms can work, but that your mixture of them creates "bumps"—I'm knocked out of the film each time we hop genres like this. You can, absolutely, jam genres together, but they need to feel cohesive.
- Page 50: I *love* the Tommy stuff!! That his teammates only pretend he can play and let him think he's won is *glorious*. It feels totally cohesive—human and daft at once. A school that's elected to maintain a big lie to make a kid feel good. A mascot. I grasp the backstory, every day before this one, without much explanation.

The sad thing for me—as the writer, and also ultimately as the director—is that the scene we filmed seemed to me a shallow, half attempt at the big vision. It was about the scale of the setting and the overall feel. It's not bad, but it falls way short of the vision I had. And when it was such a funny scene, I feel a little down about it.

The same is true of the two-page monologue for Principal Joyce. No one does long monologues in film anymore, but I wanted to write something that an actor, any actor, would read and know they wanted that part; a monologue like that can live on beyond the film. I really enjoyed writing that scene, but again, the reality is that in the film, due to setting and the manic shooting schedule (more on that later), we only get to about 90 percent of where it should be.

I also really loved writing the Magda Goebbels flashbacks. They're an "on the edge" type of writing. There is an element of bad taste about them, which I actually really like. While writing the first draft of the script, I had discovered that Magda Goebbels, the wife of Josef Goebbels, Hitler's propaganda chief, was possibly the world's most infamous solitaire player (or patience as they call it in Europe). The story goes that in the final days of the war, when Hitler and Goebbels and others were trapped in their bunker in Berlin as the Red Army closed in, the leaders of the Nazis decided to take their own lives before they were captured. The Goebbels family were desperate that their children should not fall into the hands of the Russians, who would subject them to all sorts of horrors. So Magda drugged her children and then poisoned them. She returned to her room in the bunker and played solitaire before she and her husband also committed suicide.

To go there, to that time in the bunker, for me as a parent and the world's worst self-censor (remember, I was suspended from school for publishing a school magazine that crossed certain boundaries), gave me concerns. Still, I needed to show that competitive solitaire was a thing with a history, and she was the best way for me to do that. I brought the time of the scene forward to 1944, so it wasn't actually that fateful day with all the horrific realities of it. I gave her lines to speak, however, that audiences will know refer to those later events. Too far?

I asked Cory very early on if it was too much, too risky. He thought not. So I kept it in. It was clear that the actress needed to be spot on with the comedic elements or they could end up being just random pieces of sick humour. Josephine, my wife, happens to be one of the finest comedy actresses I've ever worked with, so when we came to reshoot those scenes in post-production, I managed to persuade her to end her thirty-year retirement from acting to bring Magda to life.

Speaking of characters, there are a number of them I particularly loved when writing. Joe, obviously, is the stupid and funny one, equipped with great one-liners. Natasha was originally a one-scene part, written to give one of the young people from the workshops some screen time. Andrew Ellard noted that she was a great character, and so she became much more prominent. But then we were desperate to find someone right for the part. We were blessed to find Breanna Roy.

Principal Joyce remains one of my favourite characters. He's a blend of old headmasters from my own school days and the headmaster from Alan Bennett's *Forty Years On* plus a few smidgens of many other people we see today wading unsuccessfully through the minefield of political correctness and modern-day liberal thought.

But it's all about Cormack and his friends. For all the scenes that fall short in the final film, there are others where the writing and acting come together to show a troubled boy and the strong bond between him and his friends. That is success enough. Or is it?

I felt from the start that there was more to say about the forty-plus characters I created, most of whom only get a few minutes to hint at their complex personal stories. Could there be a sequel to *The Only Game in Town*? Possibly, but obviously we'll have to wait for the film industry to be on the brink of collapse again before we consider tackling that!

The potential for a sitcom—either a TV or web series—has always been there, and as I write this there are very developed plans and even some scripts for thirty-minute episodes that see Cormack battle entropy to put things right, just as he puts the cards in order when he plays solitaire. Watch this space, or the web, for *The Only Sitcom in Town*....

We're coming to the end of The Writer's Tale. If this film had been made by another producer, this would be the end of the book.

So tell me. What do you, dear reader, want from this book?

If you want this book to be a "how to" guide for writing a film script, here are a few tips, in no particular order:

- Write, write, and rewrite.
- Never be satisfied with the end result.
- Find the actors who will play your key characters and work with them if you can—the relationship between writer and actors became very strong during our workshop process.
- Get the best script consultant possible. Don't do it on the cheap.
- Be brave and stick to your guns, but be flexible enough to hear the sound advice and take the hard notes.
- Use proper writing software such as Final Draft.
- Don't be afraid to send your feature script to producers.

If you want this book to be an insight into the hell of making a film—anywhere, but particularly in Nova Scotia in 2015—then read on.

If you want this book to be a murder mystery, you've made a huge mistake buying it.

If you want it to be *Fifty Shades of Grey Hairs* you should read the next part—the stress is enough to turn anyone's hair grey.

PART TWO

THE PRODUCER'S STORY

GETTING OFF THE GROUND

So what is a producer and when did I first become one?

The producer is the first one on to a project and the last one off. You possibly never really get "off" a project. Long after completion there will still be forms to fill in, especially in a country such as Canada with a tightly regulated industry, where the government and its agencies are heavily involved. I produced a feature documentary for the BBC in 2012; five years later there is still work to be done here and there. I have to say that for most producers who haven't yet had that big financial success, the hourly rate is in the single cents. There is more work than fee, but with each project, you hope that it makes enough to give you time to work on the next potential box-office smash.

The producer runs the project. There may be more than one producer, each bringing something to the table: financing, connections to talent, expertise, facilities. The producer is the person who "owns" the script. He has either paid for the rights to it, or an option, or—because he happens to be the writer—it simply belongs to him.

A writer may end up being a producer on a project. Many years ago I wrote a children's feature film. I hoped I'd be able to produce it myself, but when I shopped it around, the best I was offered was a notional producer credit. My ego wasn't satisfied with that, and I walked out of the production company's plush offices determined to do it my way. I could have boosted my career by about ten years if I had accepted that at that point in my life "written by" and "associate producer" were both decent achievements. Yes, you need to be stubborn as a producer, but you also have to pick your fights.

The producer finds the funding, hires the director, engages staff and crew, builds the team, and makes all the pieces slot together. I became a producer almost by accident.

You already know that I wanted to direct, to tell the story the way I wanted to. For fourteen years, since leaving college, I had worked in theatre, honing my directing skills. But I had also been producing many of the shows and tours that my companies went on.

Theatre-in-education tours didn't really have huge budgets or demand much in the way of financing, but the basics of planning, team building, promoting, and scheduling different elements and different locations were all aspects of producing that—by virtue of no one else wanting to do it—fell to me. I thought, in the early 1990s, that my rudimentary knowledge from the world of theatre producing was sufficient to transfer to the film world.

It soon became obvious I was completely out of my depth as I touted my children's feature film script around the country, hoping someone would trust me with the budget to do it. I was learning as I went along, cutting my teeth by dealing with top international agents and lawyers in New York to secure, at no little expense, the rights to the book the script was based on.

I signed up for courses through the Independent Film Workshop, back before they evolved into the fabulous Raindance Organization. (Seriously, if you have designs on being a producer you should join Raindance. They are a truly international set-up and provide all sorts of helpful stuff, training courses, and of course the fantastic Raindance Film Festival.) I joined the New Producer's Alliance. I Studied Producer's Alliance for Cinema and TV (PACT) agreements. I networked. I attended one of the Dov Simens 2-day Film Schools—the same school that taught Quentin Tarantino and launched so many filmmaking careers. Integral to these courses are the live pitching sessions and weekend workshops on how to get your hands on money to make a film. I rubbed shoulders with the rich and famous (or at least those wanting to be). I did learn, though, that producing films would be unlike producing theatre, in just about every way.

Still, I was learning. And the first thing I learned was to swallow my pride. I wasn't going to do this on my own, and certainly not a first feature. In essence, your next project can only be as big as the money you can raise. If that is fifty dollars, then that is what you spend on your project. There is no point dreaming about a ten million dollar budget if you have three hundred dollars in the bank and need to put food on the table for ten screaming kids and several women who rely on you. (That wasn't me by the way, but you get my meaning.)

As the script I had was a children's film, I felt that I needed some specific guidance regarding that particular genre. That's not to say I didn't have a handle on entertaining children. Much of my theatre work for more than a decade, by this time, had been with and for young people. One of my last stage roles as an actor was as Baloo the bear in a stage adaptation of *The Jungle Book*. Keeping a theatre full of small children engaged for two hours is no small feat. (Having a huge, cuddly bear costume helps.)

Since the 1950s, there had been in the UK an organization that fostered family feature films. The Children's Film and Television Foundation had a long and highly respected track record of helping to finance and produce films for the most demanding market. I contacted them and sent my script. I got some good feedback from them and even got to speak to executive Grainne Marmion, who at the time was also at Red Rooster Productions, where she was producing the hit film *Martha, Meet Frank, Daniel and Laurence*. There was a long conversation about the merits of the script, and a phrase was used that has been applied to many of my plays and film scripts: "Funny, light, charming." As a writer I took the phrase as a compliment, but as a producer what you want to hear is: "Funny, ground-breaking, box-office smash."

Next I was heading up to Newcastle, for a meeting in the BBC offices of Tony Baker, a top TV presenter and producer of many hours of film and television. He'd put a call out for family films, and I thought mine should fit the bill. He liked it and I drove north the entire morning for a chat with him. We seemed to be on the same page, but it didn't quite fit the bill for what he was looking for. I started to attach some names and spoke to the agents for John Leslie, Billy Connolly, and others.

I'll end that story here, as all you need to know is that over the course of the next few years I learned about the way the industry worked in the UK, made some good contacts, improved the script, and dealt with agents and lawyers on two continents. It cost me a lot of money, but really, there are no courses that teach those things, and at some point you have to pay for your education. That's the way I looked at it. That script has long been gathering dust in a dark place, and all that is left as a reminder of those far-off days is the name of my company, which alludes to the title of that children's book that started it all.

I learned that a producer really can't have just one project to work on. A producer needs several projects, all at different stages, to enable him to keep working. The alternative, and in those early days this applied to me, is that you are doing it in your spare time. You are a part-time producer, or an unpaid one.

There comes a point when a part-time producer can no longer cope with the workload and either has to give up on some of the projects or take that plunge and become full-time, and bugger the consequences.

It's a tough decision to take. You would have to be very brave to take that leap with small children living at home and a mortgage and all the rest. It would certainly need to be supported by some success with one or more projects that at least proves there's a viable income to be had. But essentially you are giving up regular paid income and security for a life of long periods without fees and a much reduced standard of living.

I spent the years from 1995 to 1999 pushing a number of scripts at broadcasters and production companies, without much success, but I was able to do so because I left full-time work and established my own media training company. Now at least there was someone providing training courses in producing: me! I ran courses and services through a number of colleges and travelled the country for the Open College Network.

Even when I was "working," I was making film contacts and expanding my own learning. For instance, I provided college accreditation services on national media courses, and it was while doing that in Quorn in Leicestershire that I came across a young man called Paul Allen, a very talented filmmaker who has since worked on a number of projects with me.

Every month it seemed I was learning more, taking bigger steps, meeting key people. In short, working for myself bought me the time and flexibility I needed to run off to meetings whenever necessary or go off on a low-budget shoot somewhere.

I co-produced a couple of ultra-low-budget films and worked on live and recorded TV for a cable channel in Leicester. There was also at that time an active film community in Leicester, and the LineOut Centre had cameras and edit suites. Similar co-op organizations exist here in Nova Scotia, enabling people to cut their teeth on projects and get support and equipment when they need it.

In 1996, while pushing *In the Air at Whitby* closer to production, I made some trips to the Central England Screen Commission and got on really well with the commissioner Phil Nodding. Phil is another of those all-round good guys in the industry, and he gave me a few projects to do for the Commission—mainly to keep me out of his office, I think. I was happy to do anything to help boost film and television productions in the region, one blessed with great locations such as the Great Central Railway and scores of historic buildings.

Phil later went on to do his master's in screenwriting and is now a lecturer in screenwriting and production planning at Nottingham Trent University. He won a Royal Television Society award for writing an episode of *Shameless* in 2006 and has a growing list of screen and radio credits. I hope I'm not wrong when I say Phil always seemed to enjoy *In the Air at Whitby,* and I have high hopes that he will be part of the team that turns *The Only Game in Town* into a sitcom.

Through Phil, my work at the Screen Commission, and pushing *In the Air at Whitby*, I met other people who have in one way or another supported my work or inspired me. Mark Herbert was Phil's counterpart at Screen Yorkshire and was helpful in planning the production of *In the Air at Whitby*. Mark now runs WarpX and is a highly respected producer.

Top director Shane Meadows used to bounce around Intermedia and the Broadway Cinema in Nottingham, full of intensity and drive to get his films made. It made me question my own drive and just how much I wanted to make the film. (The answer comes later.)

In short, I was working in the East Midlands at a time when the film and TV industry, and some of its key talents, were all finding their feet. This was a huge shift away from London as the only centre of filmmaking in the UK. In Nottingham and Leicester in particular were enough creative individuals to make the East Midlands region a vibrant filmmaking community.

In 1995, as part of the New Producer's Alliance, I was invited to a cast and crew premiere screening of Vadim Jean's *Clockwork Mice* in Leicester Square. It was the first time I'd been to a major cinema event, with all the glitz and glamour of a West End premiere. The film, made for a modest budget, took around £70,000 (around $150,000 in those days) at the UK box office and had a clear financial plan geared around a festival release to win awards, which increased sales to TV around the world. It was an example of a film made in Britain to fit the small screen. There is nothing wrong with that approach. The film included in the cast some household names of British comedy and light drama: John Alderton, James Bolam, Art Malik, and the great Ian Hart.

The film was produced by Paul Brooks and Metrodome Pictures. I met Paul briefly and there was the customary email exchange afterwards, which went nowhere. But I had decided that if I was serious about producing, then I needed to benchmark my career against producers such as Paul. Check him out!

The man has produced more than fifty films since 1992, with just short of another twenty in production or development right now. Paul is nothing if not prolific. You will also know many of his films, not least being *My Big Fat Greek Wedding*.

The course I ran was called The Producer's CV and was delivered through various learning centres in the UK. At its core was the notion that producers need to be a certain type of person to succeed, not really a student of one area of practice or another.

Essentially, if you want to be a producer, ask yourself these questions: Can I live without a regular income? Can I budget all aspects of my life—business, social, family—over long periods? Do I take risks? Do I like to sleep? Do I have lots of external demands on my time? Am I happy with the fruits of my labour putting others in the limelight? Do I panic?

Benchmarking against someone whose career you admire is essential in any line of work. But so too is recognizing your own shortcomings. I am a risk taker. Too much so. In business I need to have partners who can rein me in from time to time.

A producer needs to have elements of the shameless self-promoter about him; he needs to be Barnum and yet at the same time he cannot believe his own spin. He needs to be ambitious yet realistic. A producer may need to be ruthless; I am far from that and hope that in the long run I can just about avoid the sharks in the lions' den (to quote Joe in the film).

So how did I become a producer?

It became clear that not only was I capable of doing the job, my personality was almost precisely what was required. I had cut my teeth on stage plays and tours, ultra-low-budget films and local TV, I had studied with textbooks and workshops and training courses, I had heard from the people making films about the process and the business, I had practised by producing short films, and I had observed successful people in the industry in order to glean nature and habit.

I had also found a good project to work on and negotiated rights with teams of New York lawyers. I felt that I was truly ready for anything.

Keep Going: 1996

People need to understand a little about the film industry and how it is a huge undertaking to get the juggernaut that is a production off the ground. You can go for years and never get the cameras rolling, but once you start you just have to keep going.

That is important to remember: "Once you start, you have to keep going." Let's say you start shooting your film, maybe 10 percent of it. That's 10 percent of the budget, so on a $2 million film, that's $200,000. But it won't be the first 10 percent of the film. It will be scenes from here and there that have no chance of showing a cohesive story as they are. No one shoots a one-hundred-page script with the first twenty pages (okay, someone will do it, but really, it's highly unlikely).

Imagine your script, neatly typed and correctly formatted. Each page is roughly equal to one minute of the finished film. The script is made up of scenes, and the scenes take place in one location or another. Scenes themselves are broken down into shots, but to save time and money, when you shoot the film, you want to shoot all the scenes at one location in one go—even if in the film they take place on different days.

The whole thing gets more complicated during scheduling, when not only do you have to figure out when you can use a particular location, but also when you will have the right actors available. I was as committed to using the young people who had thrown themselves into the film as I was in getting access to a particular location. Scheduling was easily my biggest headache right from the start.

Still, in theory, moving through your locations to shoot scenes in that way inevitably means you can have been in production for five days and have little more than random snippets of the film.

To stop production of that film is essentially saying goodbye to $200,000. You have nothing of any value that you can use to recoup what you have spent.

So you will not stop once you have started. Which is why, when you "greenlight" the film, you must be certain. The finger poised over the trigger must be true. Squeeze it too soon and you could be facing financial ruin. (Remember this, please, for what comes later.)

When trying to understand the how and the why of *The Only Game in Town*, this next part of the producer's story is critical.

In 1996, I was about to start shooting my comedy script *In the Air at Whitby*. It had a huge cast, different settings, and locations around the East Midlands and North Yorkshire coast. I'd pulled together the contacts I needed, got some very talented people behind it, and built up the self-belief necessary to power through.

Colin Vearncombe, the velvet-voiced singer-songwriter of hits such as "Wonderful Life," became more than the writer of a theme song for the film. He had fallen in love with the script; he told me he'd been on the verge of kicking the business until he read the script and was in hysterics and was inspired to write the song "Famous" for it.

Phil Nodding, who went on to win awards for his own writing, had helped with locations and had made connections for me to Mark Herbert at Screen Yorkshire. I had a cast full of young talents from the world of amateur and professional theatre.

My finger was placed on the trigger and we were inching closer to the moment of truth. The financing would have been tight. It would have been shot with deferred payments and calling in every favour I had, everywhere. Equipment would have been begged and borrowed and stolen. Much of it would have been shot "guerrilla style." As Wikipedia explains, "Guerrilla filmmaking refers to a form of independent filmmaking characterized by low budgets, skeleton crews, and simple props using whatever is available. Often scenes are shot quickly in real locations without any warning, and without obtaining filming permits."

There is a danger to such an approach. I knew this from experience.

A few years earlier I was part of the team that put together a post-apocalyptic zombie film, well before such things became the mainstream success that they are today. We shot it guerilla-style, filming on disused rail tracks outside Leicester and even in a back street just off the main drag.

In those days I was still young and handsome enough to be the young and handsome lead. For one scene I was to be hit by a speeding car. There was no cordon at the end of the road, and the safety officer and stunt coordinator were...well, I don't think they were ever employed.

So with cameras rolling...no wait! With the *camera* rolling, the plan was to have me stagger into the road, look up to see a car driving toward me, and the car would stop—hopefully before it hit me—and we would dress a dummy in my clothes, have the car speed down the road again, and throw the dummy at the windshield. In the edit, no one would know the difference between me and the dummy. (So successful was this, that the dummy has been living as me ever since, while I sat in a box, waiting to be thrown off a cliff or trampled under galloping horses.)

So, the plan was to throw a dummy onto the car and make it look like me. The first car I stepped in front of wasn't our car and narrowly avoided wrapping me around his wheels. The driver leapt from the vehicle and prepared to beat me to a pulp for making him avoid running me over. There's a sort of urban logic there somewhere. I was quick to point at the camera, because of course, if we have cameras there then the world is all right and it excuses all sorts of behaviour. He agreed and went on his way.

When the real car came, we discovered the vehicle had failed its motor vehicle inspection a few months back and the brakes were shot. For the next four takes, the car sped at me unable to come to a halt on the chalk line that denoted its mark and the point beyond which I had to leap for my life.

Eventually, the driver was told to drive slow enough that he could stop in the correct place—"We can speed it up in post." All that was needed now was for me to take off my jet pilot's jumpsuit and put the dummy in it.

No one had told me about this bit. So I'm in a back street in Leicester in my underpants while my clothes are on a jumped-up Guy Fawkes effigy. You don't need me to tell you my life could have been very different if the wrong person had walked around the corner.

Still, the dummy did the job and I'm happy to say that my character, despite being hit so hard that last week's newspapers came out of him, survived to tackle a host of brain-eating undead on the outskirts of Leicester.

Guerrilla-style filmmaking is not for the faint-hearted; you can run into trouble. I guess if you have no money you can't be sued, but I'm a stickler for rules and would always prefer to get permission. In my opinion, if you need a particular location but can't afford to pay for it, it's better to ask them politely. Tell them your film is unfunded—even lie through your teeth and tell them it's art—but most people will try to help. (This may not be quite true nowadays; many public buildings are so scared of being sued themselves that insurance policies for filming on many sites are prohibitive for the broke filmmaker.)

So, back to 1996 and *In the Air at Whitby*, a low-budget film but, as usual, one with big ambitions. Not least of which is evident in the sequence where the main character has his "road to Damascus" moment and cures his fear of flying while taking control of his life. This takes place with him wing-walking on a biplane—virtually impossible for a budget of this nature, but we found the team of the Crunchie Flying Circus to be great sports. We wouldn't have to force our lead actor onto the wings of a high-flying acrobatic plane, nor would we have to strap a dummy to the wings and film him as his straw and magazine insides departed through the gaps in his ill-made costume. No, the wonderful people at the Crunchie Flying Circus, including the suitably named professional wing-walker Helen Tempest and her partner, Tanya Gaze, would be in the film in the long shots and the aerial sequences high above the ground, and we would film our lead actor, Chris Batten, from the ground in close-up for his facial reactions. "It will all come good in post!"

So *In the Air at Whitby*, a comic tale based on a true story and set all over the East Midlands and North Yorkshire, was about to be greenlit. The point of no return was upon us.

At that moment, a producer far more experienced than I read the script. It had him in stitches. "I read it on the train; I was laughing so much people must have thought I was mad!"

Others read it, and suddenly there was an option on the table and the chance to make *In the Air at Whitby* for a real budget, to give it the production values it needed. The target moved, my finger hesitated on the trigger, and the moment was gone.

When you halt a project that is about to go to camera, you let down all those who have worked with you to get the film to the brink of production. And there were many. In the cold light of day, you feel the sadness. You missed your chance. I was prepared to take the risk, but when I saw that someone else was willing to steer the barrel over Niagara Falls, I was happy for them to roll with it.

As so often happens, the option deal came and went and the time for doing the film melted away. It comes up every now and then, but it was of its time, and all those whom I would still want to be in the film are twenty years older and no longer right for the characters in the story. I lost my one and only chance to make my film.

I sat with Colin Vearncombe at his home in Schull, Ireland, in 2010. "What happened to *In the Air at Whitby*?" he asked.

I felt ashamed. The script had inspired him to get back to writing in the mid-1990s and, against his manager's better (and correct) judgment, he had given it time and joined in for the ride. He would have been in the film, in a bandstand in Nottingham performing a version of Scott Walker's "Make it Easy on Yourself."

"I don't know…nothing," I said, hiding my eyes from those piercing blue ones that would fix you and search you for—and find—the bits that made you a good person, no matter how small. "I think the moment has passed for it. But you never know. I'd like to think I could still make it." I was faking hope.

"You should!" he said. And that was it. I should make it. I should have made it. Dragging a film around that you almost made is a great burden. It's the worst feeling a producer can have.

The pivotal point in my producing story was 1996. I shall never again be knocked off course. From now on, whatever the film I start to make, I will finish it!

8

SCI-FI, COMICS, AND SHOPPING TELLY

So my first two forays into what I would consider "true" producing—that is, being the chap who is on right from the start, it's totally my baby, building the team, getting everything done—had ended in the long, slow death of a failed film. It's true that no experience is completely without value, and I had learned plenty and made some great contacts in the business, but there was nothing to show for three years pushing and shoving treacle up a hill.

Well, not nothing. The children's film left me with the name of my film company—Simple Films—and *In the Air at Whitby* gave me confidence in my stories and planning. I would just have to get up and go again.

I also recognized that it could never be just me. I had many of the qualities needed to produce a film, but not all of them. There needed to be a wiser business head in there somewhere. So I turned to my best friend and former drama class partner, Phil Marriott. Here was someone who knew numbers and business, but he also had that sense of humour that could see both of us break into fits of laughter like school kids. Anywhere.

I went back to basics. Short films. Corporate films. Things were going well; I still had my training courses and a self-employed lifestyle that gave me the flexibility I needed. I had also ventured into the world of publishing and produced "pamphlets" here and there. Then I had an idea for a sci-fi film that I needed to flesh out.

I began talking to artists, and the concept for my sci-fi comic *Cyborg Warriors* was born. I also devised a TV game show version, something along the lines of *Gladiators* with teams and sci-fi settings.

We did a lot of work devising the TV show and it attracted one of the top companies in London. There were long discussions about it, and then after about a year all went quiet. Two years later, a TV game show was aired that was clearly ours. The company that produced it was run by a chap who had been at the original production company we were talking to at the time but had since left.

As a producer trying to break into the industry, there is little one can do about such things. To kick up a fuss could mark you out as a troublemaker. Who would want to see any of your ideas if you went around suing people? Hiring an entertainment lawyer to fire off a warning letter would have cost more than I could afford. (Please note: This is why so many production companies have on their board a lawyer, someone who is able to run off letters like that as part of his or her stake in the company.)

Watching something on TV that was so clearly your idea and so clearly stolen is a real kick in the teeth. The whole reason I had gone down the road of comics, trading card games, TV shows, and films was to show that our idea came first and there could be no arguing about it.

Cyborg Warriors broke me financially too. In the days before on-demand printing, the costs of producing colour comics was massively high. I'm never the sort to balk at such things as cost—and anyway, the plan was sound. Great artists, great stories, and the security that we'd protected our copyright by publishing the comic.

The bright future that we felt we were embarking on was heralded by the Year 2000 rockets we sent flying over Lochcarron in the Scottish Highlands. This was our family's favourite place on earth—a cottage at the end of a narrow trail on the side of a Scottish loch surrounded by mountains. Where else should we spend New Year's Eve at the turn of the millennium? It seemed like a fantastic idea: the four of us—Josephine, Oliver, Charley, and I—each had a huge firework sky rocket, on which was our wish for the coming year and century.

I'm pretty sure that back then, not one of us had even the slightest dream that we would be emigrating to Canada. My wish was for happiness, health, world peace, success in the film and TV industry, and for *Cyborg Warriors* to make me a millionaire.

I wasn't to know it then, but the dream lasted barely longer than the trail of sparks that scattered over the icy water.

By the time we returned home—five hundred miles in a rental car with our own car following on a tow truck after its brakes failed coming down the Bealach na Ba (has anybody else had a five-hundred-mile breakdown tow?)—the promise of the year 2000 was fading fast.

The *Cyborg Warriors* comics had failed to sell in the vast numbers required. We would soon find out the TV show had been stolen. The contract I had with a magazine publisher was about to end in acrimony. Work was in short supply. Money even shorter.

For those of you that don't know, Shepshed sits in the heart of England, about as far from the sea as you can get in any direction. Heading north or south is easy in England. But if you want to head across country it's a different story. Peterborough is about eighty miles east of Shepshed. There are many different routes to take, but none of them are quick or easy. Some are downright dangerous.

Despite this, when I saw a full-time job advertised with a new TV channel in Peterborough, I put my suit on and headed east. What I found was a building site on a sprawling industrial estate on the outskirts of Peterborough. The channel was due to launch in a month, and the studio hadn't even been built. I met the head of broadcast, Mark Thatcher (not the son of the former prime minister), who somehow was managing to stay calm. I wasn't what he wanted, but he was desperate and time was short. There was so much to be done and very few people to do it. Most of the "real" professionals would only be turning up after launch, in case the station never made it.

Mark is one of the top guys in the world for what we would call "direct response TV," which on the face of it could be called shopping telly. He established the first QVC channel outside the US. QVC are the undoubted big boys of shopping channels, but with Ideal World TV, Mark had a bigger vision. Ideal World grew out of the mail-order business Shopping Direct, but Mark wanted the station to blur the lines between entertainment and selling. He wanted to sell things that no other shopping channel—and certainly not QVC—would think of selling (or be able to sell). I remember selling a fragment of Apollo 17 and some moon rock in a presentation case.

I like Mark Thatcher immensely and am forever grateful he took a chance on me and put me in a place where I could learn and run with some ideas.

But that would be later. Right now, in the middle of a work environment that more closely resembled an assault course through a warzone than studio and office space, this new channel with plans for 24-hour broadcasting (and selling) needed a schedule of programs and a warehouse full of products to sell.

We launched on time. Sold an Audi TT, which was and may still be the most expensive single item ever sold on UK shopping channels. They were exciting days, and the on-screen talent was full of the industry's big hitters: Paul Lavers, Debbie Flint, Steve Whatley (sadly no longer with us), Ellis Ward, Gary Ashburn, Shaun Ryan.

There was some great talent off-screen too, with a crop of young producers and directors. Most of that early team I am still connected to—all have moved on, but we all share the memories of some months of madness in the Eastern Industry, the sprawling industrial zone on the outskirts of Peterborough. I'm sure all of them will agree, though, that Mark deserves huge respect for driving this project through. Many questioned his sanity, everyone questioned his colour choice for suits, but no one could question the energy, vision, and skill required to pull it off.

I was allowed to film some promos and develop an idea by which we could use the facilities to train young people. But mainly I was planning and scheduling programs about *Pokémon, Star Trek, Star Wars*...basically everything I was interested in. I developed program slots that sold art, collectibles, music, and all sorts of strange one-off objects.

In my spare time I continued to make short films and write, but spare time was hard to come by. Travel to and from work took three hours a day, if I was lucky. There was an attitude from the station owners that essentially frowned on leaving the studio. "Why on earth should you want to go home? This is a 24-hour station!"

Sometimes I would leave so late it wasn't worth going home, and I discovered a nearby hotel that was super cheap and basic; I had no idea such things existed. But when all you needed was somewhere to lie down and then shower in the morning, it had to do.

I wasn't one of the young up-and-coming producers at the station. I'd already upped and come and was by no means young anymore, so the desire to burn myself out had long been burnt out. I had a wife and two children and a home that I loved. I needed to be there.

I came home late one night and slipped into bed just to feel my sheets around me. I left in the morning before anyone was awake. As I opened the car door I looked up to my son's bedroom window to see him standing at the window with a sad look on his face, waving at me weakly.

Something needed to change. But I wasn't sure what. Mark had suggested that we would have to move closer to Peterborough. That didn't seem like an option.

I tried different routes to and from work. One day, while driving along a winding road, I came across a view that chilled me to the bone. Two grain silos stood ominously in a field somewhere between Melton Mowbray and the A1. A voice inside me whispered, "This is where you die."

Brushing it off, I continued to work but made sure I didn't take that route again. Until one cold night in November, leaving work late to find the traffic was snarled up in all directions, I slipped off the A1 and headed home toward Melton. Ahead of me I could see emergency vehicles under the dark outline of the silos. My heart skipped and then relief came over me. The diversion signs placed after the earlier accident skirted me around the silos, and I made my painfully long way back home.

The next morning, confident that I had cheated death by being a few minutes late to whatever accident had happened, I drove to work. Winding down a country lane, ahead of me a car inched out of a junction from a dirt road. I eased off and waited to see what he would do. He stayed put so I accelerated again. When he shot forward, there was nothing I could do to avoid him. He hit me side on and threw my car over the road, into a telegraph pole, and then into the path of an oncoming car before I ran right off the road, into a ditch and upside down.

Just around the bend the two silos watched as I hauled myself from the car, disoriented and having expected to die at so many moments during the crash. I collapsed on the ground. The driver of the car I nearly hit, who I later found out was a guy called Donald Sang, walked over. "I didn't think I'd see you get out of that one!"

The driver who hit me walked over, saw I wasn't dead, and walked back to his car to drive off. Donald prevented the driver from leaving until the police had come, and stayed with me until I was confirmed okay and taken home.

Things became bad after the crash. My body had been tensed for impact and thrown all over the place. I was lucky nothing was broken, but by the time I got home I was struggling to move. But that wasn't the worst of it. I was reliving the incident over and over, wondering how I survived a crash that completely wrote off the car. I missed a head-on impact with the telegraph pole at 65 mph by inches. I missed running head on into Donald by inches and thanks to his own quick reactions. I missed being impaled on a fence post by inches.

It took a long time for the physical pain to leave me. But it took longer for the emotional trauma to go. I was the worst car passenger in the world. And I couldn't drive for myself.

I lost the job at Ideal World and had to think of doing something else. Something else that wouldn't require driving. I ended up running the marketing for a scientific equipment manufacturer within walking distance from home, the best job I've ever had and the finest company and people I've worked for.

I made a pledge that there would be no more producing. I was true to that pledge for about three months, until two of my former students from the Open College film course knocked on my door and asked for help producing a short film. *The Trumpeteer* was so enjoyable I toyed with the idea that I could do more.

All this time, Phil had humoured me despite our company making no headway, not least because neither of us had the time.

This is important. For any young, aspiring film producer, this is the bit no one tells you. I have been in the position myself, working a nine-to-five job, looking after a home and a family, trying to find some time in between to do my own stuff. It takes a great deal of selfishness to indulge your desire to fill whatever spare time you have with the TV and film things you are driven to do.

Looking back, it was grossly unfair of me, and I have to admit in later years I've often wondered if I should have given that time to friends and family.

I have also been the owner of a company (several in fact) that has secured private investment. The money was incidental to the plan, because what any small company needs is hours. Unless the investment is huge enough to pay the salaries of some permanent staff for a year to get things moving, what you hope for—and what I wanted from the shareholders—is their time and energy.

Producing anything is a long and thankless task. The lawyer involved in establishing Simple Films way back in 1997 said to me, "Let's hope you have a good business, because otherwise it's an expensive hobby!"

Having a team of shareholders, directors, or partners that are as keen and energetic as you are to get things moving is vital. In fact, you can do it without the money if you have a big enough team and wide enough range of skills within it.

I asked of my financial partners that they spare me a few hours a week. If each of the four of them put in five hours and I found twenty hours a week myself (I never need much sleep!), we'd have forty person-hours a week—the equivalent of a full-time person pushing the company forward.

It never happens like that. Everyone is busy. No one has spare time. It's a shame, because people can miss out on the fun and exciting and eventually profitable parts of the producing journey. In the end though, it's all about work-life balance and what is ultimately important to you. For me, producing—or simply pushing a project until it either grinds to a halt or it gets made—was a force in me that I could never ignore.

There is another side to the same coin: when you produce a film and effectively get in the business of buying other people's time and skills, the question of how much time becomes as big an issue as how much skill and talent (and experience).

One way this can impact on your film might be the need to secure certain cast or crew; you need to make sure they blot out any other commitments during the period you need them. This again requires that you have a fixed schedule. For *The Only Game in Town* it was not only impossible for me to demand exclusivity of people's services, but it was also unfair. Asking people to keep three months or more free from everything else just so they would be available those few days when we managed to get everything else in place was something I wasn't going to do. I just had to accept that the difficulties of scheduling were not going to get any easier.

Buying someone's time on an exclusive basis costs more money, as I found out much later on, when the film began to struggle for cash. If you can't pay for exclusive services, then everything slows down.

Advice for any aspiring young producer? If producing is what you really want to do, you have to find a way to grab back more and more of your time, which means giving up more and more of the regular income (and please see the previously stated requirements for a producer). You will need to rely on less income, and less frequent income. If that isn't for you, then do not try to be a producer.

So it was that for several years, Phil and I battled through on no time and no money trying to make things stick. The little money I had had been put into protecting *Cyborg Warriors* in comic form, only to see that stolen from under our noses.

I was at the stage where I would have to either accept that nothing was going to stick and that I should resign myself to having what was, for me, a great job, or make some major change in my life and bring the focus back to my creative goals.

If anyone has ever walked away from a great job with a great company and great prospects to take a leap of faith into waters unknown, then I take my hat off to you. I'm always fascinated by such people.

Once the thought had gone through my head just once, my usual risk-blindness took over, and I thought that the answer was simple. If I wanted to correct the balance of working for someone else and working on my creative ambitions, then I needed to give up working for someone else.

I am lucky that Josephine is something of an adventurous spirit too, and together we explored how we could make such a change to life and work. Moving to Scotland had been a long-time wish. But try as we might, we couldn't get the numbers to work out, in terms of having a house in the right place and cash to operate a business—or buy time to get the film company going. We would have to think outside the box—or at least, outside the country.

It was sometime in 2003 that the family move to Nova Scotia became a serious consideration, and we applied for permanent residency, never ever having been to Canada, let alone Nova Scotia. Three years later, we turned up in Chester Basin on the South Shore of Nova Scotia and knew no one and began the process of settling teenage boys and finding our way in a new country.

Again, all of that is a different story. Suffice to say we left some great friends behind but made some great new ones in Nova Scotia. We left behind parents, and there will always be regret about that. The challenge has been tough, and it's far from over, but we have managed to keep smiling.

Having established Simple Films in Nova Scotia, supported by a group of investors and a board of directors with plenty of business experience behind them, I produced and directed more shorts and made a few interesting documentaries. The purpose was to find out who we as a company could work with on future projects, and, as stated before, to give us time to see where we were placed creatively in Nova Scotia. The projects were little testers if you like, getting to grips with a new country and a new way for us to see the world. One of the first projects we did was *Painting the Wilderness*, a profile of Canadian wilderness artist Mark Brennan. What a great way to see parts of the new country!

I met some talented people in the business here. I picked a project by a Nova Scotian writer and touted it around to see if we could get funding. By the time I had added up my time, lawyers' fees, and option fees for several years, the project had cost a lot of money and no one was buying.

I was starting to get disgruntled and couldn't see a way forward with any of the big projects we had lined up, despite making great connections around the world.

I have two major failings. One is I am a really bad judge of character. I give people the benefit of the doubt and take them at their word. The second is that I have no sense of risk. I'm an opportunist and am prepared to take huge gambles on people and projects.

In the early years of producing in Nova Scotia, I fell foul to several people who were adept at drawing people into their web of schemes and projects that were being "oversold." Producing is a blagger's profession. You are always talking your project up, selling the "big name attachment" who isn't really attached. I'm not saying I never "talk up" my projects, but invariably I will add provisos and caveats. To me, a producer should be able to find enough selling points in the project without invoking names of people that will never actually have any involvement. In my experience, for us at the bottom of the ladder, there's little advantage in overstating your position.

Sadly, there are many who will. I have been overstated to and I have been the person "added" to a project to make it appear bigger than it was. I have not enjoyed either situation, and when everything settles down, if all that's lost is a bit of reputation and a lot of time, that is bad enough. But I am very susceptible to people adept at worming their way in to one's confidence. I made some huge mistakes with personnel and employment, which have cost me financially and set my career and project plans back years.

Please. If you have someone in your life with more sense than you when it comes to people, don't just listen to their opinion, give them the role of making all such decisions for you. I do now.

Shortly after a particularly depressing episode that had cost me a lot of time and money, I was approached out of the blue by a Scottish company with a BBC contract for a project about the Skye Bridge. They wanted to see if we could co-produce and make the project something bigger.

All the way to Canada to make a project about the Skye Bridge, a bridge that we had crossed so many times. Uncanny.

We looked at the budget, found a source of financing, and went for it. We established Skye Larke Productions to produce *The Bridge Rising*, and out of that came a wealth of experience that we have since built on. Through it, we found a team of people we could work with again on other projects. *The Bridge Rising* didn't make a lot of money, but it showed the quality of work we could be part of.

It was *The Bridge Rising* that paved the way for a chance to produce our own feature film. To keep the budget as low as possible, I decided not to buy a script from another writer. I had plenty of my own. But which one?

Out of the bottom drawer came *The Only Game in Town.*

9

THE RIGHT PEOPLE

It's a wonder I don't have multiple personalities. No sooner have I written something, than the producer side of me is looking for ways to make it happen. I need to make it clear that I didn't give myself any special treatment with this script. I'm able to distance the writer, precious about his latest work, from the needs of a business person, and, essentially, the film's main investor. So although I didn't have meetings with myself to discuss details, I worked through the questions and answers constantly.

As a producer, the first question is: can I make this film? There are many sub-questions that feed into the answer to that question, such as: Can I raise the budget? What is my own schedule like and what does the project timeline look like? Do I have the right people?

For me, the "in my head" budget was going to be around $150,000. That seemed within reach. The budget for *The Bridge Rising* was over $300,000. And even with my poor track record of people choices, I felt confident that I knew enough actors and industry professionals to make this work for a very modest fee, while looking great.

Of course, one of the key factors in the industry is the schedule. That starts with my own schedule—do I logistically have the time to devote to such a project? I have been a full-time producer for several years now, but that means there's always something to be done on one project or another. We had just come out of *The Bridge Rising* TV version in 2012, and the feature film version, which was ready for release by summer 2013. Allowing time to complete paperwork, get my breath back, and finish a couple of small projects, it looked as though I would have free time at the end of 2014 and into 2015.

Cory's schedule too looked fine, although he had some other directing projects lined up and another season of *Trailer Park Boys*. The hit show was preparing for a shoot in early summer 2015, and as it turned out he was down to direct some of the episodes of the latest season. We hoped to have everything done by the time his commitments to *TPB* came to the fore.

I was learning the downside of having a popular and in-demand director, though. Matching the sporadic shooting schedules of young people, schools, and Cory Bowles continued to plague me.

The final schedule to which we nailed our colours needed to take into consideration the young people we had been working with. As the workshops came to a close in autumn 2014, I had built a schedule that used the school locations during evenings and weekends and didn't put a huge burden of time on Cory. I was acutely aware that we would need to start shooting scenes very soon to allow some of the older young people the opportunity to be in the film before they went to university or out West for work. The schedule would need to be flexible enough to allow the forty-plus young actors to work on it, and I was conscious that the ultimate deadline for many of the young people was August 2015, after which time we might lose them for good.

For Cory, his *TPB* commitments meant we needed to aim to complete our shoot by the early summer of 2015. On that basis, it was clear we had a schedule that worked.

I discovered a great little online tool called Scenechronize that helped with the scheduling and scene breakdown (picking out all the elements needed to make the scene). I had forgotten until now just how many times I logged into Scenechronize to build a new schedule.

Schedule and team. Time and people. That's all it is. And the team was coming together. I was surrounding myself with people I felt comfortable with. Cory Bowles directing, Craig Cameron my executive producer and mentor.

My friend Colin Vearncombe read the script. "I laughed out loud. I was too ill to laugh, but I still did." I had been looking for projects to do with Colin for a while and was pleased when he offered to do the music for the film.

Scheduling the use of the school would be important. Careful planning was required to use the facility, Brian as an actor, and the young cast members, most of whom were school age. Brian and I went to great pains to create a schedule that would work.

I brought in Ashley King as director of photography (DoP). Ashley had worked with me as DoP on *Broken*, and through his work as an instructor with daVinci College he had a team of past and current students that could crew almost the entire production.

Using college students meant that we needed to work with daVinci College to ensure the film timetable didn't interfere with their regular program. This led to a few more schedule changes. To clear all this and to provide much of the grip and lighting gear for the production, daVinci College Head of Media, Fateh Ahmed, came on board; with what he was bringing to the production it was only right to offer him a producer credit.

In a very short time, we had a good creative team, a decent production crew, and even some of the key adult cast. And as Cory and I continued to do workshops along the North Shore throughout 2014, the number of young people willing and able to bring the characters to life continued to grow.

So by the autumn of 2014, the film was no longer just about me. We had a team, one good enough to make this happen.

A Market for the Film?

Somewhere in the Producer's Handbook, it will talk about marketing and selling the film. You may be forgiven for thinking that I was going to make a film "because I wanted to" with no thought of selling it. You would be wrong. Within every decision taken during the planning stage are the questions: Does this help it to sell? What is the market? How much can I expect to make on this film?

The budget goes hand in hand with financing. Can I raise the money I need to make the film, and if I make it for that, who is going to see it?

The makers of low-budget films often throw everything into making the film and leave nothing for marketing it—festival entry fees and so on. While the industry agrees that selling a low-budget film is very difficult (possibly because low-budget often equates to low production values), it's also true that if you have only spent $200,000 then it must be easier for you to recoup that smaller amount of money.

I was pretty clear in my head about the type of film we were making and what could be expected with the kind of budget we had. *Clockwork Mice* was made for a similar budget and recouped through a series of television sales to different regions. With TV licences for well-made films ranging from $30,000 to $150,000, there is a level of comfort for a producer such as me. The film was very mainstream too—no sex, drugs, gratuitous violence, or foul language. It would be an easy sell to overseas markets.

In the back of my mind, however, was the Holy Grail of all filmmakers: the theatrical release. For a film to really generate interest and have a chance at the big money returns, then we had to try to get a theatrical distributor.

The film I was benchmarking against was Bill Forsyth's brilliant *Gregory's Girl.* Made for £200,000 ($400,000), it took in over £25 million ($50 million) at the box office. With the right distributor, the right film could be a similar breakout success.

The Only Game in Town bears a lot of similarities to *Gregory's Girl.* The young cast, the workshop preparations, the teen romantic comedy and first love storyline, the budget level. Both have a gentle, offbeat, quirky storyline with likeable characters. The script, I was told, "reads like a Bill Forsyth film for Nova Scotia." The goal was—and still is—to match *Gregory's Girl* with box office takings too.

So marketing a film such as this requires thinking on your feet and a constant re-examination of the changing potential routes to sales success. A TV pre-sale here could take the pressure off, but might it reduce the interest from a distributor looking to maximize its own sales? If you pre-sell to one or more key television broadcasters, you are taking away from a distributor's market.

Still, I was aware that Super Channel had been a valuable outlet for other Atlantic Canadian films, so when, during the Strategic Partners industry sessions at the Atlantic Film Festival, I met Marguerite Pigott, Head of Production at Super Channel, I discussed *The Only Game in Town* with her.

I always think life must be hard for people in Marguerite's position. Everywhere they go, someone wants to accost them and try to sell her what is very likely to be a poor film. I saw the pale grey shutters over her eyes as she kindly listened to my opening pitch: "Teen with Asperger's...competitive solitaire...comedy...romance..."

But when she found out my aim was to make a *Gregory's Girl* for Nova Scotia, her eyes lit up. *Gregory's Girl* was her favourite film. On that basis, we explored the marketability of *The Only Game in Town.*

You know that comedy is all about...timing. The same can be said for the film industry. I have networked, cultivated friendships and connections with industry decision makers and included them in my long-term plans, only to find that these people move on to another company, or retire, or have a baby, or discover a burning desire to find their inner soul in the foothills of the Himalayas. The timing of your connection with a distributor or broadcaster is as important as the project you pitch to them.

If there is one problem with running a film company based in rural River John (as with trying to run one in Shepshed), it's that we are so far away from the centres of the industry that we are not meeting the insiders every day in this bar, or at this conference or that party. If the wheels of industry move more slowly in Halifax, Nova Scotia, than in Toronto or New York, they are rolling backwards down the hill in Shepshed and River John.

By the time we hit production with *The Only Game in Town*, Marguerite had left Super Channel. At time of writing, we may indeed return to Super Channel with our finished film, but we're holding tight for now, still with our eyes on the big prize of theatrical release with a distributor with full access to all the key territories.

The film with its concept and devices, characters and quirks, lends itself to quirky marketing campaigns. During production and as we first began post-production, we ran crowd-funding campaigns, which we used to spread the word as much as raise funds. We produced perks like The Only Wine in Town, courtesy of Jost Vineyards, and packs of playing cards, and all of these things and others will come into their own once we approach release or screenings. These are promotional gimmicks. They don't sell the film, but they help to raise awareness.

The music I have always seen as part of the film is as much a part of a marketing campaign as a creative choice. The soundtrack—if I get the one I want—will have tracks by artists from the UK and Europe and the US. This is deliberate. Creatively, the visuals should look like Nova Scotia, but there should be something that sets us slightly out of place, in the way that Cormack is slightly out of place in the world. Not using East Coast rock or Maritime fiddles is a way to create a world that is—and also isn't—Nova Scotia.

But from a marketing perspective, the music tracks I've chosen will open up the film to audiences outside of Canada. Utilizing the fan base of key artists and musical genres, we could spark interest in the film where most Nova Scotian films don't reach.

As I write, we're coming to the end of post-production, and we have placed the tracks I want to use, where I want them, and they really work. They add to the story; far from being a marketing gimmick alone, the music will play an essential part in the final film.

How do we find an audience for the film? Well first we have to understand who our audience is.

At this stage, I am not interested in looking at market segments and audience demographics. What we have is a very mainstream film, and while I want as many people as possible to see the film, I am not in a position to get those people to see it. The gatekeepers to the information I want to get out there are distributors and broadcasters. The first part of my marketing—finding out who my customers are—will be to find distributors and broadcasters who want this type of film, perhaps have a connection to Maritime Canada, have an appreciation for teen romances, and are big enough to achieve the goals I have for the film.

Yes, as part of my later discussions with said distributor or broadcaster they may well ask me for our target markets and niches that we've identified and so on. That's fine, but surely if you're handing your film over to a distributor who is going to take 40 percent of the sales (and they won't even agree to discuss things with you if they don't like the film and think they can sell it), surely what you are paying for in that 40 percent is their ability to market your film.

I am a qualified and professional marketer, but beyond knowing that there are many people around the world who would love to see *The Only Game in Town* it's not my job right now to figure out how to reach each one individually. Should we fail to find a distributor and have to go the self-distribution route, then we will need all of my marketing skills and all the help of publicists and social media gurus that our crowd-funding can afford.

I know many producers will raise eyebrows at this. Certainly government agencies in Canada have a check box that asks for "marketing strategy," and a producer must spend ages drafting something that—unless he's working on a narrow genre movie, or self-distributing—is at that stage a total waste of time.

This comes back to the first part of the book, where I pointed out that filmmakers don't wander around aimlessly in a void and suddenly decide to make a film. A true producer is always going to have a feel for the types of films he can produce and sell. He won't embark on such a massive venture without right at the very start asking himself, "Am I going to go broke making this, or can I make some money?"

I wonder if Alfred Hitchcock was asked for a marketing plan when he decided to make *Psycho*. I think the whole obsession with such requests in the industry stems from the idea that filmmaking is an art form carried out by part-time creative people without any sense of finance or business.

The marketing strategy request is the government's way of addressing the situation where an artistic filmmaker shows up asking for funds he or she has no idea how to recoup.

Disagree if you like. But has any filmmaker in Canada been refused funding because the marketing strategy they submitted is totally fanciful or ill thought out?

Anyway, enough said. Here's my marketing strategy for *The Only Game in Town*: Make it. Make it good. Sell it. (Actually, I did a marketing strategy. Why? Because it's important to think about these things and to be aware of them right the way through the project. And because this is Canada, and I know that at some point, someone is going to ask me for one....)

There is of course another aspect of marketing that I ought to tell you about. While in the early days I was assessing potential markets for the film, I was also trying to secure financing, and in the case of this film the intention was to secure a great deal of private financing.

I often get asked about the company name I used as the vehicle for the production: Only Me Productions Limited. Yes, there is that connection to *The Only Game*, but over the years I have had to form a number of companies as the vehicle for one project or another, and in all cases, the companies have really been only me. Only Me Productions was established with a share structure to encourage other private investors, and indeed we began the process for using the Nova Scotia government's investor tax incentive schemes. So, with my typical sense of irony, for a company that would not be only me, I thought I should call it Only Me Productions.

My point is that the company itself became something to "market" and "sell." So my early strategy not only included looking for potential distributors, but also, completely separately, potential investors.

Private investment in films just doesn't happen in Canada. It's kind of understandable. That kind of structure has never been there. The industry exists on development funds and government incentives. As such, Canadian films have never been judged by how much they generate back for investors. That's fine too, but it does mean that should anyone try to bring in outside investment, they will be scared off by the slim returns historically generated by Canadian films. Recently I have been talking to the producers of some of Canada's biggest TV franchises, and even they scoff at the idea of trying to persuade a private investor to invest in their productions.

I'll refer to the 2015 Nova Scotia Film Tax Credit debacle later, but meanwhile I will say that I could see the reasoning behind reducing the tax credit, perhaps in phased amounts over the next ten years. Ideally at the same time the government would support schemes and incentives for private investors, which could gradually take up more of the financing of Nova Scotian films until the industry could demonstrate that films can generate a decent return on investment.

I am prepared to be laughed out of the province for this view, but let's be honest—if the industry is solely reliant on government schemes of one sort or another for its very existence, and if as we saw in 2015 those incentives can be removed on a whim, the industry itself should look seriously at how it can avoid such things ever happening again. One sure way is to build a new, independent funding system.

No, it wouldn't fund every film. Yes, some people would have a better chance of getting funded than others. But you know what? That is exactly the situation we have now. There would still be a place for public funding and broadcaster envelopes and all the rest of it, but the industry could have long-term stability, and the drain on the taxpayer would be reduced.

EMPTY PROMISES

Despite the deals we were doing for gear and personnel, the budget, once we started to populate the spreadsheet, crept up to around $250,000. This was to be expected. There were forty-plus speaking parts and thirty locations. Everyone had to be fed. Everyone had to be paid.

Dov Simens, in his seminars on making low-budget films, instructs first-time directors to have four actors, in one room, and kill them one by one. If you don't like blood and guts, have them talk about love or death. My first feature: forty-plus speaking parts, forty-plus extras, thirty locations.

Dov, bless him, also suggests that if you can't pay people, you *must* ensure you feed them. Well that's a given, but I was setting out to make the film as I felt it should be made. No deferred payments, everyone fed, everyone paid.

The minute we talk about paying people the question arises: union or non-union? The pay rates in the industry for low-budget films do not in themselves have to be prohibitive to producers. In fact, in many cases, our pay rates were well above union rates. What steered us to non-union was the work conditions that we would be dealing with. If your key crew stops work just at the moment when your young actors have peaked in rehearsal, you miss it. There would be reductions in the hours we could work in a day, and that would mean extra days shooting and extra costs. If we had gone union, we would have had to pay fringe benefits and fees. The cast would have had to be slashed to achieve this structure, and many young people would never have had the opportunity.

And that was the most important factor. If we went union, then we could only use young people who were union actors. The vast numbers of highly talented North Shore young people would have been replaced by actors from outside the area.

This next statement will hurt. We worked for a year with our non-union young people but also had amongst those workshops from time to time young people and adults who were in a union. The non-union youngsters were better by miles.

That isn't always the case, and there is no real connection, it's just the way it was for us. With one exception. A regular at our workshops was Mia Perry, a very talented young girl with drive and ambition to make it in the industry. Mia was union registered and as a result couldn't take part in our film. She has since gone on to perform in Leah Johnston's short film *Ingrid and the Black Hole* playing a young version of Molly Dunsworth.

There will be more on the union/non-union dilemma later, but for now, let's just say that it was a foregone conclusion, with the type of film we were doing, the numbers involved, and the age of most of the actors in the film, we would be non-union. And as I explained, it wouldn't save us anything.

With a budget of $250,000 we had three key elements to raising the financing: a Nova Scotia tax credit upon which the industry had been built for more than a decade; strong indication of financial support from a group of high net worth individuals; and finally the real possibility of early sales to someone like Super Channel.

We were able to secure debt financing to cover the delay between production and the receipt of tax credits—the industry norm—and had prepared prospectuses for private equity providers. Amongst the potential providers of equity were Film and Creative Industries Nova Scotia, which used to be Film Nova Scotia, who had an equity fund that Nova Scotia producers could tap into to fill small gaps in their financing structures.

In October 2014 I returned to Nova Scotia from a trip around Europe, armed with a seemingly certain source of private finance and the feeling that the future was bright. I prepared to move forward with the film.

I had also launched a new film festival for the North Shore region, the Sunrise Film Festival, with impresario Troy Greencorn (Stan Rogers Folk Festival, the East Coast Music Awards, deCoste Centre), and although our team thought we were totally unprepared, I decided to launch the festival with a date of October 2015 and put out a call for submissions from all over the world.

"What are you doing?" Josephine demanded. "You're taking on too much. You're doing *The Only Game in Town* and now the festival!"

I smiled at her. "Don't worry. Cory is directing the film. My main work as producer will be over long before the film festival starts to get busy. Everything will be all right."

"Don't come crying to me when you're up to your neck in it. Besides, you will end up directing the film."

Oh she of little faith...

By the time we reached October 2014, the budget had been set. The creative and production team was on board. The young cast were ready to start. Locations were approved and the schedule was just about hanging together. The financial structure was in place, and all we had to do was call in the promises of funding. There are elements of risk in everything we do. I've already said that my aversion to risk is perhaps less than other people's. But is it a risk when you've done your homework, put everything in place, made the deals?

There had been, throughout 2014, an element of doubt in the Nova Scotia film industry, caused by a report on taxation in the province written by government consultant Laurel Broten for the McNeil government. The uncertainty that the impending report caused was already having an effect on production. Film producers like Mark Almon were lobbying hard that the report should not lead to damaging changes for the industry.

Broten's report, released on November 19, 2014, included a recommendation that Nova Scotia scrap its Film and Television Production Tax Credit. This caused uproar, and while many other elements of the report were panned around the province, producers sought assurances from the provincial government that the tax credit would remain in place. When Premier Stephen McNeil announced a little later in November 2014 that there would be no change to the present system of tax credits and industry support through Film and Creative Industries Nova Scotia, a collective sigh of relief was heard all over the province. The premier pledged to keep it in place and review it again in five years. That is precisely the sort of stability that the industry needed; given the general three-year cycle for film development to production, producers could continue to plan for the future.

For me, and Only Me, that was the last bit of uncertainty dealt with. The last shadow of doubt had been removed from the plans. The potential investors who were holding back because of the possibility of a lack of funding from provincial government could now be convinced that all was well. In truth, once I'd got the investors on the hook I had been slow to reel them in simply because of the doubts Broten's report cast. I had met with some high net worth individuals, and only now did it feel right to "seal the deal." Only now, since the premier of Nova Scotia, no less, had declared in public that the one reliable funding mechanism for Nova Scotia productions would be unchanged for five years.

In late November 2014, there was really no need to wait any longer. We could start production on the film.

The Green Light

So we were comfortable that we had the financing. We had interim financing to bridge the gap between expenses and tax credits and sales, and had a strong business structure for the private financing that we had lined up. Perhaps a little from the Film and Creative Industries Nova Scotia Equity Fund would top it all off.

Our schedule was going to be all over the place, and we were using young people, schools, and other locations that would require special arrangements.

When we went to greenlight the project in December 2014, everything looked like a plan coming together. We shot some key scenes—our first stab at principal photography—on December 13 and 14 and knew we could use them immediately as the evidence of intent, ability, and quality to persuade any wavering potential investors.

To get the ball rolling until our investors came good with the cash, we had taken 10 percent of the financing and worked out our schedule over the winter. More scenes were shot, an actor here, an actress there, allowing us to give screen time to the young talent we'd discovered and nurtured.

Remember at this point I received Andrew Ellard's script notes, and to make the necessary changes to the script—and to allow for the usual bad weather of January in Nova Scotia—the schedule was once more revised and we aimed to shoot more scenes in February.

I met with investors during February of 2015, but more rumblings were going round about the upcoming provincial budget. Investors still held on to their money, despite me repeating the premier's words of just three months earlier: "The current tax credit is safe and will be reviewed in five years' time."

We pushed on, secured an ice rink venue. We had trouble getting Cory's schedule to match that of the young people and the random venues, and I had to direct a couple of shoots. At this point I should have sensed the growing uncertainty that had never really gone from the rest of the industry (and hadn't filtered through to us rurally based producers) and that in turn was making it hard for Cory to say that he would definitely be available for this day's shoot or another.

At the end of March, I visited Film and Creative Industries Nova Scotia hoping to speak about the equity fund. Linda Wood, in charge of equity funding, wasn't in. I also discussed the tax credit Part A application (the bit we do to show to lenders and funders that we can expect a certain level of tax credit back) with the tax credit officer. All was good.

On April 2, a week before the provincial budget that was so anxiously awaited in the industry, I wrote to Linda Wood to arrange a meeting to discuss equity funding. My investors were understandably nervous and still argued that the situation was far from certain. If I couldn't secure the private money, then the Film and Creative Industries Equity Fund might now be more important. I needed to get the ball rolling with that.

Linda wrote back to suggest we set a meeting for the week commencing April 16 when she returned to work after being away.

Scheduling Cory to direct any scenes was becoming impossible. The ripple effect of nervous producers pushed his other projects around, and of course, as a low-budget project, we would always get the raw deal. Having pushed scenes back again to fit his schedule, we then had to find different locations for the next round of scenes.

We began to struggle to line up the school, young people, Cory, and other locations. I was under increasing pressure and was continually trying to remain positive about the situation in the film industry so that the investors we had spent so long putting on the hook would finally give us their money.

We had spent the first 10 percent of the budget and had some really nice scenes. Looking back, there were all sorts of warning signs, but my head was down and I was blind to everything else outside the daily effort of the film itself. And therein lies a major problem. And again, quite possibly everything that ever went wrong with this film is down to me—only me. I come from a working-class background. All my life I've had to fight tooth and nail and twice as hard to get anywhere or make anything happen. When the going began to get tough at this point in the production, others may well have recognized something wasn't right. But to me, this all felt normal. Having to deal with obstacles was normal operating procedure.

The provincial budget came out on April 9, 2015, and there was utter dismay in the industry. The tax credit system that would "continue unchanged for five years" was trashed. The Liberals passed the Financial Measures Act, effectively ending the tax credit system as we knew it and dealing a death blow to Film and Creative Industries Nova Scotia.

The government press release stated: "The Film Industry Tax Credit will give companies the first 25 percent as refundable, but the remaining 75 percent of the credit will be applied to any taxes owing. These changes take effect July 1, 2015, to ensure projects currently in progress can continue."

The provincial government had chosen to follow Laurel Broten's report—a report that drew criticism from all sides on many topics—and to listen to the Department of Finance, whose axe-grinding about the film tax credit had become an obsession, instead of really assessing the benefits to the wider economy of such a device. Tax credits are economic drivers, and other provincial—and national—governments know it.

Our next scenes were instantly cancelled. I want to try to show you what this felt like; it's hard for me, some two years later, to get my head around the turmoil that was going on.

Let's think of analogies that might work. You've spent two years building your dream house, got the expensive architect's plans, spent money on the materials, paid labour for subcontractors, built the main supporting walls—then a storm comes, and while you're standing in the middle, trying to shore up one wall after another, everything you so carefully put in place comes crashing down around you.

I'll give a better, more telling analogy later, but whichever analogy you prefer, they serve to show where we were in our production. We had started. Whatever definition the government agencies later decided to put on it, *The Only Game in Town* had already begun production. We had spent $25,000, we'd shot scenes and committed to many more. In all the government releases they confirmed that productions that had "started before July 1" were considered eligible for the now defunct system of funding. They provided no definition for "started" other than "have you started?"

Remember, the definition stated by the government—and one recognized in the industry—was: "Principal photography begins with the first day of shooting of significant scenes which involve the main photography unit, e.g., in drama, scenes with actors rather than simple establishing shots."

When we approached the Department of Finance to make them aware that our film would be coming through under the old system, they told us that their definition would also include "how much principal photography had been done." Effectively, then, although there is a definition that everyone in the industry has agreed on, the Nova Scotia Department of Finance chose to make an arbitrary change.

So here is my preferred analogy for our production at that point, along with our state of mind: the Corryvreckan. Situated off the west coast of Scotland, the Corryvreckan is the third largest whirlpool in the world. For a while *The Only Game in Town* cruise ship had drifted leisurely over calm waters, enjoying the scenery. Then the tide changed and the cruise ship's engine had to work that little bit harder to maintain position. Then the Corryvreckan kicked in and the water chopped and crashed, dashing other film boats against the rocks. The novice skipper at the helm of *The Only Game in Town* moved his eyepatch to cover his one good eye and believed he could navigate right through the maelstrom.

With each revolution of the great whirlpool, the ship came closer to destruction, but still the crew (and the cast) steered as if it was their last chance. And let's be fair, for many, we knew it would be. After a year's work on the project, many young people would be unavailable to make the film after this summer, they would be elsewhere.

The skipper had already lost one ship, he wasn't about to lose another.

This is what it felt like. Not a house crashing down, because there was no visible sign of destruction. It was as if we had sailed the boat to where it should have been, but at that moment, when the Corryvreckan began churning the water, it was all we could do to stay where we were. You could sense the pull of an overwhelming force, dragging you under, ripping the rudder from your vessel.

The Corryvreckan happened to the Nova Scotia film industry in 2015.

On May 5, 2015, while we were all still reeling from the news about the tax credits, the government issued a statement from the Finance and Treasury Board reiterating the position stated in budget announcements in the press, saying: "Productions that commence principal photography before July 1, 2015, will receive the tax credit based on current rules."

The same document—and this was sent out to clarify the position, to be the final say on the matter—went on to say: "If principal photography does *not* commence by June 30, 2015, then these productions will not be eligible for the FITC under the current rules." Anyone who was paying attention at the time will remember those words, that clarification, without caveat or exceptions. Had our film commenced principal photography before July 1, 2015? Unequivocally "yes."

Marc Almon and Screen Nova Scotia, which suddenly found themselves centre stage in the unfolding drama, lobbied the government hard to make the old system available to all productions that happened in 2015. Had this been agreed then every other problem we faced would never have arisen. How lovely it would have been at that point to be able to sit with the agency that oversaw film and TV production in the province. What we needed was to be able to talk to Film and Creative Industries Nova Scotia to get a decision from it about equity funding and the actual position of our film.

But—and this is a big but—the government had closed Film and Creative Industries Nova Scotia with its announcement of the slashing of the tax credit. There was no one to talk to. No agency to say one way or the other whether your project was safe. All we had to go on was: "Productions that commence principal photography before July 1, 2015, will receive the tax credit based on current rules." The equity strand I wanted to speak to Linda Wood about was no longer available. So now I'm running around, trying to convince people, investors and the team, that all would be okay, because, quite clearly, we had already started production.

At the end of 2014, I had found myself as a go-between for a multi-million-dollar industrial project looking to move to Nova Scotia. I had seen the way the owners of the project intended to retain equity in it by debt financing, and I thought that on a much smaller scale, I could do the same thing.

We had already had to secure interim financing to cover the period between production and the refund of production tax credits. It wasn't a huge leap to increase the amount of interim financing to cover the equity gap and simply push on with production. The equity can be sold at any time, and in fact the further we got in production the less risk there was for investors, so it seemed like a common-sense step. I knew the tax credits would come in at some point. Why shouldn't they? And I knew that the finished film would be a huge financial success. I also knew that at any point along the way, investors could still come on board. There was nothing to worry about.

Of course, I was always going to think like that. I would always take the risk. I was also a prisoner of my own past and was determined not to pull the plug on another film. And there was also the government promise: "Productions that commence principal photography before July 1, 2015, will receive the tax credit based on current rules." The government hadn't gone back on its word before, had they? I was trapped by history and ego.

Convinced that we could still make this film while the Corryvreckan lapped at our stern, I rallied the crew one more time and tried to rewrite the remaining schedule for the umpteenth time.

On the back of the tax credit decision and what was more important, the closure of Film and Creative Industries Nova Scotia—which meant a lack of any advocacy for the industry—a whole world of unknowns came into play. No one likes unknowns. Investors don't like unknowns. The resulting turmoil had caused schedules on all productions to slip. Every day I was nailing a new list of shooting days to the wall, only to see it unravel by mid-afternoon.

Our director, Cory Bowles, was having no easy time of it either. I discussed the situation with Craig Cameron. "It's just scheduling," he said. "Everyone's struggling."

We were feeling the pinch though. Our locations were mostly in a school. Schools close at the end of June. We would run into trouble getting locations and even some of our cast if we ran into the summer break. We really had to go now.

Please remember, we're also in the middle of the Corryvreckan whirlpool. Trying to schedule is hard enough, but government decisions were spinning the waters around us, pointing us one way and then another.

Throughout March and April, only a few minutes of film were actually shot against a planned fifteen minutes. Things were only going to get worse.

Events were unravelling faster than I could keep track. Looking back now, the chronology of events is hard to pick through. Thankfully I logged discussions, meetings, and emails. I remember feeling confident that we had everything lined up. Our main shoot would recommence in May, a few scenes would still need to be shot in June, but all would be good.

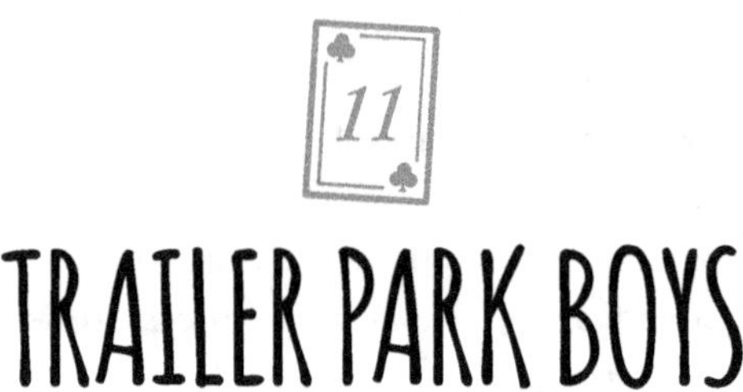

TRAILER PARK BOYS

Let's get one thing straight. We moved to Nova Scotia in 2006. We didn't know about *Trailer Park Boys*. We did chance upon a couple of old friends in Loughborough, shortly before we emigrated, who told us about this really funny show they had seen on a trip to Canada. Other than that, we were totally ignorant of the status of the show in Nova Scotia.

We spent the first three months of our life in Nova Scotia in a place called Chester Basin. Oliver and Charley attended Forest Heights High School. Within a couple of days Oliver had sparked up a friendship with a girl named Molly Dunsworth. We visited her home a few times. I met her father, John. He was one of the first people I met in Nova Scotia who wasn't tying to sell me a house. He struck me as a nice, genuine, and unassuming man. His arm was in a cast after some bizarre accident, and we chatted about Nova Scotia, family, houses, and home.

Those three months were a blur, and we moved to the North Shore. I only later discovered that John Dunsworth was an elder statesman of Canadian theatre and one of the stars of *Trailer Park Boys.*

At some point we had reconnected, and early in 2015 I approached John to play Principal Ambrose Joyce, the part I'd written with the huge monologue. I sent him the script (remember, I was always nervous about Canadians getting my humour in this script). After a few days, I checked back in with him, to see if he'd read it.

"Got halfway in and my mind exploded. Will finish and get back."

His mind exploded? What had I done to him? I enquired gingerly, "Exploded in a good way?"

His reply: "Some off-the-wall funny brilliance, and I'm only halfway through." I'll just leave that hanging there for a moment or two. "Some off-the-wall funny brilliance!" said a man famous for his off-the-wall funny brilliance. Then John provided an entire backstory for Principal Ambrose Joyce, which one day, we simply must explore. John was a gem. A generous creative person and a voice of reason and experience. I couldn't wait to work with him on set. We began scheduling him for the part.

On April 29, Screen Nova Scotia, who were increasingly filling in the void left by the removal of Film and Creative Industries Nova Scotia, organized a meeting to give updates to the industry about the rapidly changing landscape. There were a lot of people there. I had felt as though I wasn't giving enough support to the cause, but after all, I was in the middle of a production and time was hard to come by.

I met with John Dunsworth and we joked about the script and talked a little about scheduling. He introduced me to a few other people, talking of my project in the best possible way. I met with Cory at the same event and we talked about the next set of shoot dates. Both John and Cory explained that because of the industry turmoil, their *TPB* schedules were in disarray, but they would be confirmed soon.

On May 6, I met again with investors and did a reasonable job of convincing them that Cory had now been joined by John Dunsworth, meaning we had two bankable names on board.

Cory Bowles Bows Out

Having finally been able to pin down a string of May shooting dates, starting May 15, I woke on May 8 to an email from Cory with the subject line: Regrets. I knew already that the turmoil in the industry wasn't just affecting me and my film; there were many others trying to navigate shifting schedules and contractual commitments, not to mention family needs.

Still Cory's email came as a hammer blow. The main reason he was sending regrets: "*Trailer Park Boys* has moved until the end of June, and therefore my ability to get a strong prep would be less than ideal."

Cory could not direct our film because of his commitments to *TPB*, whose schedule had been affected by the government changes. Cory would be heavily involved in the new season of *TPB*. As director he would need lots of time to be fully prepped. The doubts over the tax credit had meant that sensible producers—or at least producers who were to start production—had sat back and waited, letting their schedules slip. Now, the period that they would be shooting created a conflict for Cory between our sporadic shoots and the prep time he needed for *TPB*. I don't know for sure, but it may also have created a conflict in an exclusivity clause in his *TPB* contract. Essentially, he knew that if he was still thinking in depth about *TPB*, he wouldn't be able to give everything he needed to give creatively for *The Only Game in Town*.

I could have shown faith to Cory, ignored the scenes we had already shot, given up on the attempt to shoot the film before the end of summer 2015, and accepted the fact that most of the young people would not be a part of it when we came to do it in 2016.

I also knew deep down that a postponement of the film essentially meant the end of the project, as it had with *In the Air at Whitby*. In the end, two burning desires—not to have another stalled film and to give the young people their chance to shine—won through. I only regret it because I so wanted to work with Cory.

Cory's departure gave me much to think about. I quickly ran through the options of available directors who could come on at a moment's notice and take it from there. Cory had written, "That being said, I have and still am inspired by the work you've done in the community, and you've built an incredible blanket of trust with the team and cast you have pulled together. And I think that you would be the best possible person to direct this film."

I didn't agree. We went ahead with a day shoot at a local ice rink that had proved very difficult to book, and I couldn't face going through that again. Getting an ice rink to film in in Nova Scotia was far harder than I imagined. I scrubbed out the rest of the schedule once more to give me time to find a director.

The young cast had been tested with scenes from *The IT Crowd*, and it was clear that kind of humour would work with them. Having had some success with my dealings with script consultant Andrew Ellard, who had worked with Graham Linehan on *The IT Crowd*, I approached Graham himself to direct—and got a swift refusal from his manager. I asked a few others, but it soon became clear that whether or not Cory's faith in me as a director was founded, if I wanted to make this film before the summer was out, it would have to be me directing it.

I now needed the time to do some director prep for the rest of the production. The schedule was once more thrown to the dogs.

We are coming to the end of The Producer's Story. At this point, the director should be the focus of the project, and the team that the producer has built should be running with it.

There would still be work for the producer to do. Certainly in this case, there was still the hoped for input of private finance. Telefilm, the agency responsible for the development and promotion of Canada's film industry, had heard about the film through press releases, and I had been contacted by the person overseeing investment in Atlantic Canadian productions. We chatted for a long time and I was advised to come to them for financial assistance to help in post-production. We couldn't get production funding from them, as we had already begun shooting. (Again, please note that: Telefilm couldn't give us production financing because we had already started production.)

Nova Scotia Business Inc. (NSBI), whose new top dog ironically was one Laurel Broten, had been appointed by the provincial government to administer the replacement scheme for the old film production tax credit system. As part of my ongoing involvement with the planned industrial project looking to locate to Nova Scotia, I was spending a great deal of time at the NSBI offices. I met briefly with one of the new staff members seconded to the new film department and, finally having someone to talk to about the situation, asked about the procedure for applying for the new fund that would launch at the start of July 2015. This was an incentive fund, not a refundable tax credit. Productions needed to apply and be pre-approved for funding.

"But you can't apply for the new fund, Stuart, because your film has already started production."

Although I was reluctant, appointing myself as director was really the only sensible option for the film now. It would have been a difficult enough task, but I was also still embroiled in producer issues that affected my ability to prep the shoot. Even though we could move forward with some confidence that the old tax credit system applied to us and our financing plan was essentially unchanged, dates continued to slip, and through no fault of our own there was the real risk that the film just would not happen.

The Same Problem

Remember 1996? The last-minute pulling out of a film production? Well, here I was in 2015, faced with the same prospect. In 1996, the much younger and more sensible me recognized that there was a future ahead, full of more possibilities to make films. Younger me could afford to walk away and fight another day. Armed with that confidence in the future, most others might well have weighed up the 10 percent of the budget already spent on *TOGIT* and called it quits. But now I am old and crusty and not prepared to wait another twenty years for a chance to make a feature.

Colin Vearncombe always said he admired in me my inability to accept the word "no." Actually, he might have been questioning my grasp of language, because he did say that I "don't know the meaning of the word 'no.'" The truth is, there was no real choice here. The film had been started and had to be completed.

My own calendar might have been very different in another twelve months' time. It was now or never for our funny film that was loved by everyone who read it.

Then we hit some new and unexpected roadblocks.

When I speak about the first new problem, I do so knowing I may lose some friends in the industry, but I can only speak about how our film was affected. I'm writing now, two years after the event, and recalling those days and the utter turmoil we were in. People probably weren't really trying to hurt us, it's just that at the time, they did.

John Dunsworth, a widely respected actor who had given so much the industry in Nova Scotia, wanted to play Principal Ambrose Joyce. We had to work around his schedule, but it was doable—apart from the fact that he was an ACTRA member. I was told that dispensation could be given by the union to allow him to play the part, and at a time when the industry in Nova Scotia was being battered to death by a narrow-minded government, one would have thought and hoped that this dispensation would have been given to a film production that was prepared to pay one of its members.

Instead, without the chance for discussion, the union flatly refused and made no offer to try to find a solution to make something work. I found that strange.

In life, there are two kinds of people: those who try to help, and those who say "no." People who hide behind rules that have been created but can "never be broken." Unions, of course, would not exist unless someone had agreed to break the rules that existed before them. My question is this: if a union is there to help its members, how does it do that by not allowing them to work on projects they want to work on?

This was a surreal time in Nova Scotia. The government, despite making hugely unpopular decisions in health, education, and the film and television industry, somehow managed to avoid serious opposition from other parties, and there were many in the province who believed the lie that the film and

TV industry wasn't worth the government funding it received. The industry called on all its supporters, organized rallies, and showed a united front from all sectors to push back. Front and centre of those rallies were the unions. Obviously. If the film industry was damaged in Nova Scotia, it was going to be bad for their members.

And yet, at the same time, the unions were involved in a battle to the death with one of the most successful and highly respected film and television companies in Nova Scotia: Egg Productions. At a time when the industry needed to convince the public of our collective cause, the unions were demonstrating against Egg. The sad eventuality was that Egg could not abide by the demands of the intransigent unions and rather than continue the fight, owner Mike Hachey closed down the company.

So we have an industry, apparently trying to save itself by demanding government money but happy to shut down one of the major employers and drivers of economic success. I firmly believe the actions of the unions at that time were a major contributing factor to the lack of public sympathy in Nova Scotia for our industry.

We lost John Dunsworth. More delays to the schedule as we searched for a new Principal Joyce. I fell back on those I knew from England: Paul Lavers from Ideal World TV in Peterborough, England, and Jonathan Kydd. Paul was the head of the presenting team and a talented stage and TV actor. Jonathan is the son of the legendary Sam Kydd and a comic actor I'd had on my radar for twenty-odd years. Jonathan was already working but would have been "over like a shot." Paul was the same.

It didn't matter. Those new delays brought something else into play.

The use of the Tatamagouche schools had been planned for around a year. It was to be the high school's swan song, as it was going to be knocked down and replaced. We'd already filmed some exteriors of the white building; it had that look about it.

Having Brian Holmes as the nasty teacher and solitaire coach Alex Crowley was a major factor in the use of the schools. But that was before the scenes were being pushed back toward the summer. Ever closer to the summer. And such was the time frame we were up against, instead of an evening here and a Saturday there, we would need whole blocks of days—an entire week at least—to finish off.

Then we met someone else who liked to say "no." I don't know the meaning of the word, remember, but I should have some sort of idea given how often I heard it during *The Only Game in Town.*

In this edition of the *Midlothian Times*, principal Joyce (Rick Shaver), is interviewed, and it is announced that the school team has reached the national final.

MIDLOTHIAN TIMES

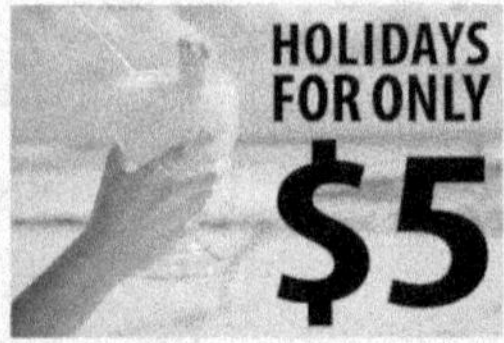

Friday 23rd July 2017 75c

There's no Times like the present

I'M A LUMBERJACK AND I'M OKAY

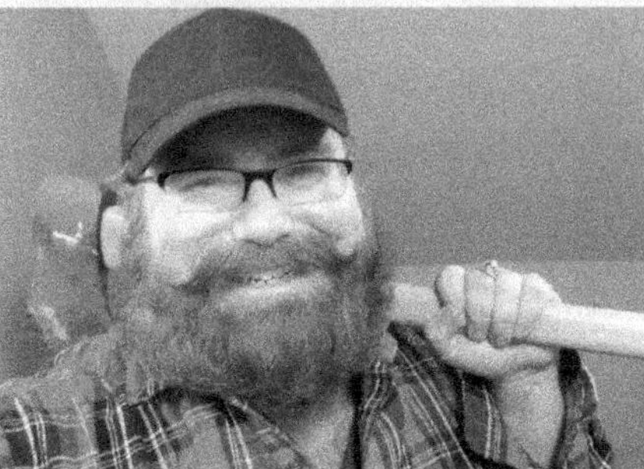

Transgender lumberjack is unfairly given the axe.

By Monty Python

One of Canada's iconic industries, the logging trade, has long been the domain of real men, manly men, men who spend all day with their chopper in their hand getting wood. This was recently challenged by several female lumberjacks who took years to become accepted into the lumberjack fraternity. It was not an easy transition with several incidents including one where a man had his pride severely hurt.

Over the last few years, it has been more widely accepted that women are part and parcel of the industry, but this has all been thrown into question yet again when a lumberjack announced he was transgender. His colleagues were dubious at first, until he started wearing women's lingerie to work. After several complaints, some from the men that it was distracting, and some from the women who were jealous because he looked better in fishnets than they did. Eventually word reached the management who suspended him indefinitely pending an investigation. After months of waiting, he was dismissed from the company on grounds of indecency. He, who is now a she, will be appealing in a few months.

Midlothian in National Final of Solitaire Championships

Giordani Bruno

Suggestions that Midlothian have been a one-man team this year are quickly rebuffed by Coach Alex Crowley. However, rising star Cormack Vertue has played no small part in the team's success, thanks to an unbeaten run that started in the very first game.

"Vertue is the key threat, and we recognise that." So says Coach Jake Chisholm of The Calgary Stamp-Collectors, who will face Midlothian in the final. "But we will have strategies in place to tackle him. We need to get in his face, under his skin. We have the players to do that."

Vertue's play this season has been flawless. "He's not necessarily fast," commented Ambrose Joyce, Principal of Midlothian School, "but he always manages to get out."

'Getting out' of course is the term for completing the full sequence of cards. Vertue certainly has an impressive record, but he will have to remain on top form to carry Midlothian to victory against Calgary, who are known as one of the fittest teams in the league.

"Yes, Cormack I'm sure will come up with another Vertue-oso performance," said Principal Joyce.

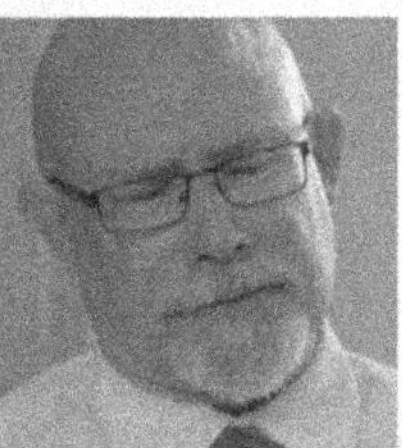

Ed Itto-reale

What does it mean to be human is a question we have asked ourselves throughout the years, but one man thinks he finally has the answer. Symon Borg, or Syborg as he likes to be called, is a pioneering scientist and liberal thinker at Acadia University. He has recently been doing research into human evolution with regards to using technology to enhance the users perception or mobility. 3D printed arms to replace lost or missing limbs are fairly common now, using muscular sensors to transfer biometric data to the moving parts of the artificial limb. Syborg has found a way to bypass the muscles and harness the nervous system using implanted technology. His goal is to create a wearable exoskeleton that can be controlled directly by the users thoughts to enable paraplegics to walk and use their arms. The research is in it's early stages at present, but the technology is real and has a wide range of uses and adaptations, allowing humans to bypass evolution and choose their own path.

Implants already tested include sensors that allow the user to perceive ultraviolet and infrared light-waves. There are cranial implants which connect to extremely sensitive microphones which can pick up noises well outside the normal human hearing range. Syborg has also developed a filter system which can be implanted in the throat with small vents at the side of the neck which act like gills to filter out toxins and airborne particles. These are exactly the sort of thing that the mission to colonise Europa and Enceladus are hoping to use to enable colonists to breathe. They are also looking to connect artificial eyes to the brain in order to filter out glare and make it easier to see in the challenging conditions on the moons. All these new developments mean that ordinary people will benefit (if they can afford the hefty price tag) and open up brand new horizons for humans to explore. Welcome to the brave new world of Syborg's.

Living in Canada is bad for your health

Lai-Ying Soanso

According to a recent survey poll by the US Tourist Commission, living in Canada is bad for your health. People have a lower quality of life than those in neighbouring countries, spending more time travelling to work, and less time at leisure pursuits. Over 55% of people polled believed that the cold weather and the lack of sunny beaches was the main reason so many Canadians were depressed. The poll also suggests that most Canadians would rather be US citizens and enjoy the civil freedom to be as rude, ignorant and downright racist as many Americans enjoy under the watchful eye of the Trump administration. 67% believed that Trump would beat Trudeau in an arm wrestling competition, despite accusations that Trumps hands were too small to make it a fair competition. 73% of those polled thought that the Canadian education system was broken and failing the people, the remaining 55% confidently stating that America was much better at maths.

The report has been criticised by many as being nothing more than an attempt to boost the moral of the American people. This is obviously false as most Americans wouldn't understand the results anyway.

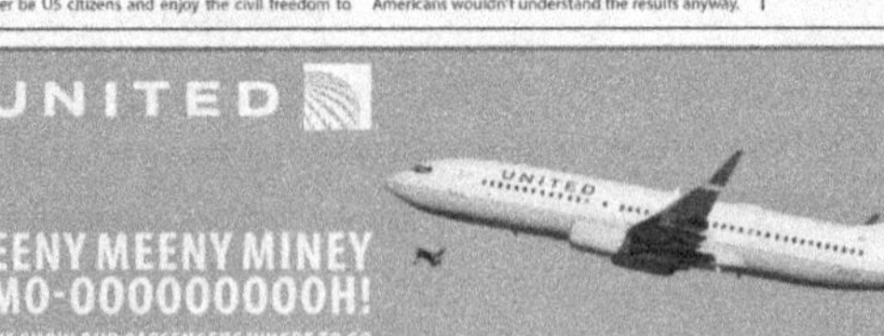
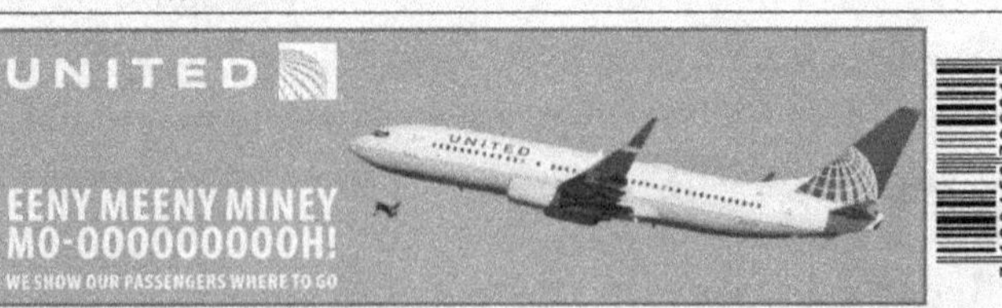

We found, in the director of operations at Chignetco-Central Regional School Board, another person who seemed to take great delight in putting up obstacles to something happening—again, something that would have benefited the many young people from his region in the film. But he had found himself in a vital position with the ability to make things easy, or the chance to make things hard.

It started by hearing from Brian that the man in question wasn't allowing us to film at the schools because "he had some questions." Telling someone "no" because you have questions but then not telling them what those questions are is the first play in the coaching manual for obstructive petty jobsworths ("Jobsworth," you ask? You know, the useless so-and-so who refuses to help out because it's "more than my job's worth").

He played everything else by the book. The deliberate use of telephone contact rather than email to prevent me having anything in writing from him. The fact that he would call the office line at seven thirty in the evening, knowing no one would be there, and leave a brief message just to make a show of trying to make contact, but then never be available when I returned his call.

As the days turned to weeks I managed to find out what his "concerns" were. He gave me all sorts of reasons why it couldn't happen, made me jump through hoops to prove this or that—all of which struck me as completely irrelevant and designed merely to delay me. At this point, delays in decisions were as deadly as negative decisions. I was certain he knew that and revelled in it.

Here is an excerpt from my Producer Diary from that period.

Our production now hangs in the balance. After managing to survive the worst that politicians can do to our industry, the fate of our production now seems to rest with one man: the Director of Operations at CCRSB. Against the wishes of the principals of both schools, and without any concern for the summer jobs of more than fifty young people, local businesses, and service providers, he has taken a stance that could see the production cancelled.

Despite calls, emails, and representations of our despair, he has refused to respond and so far has given no explanation for his negative position on the production's long agreed use of the schools for interior scenes. In twelve months of discussion with school principals, no one has spotted any potential issues regarding the use of the facilities.

His position is at odds with even the head of the family of schools board [a group of boards that looks after around eighty schools in northwest Nova Scotia] *and ironically, comes when Nova Scotia is holding a province-wide conference looking for positive action that can be done to alleviate the decline of this province—where our film project was held up as an example of precisely the type of endeavour that was needed to boost our rural areas.*

Having personally read the board's own guidelines for "use of premises," there is nothing contained within that a) prevents us from hiring the schools to produce a film, or b) requires the Director of Operations to interfere and withhold permission without giving a reason.

It may already be too late. The need to issue schedules once more to cast and crew, book accommodation, finalize equipment rental, and transportation, and book other local services has become desperate. Even if we were to get the go-ahead now it may be too late to get the production back on track. I am exploring other options. Most of them create a significant cost increase to the production, and all of them remove the production from the North Shore of Nova Scotia and the associated benefits to our community. As an example, a local accommodation provider will lose business totalling more than $15,000 as a result of our production moving out.

As of now, the man still refuses to answer calls from the two principals and has been made fully of the aware of the desperate financial situation this puts our business in. He simply doesn't care! Today alone I have made more than ten calls. He was in the office, just "unavailable."

I believe that his attitude and irresponsibility are not in keeping with the position of Director of Operations at CCRSB.

What is this man's agenda? Why is he fighting to prevent opportunity for young people and security for our local businesses? He is the same man that argues most vehemently for the closure of River John School, Wentworth School, Maitland School. How is it right that one man can rip the heart out of communities when we're all fighting for survival here? I have spent many days in recent months working with others in the community to fight for our province. One Nova Scotia, PictouCounty2020, Engage Nova Scotia—they all ask what can be done to improve our province.

Three words: Sack the man!

I got the impression that this man believed the schools to be his property and that only he and his buddies should get preferential treatment and be allowed to use them as they wish.

Looking back, it's funny—perhaps nothing more than coincidental—that the people we were right up against (or rather who were against us) in the making of our film were the people who at that time were fighting good people on other fronts too.

The unions were also fighting Egg. The government was also fighting the health sector and teachers, along with the film industry. And CCRSB was fighting small, neglected communities (the communities we were aiming to help with our film) by forcing the closure of schools, one of which just happened to be in our hometown of River John. We saw first-hand how underhanded the school board was in its fight against desperate parents and communities. We saw how they tied them up in knots asking for pointless details and sending them on fool's errands, while behind the scenes their minds were already made up.

I cannot come to grips with the twisted mentalities of the types of people who revel in obstructing other people in their work or lives. All our man at the school board had to do was say "yes, get on with it." Instead, I heard on the grapevine that he had been grumbling about how much money I would make on the project (what?!). This suggests there was a personal agenda at play. I find it strange that in the Province at that time there were people who were paid more money in their salaries and pensions from the public purse than any filmmaker has ever done or will ever do, and yet they found it easy to slam our industry.

It's been a topic of discussion only recently with another top producer who is certain that our industry well and truly lost the argument during 2015, and with that any public support we might have had.

Here I am almost three years later and my anger has subsided, and with hindsight it's hard to blame one man for forming an opinion of our industry that had become widespread.

Some of the most powerful organizations in the province are the school boards. They appear to have control without accountability. Even the Minister of Education was unable to intervene when the board refused to grant a stay of execution to the River John School. Yes, I was angry about the way we were treated when all we wanted to do was to make a film. But the way the people of River John—and other small communities—were treated by CCRSB makes me angry to this day. The system, and the people within it, needs to change.

As the very one-sided discussion was taking place with our man at CCRSB, two things began to happen. The first was the very real feeling among people involved in the film that "everything was against us." It wasn't just a feeling. We were being attacked by the government, unions, school boards, and even time itself as my young actors rushed headlong through puberty. More than a year had passed since my first meeting with many of them, and they were changing.

I decided to foster a sort of "siege mentality." I used the film's social media page to rally the troops and gather them behind the banner. The greatest army you can muster is the one with young people and their stage mums. Should war begin, no one would want to mess with them. And bless them! They were brilliant and called MLAS and the media and built us an A-list of supporters we may still need to call on.

The second was that I was searching for schools that were not part of the school board and that could be used as a setting for half of our film. Numbers were limited. Offers came in from Halifax. That wasn't going to happen. This was a North Shore film, and fifty plus young people from our region might have been excluded from taking part had we moved the production to Halifax.

I found a church school in Truro that offered to help, but it really wasn't ideal. Then we found the Tatamagouche Centre. A former school (it actually looks like the school I went to in Shepshed) and now a retreat and learning centre, we found in the manager Katja Burtis someone who finally saw a problem and wanted to find a way to fix it.

The Tata Centre was also able to provide all the accommodation we needed. No more scattered days of shooting; we would now have to pull everything together in one final spell of filming.

Remember when I said that if you want to secure a person's time exclusively it's going to cost more? Well now that we planned to shoot the remainder of the film in a solid block, we would demand exclusivity. Cast and crew needed to commit to us for their entire scheduled time.

We lost a few cast and crew members who could not now make the revised

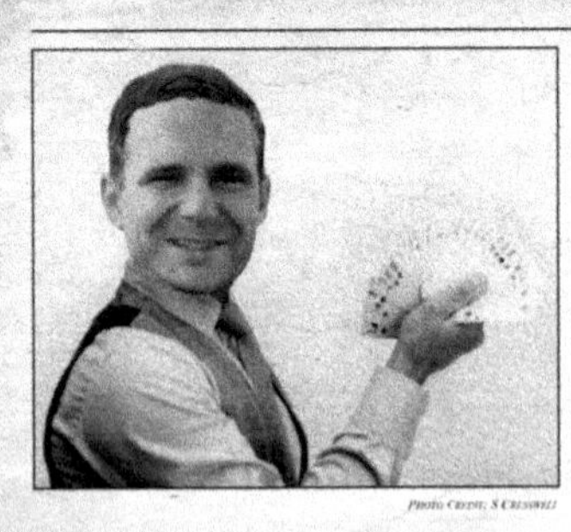

Card Supremo!

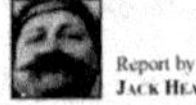

Report by JACK HEART

Amazing scenes as local boy wins the Canadian Solitaire Championships

Solitaire may be one of those games you play by candle-light when the power goes out and you have nothing better to do to most of us, but to young Alex Crowley it is a way of life.

Alex has been obsessed with solitaire for a few years now, locking himself away in his room for hours on end practising the noble art of playing with himself. It seems to have worked out well for the young man as he recently beat everyone to become the Canadian Solitaire Champion. This would be a remarkable achievement for any youngster, especially as he had to beat ten times reigning champion Jaques De Monde, but this young man did it in such a way he has set the world on fire. He claims he never fails to get out at solitaire and proved his claim in the championships where he successfully completed thirteen gammes of solitaire with such speed and ease onlookers were astounded. By the final the crowd of fifty were cheering and clapping every move Alex made. Jaques was visibly upset at the defeat, especially as Alex was lifted by his peers onto their shoulders and carried around the conference centre in a jubillant victory procession, the likes of which has never been seen in the sober world of solitaire. Alex is definitely leader of the pack.

This satirical news clipping shows a young Alex Crowley being hailed as a solitaire champion. The filmmakers managed to superimpose an old photo of actor Craig Gunn to get an authentic look.

dates, which had slipped into July 2015 as we tried to find a new school location. One of the biggest casualties of the schedule change was Brian Holmes. This meant recasting the main bad guy, Alex Crowley, and reshooting some scenes already filmed with Brian. By and large, we came through the exercise unscathed. Now we knew dates, we simply had to find the remaining adult supporting cast who could do the job and be available for our schedule.

Possibly the most demanding period of my life finally looked to be over. But just to reflect on what we had gone through. There were three major baddies wreaking havoc in Nova Scotia in 2015, upsetting people, laying down the law as they saw fit, closing down services, cutting jobs, destroying hope: the provincial government, the film industry unions, and the Chignecto-Central Regional School Board. We were fighting all three at once.

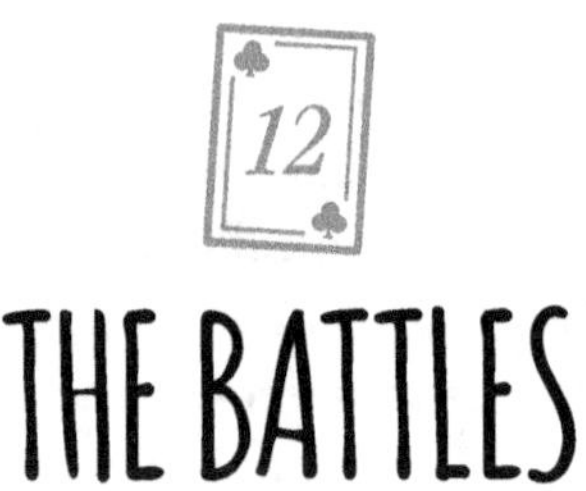

THE BATTLES

"Making a film is like going into war." There was a production manager who spoke like that on a previous project I worked on. I didn't agree. Films are fun, creative, happy projects.

Yet in 2015, every step we took seemed to open us up to another battle: an individual or an organization or a piece of legal mumbo-jumbo or a pedantic jobsworth—we had them all, queuing up to erect roadblocks, to make life difficult, to delay us, or to blow us rural filmmaking bumpkins out of the water. I was ready for a fight, but it began to feel like a conspiracy against the film—or maybe only me.

Those battles were taking their toll though. Since taking over from Cory as director, I had been on the front line as the producer, still trying to keep the production on track. That was fine, but I also needed time for my director prep.

Ashley (the DoP) and I went through the scenes, planned the shots and camera requirements, and produced really rough storyboards, but in essence, it would all be about letting the cast have fun with the script.

Janelle White became a major asset during this period; despite her youth (late teens), she took in her stride the responsibility of managing the production and supporting me. She had attended several workshops early on as a cast hopeful, but she impressed me with her unflappability and meticulous attention to detail. I asked her if she would rather be my production manager, and I was pleased when she said she would. We were working out of the Simple Films office in River John, overlooking the river—one of the finest views around—and the work became more intense as we finally began to see within the constantly changing schedule a patch of calm ahead, which we recognized as the last chance for the remaining production of the film.

Jake Chisholm was also an office regular at that time, bringing his people skills to the fore to ensure we had extras and chaperones and media coverage throughout. (Jake of course should be on screen, and he grabbed the chance to be one of the opposing solitaire coaches, even getting a few key lines in the finale.)

Janelle got herself an assistant even younger than she was: Eamon McCarron didn't let the permanent chaos of a film production office throw him, and he took on his behind-the-scenes role during production with the same tenacity. (Eamon also appeared in the film as one of the henchmen of MacDonald, Comack's arch-nemesis.)

The professionalism and dedication to their task (and dare I say "art") shown by all the young people involved with the production was in stark contrast to the inefficient and often pedantic work of many adults we came into contact with.

Yet if I thought the battles in pre-production were difficult, what was thrown at us during production was on a par with the Battle of the Somme or Gettysburg. And for much of the time, there was no one we could actually fight back against.

So we pulled together a final schedule that appeared to map out all the necessary shooting, unlike that which had gone before and nothing like the original plan, and put our fate in the hands of the Nova Scotia summer and the energy of cast and crew to stick to the task.

The cast and crew assembled at the Tata Centre. Key cast were staying for the duration, July 22 to August 6, and all of the crew too. It would be our home-away-from-home and an experience of a lifetime for many of the young people.

Josh Fifield, "Rob"

I remember the first time I heard about the production coming to northern Nova Scotia. I was in a community theatre group run by Amanda Gillis; Stuart contacted us to audition some prospective kids to be in the feature. Jessie Craig was one of my fellow group members; she would go on to play the role of Odette, and several others would receive minor roles as well.

After months of workshops and auditions I finally got word that I would be playing the role of Rob. It wouldn't be until the table read that I would meet all the major cast together including my good friends Jessie Craig, Carleigh and Andrew Halliday, and familiar faces from past workshops that would soon become some of my closest friends.

I was excited to play the character of Rob. I could see a bit of myself in him, being insecure about a tragic aspect of his life but still managing to find and stick with just a few great friends through the thick and thin. Rob is a strong person both in the writing and in his own character. Losing a father at such a young and impressionable age is devastating, but he still finds the will to go on. He fights to get his lost card back, one of the few reminders of his father he has left; he helps his best friend Cormack with the solitaire championship even after a big argument between them, and even works at the vineyard to keep his family financially stable. I hope that other kids facing tough times in their adolescence can look up to a character like Rob and find their own strength to carry on.

Getting to all stay together in the same house up in Tatamagouche made the experience that much more personal and grew the bonds between not only the cast members but with the crew as well. We were really all in it for the passion of filmmaking and to bring this story of pure friendship to life. The days were long and the work was hard, but it was all worth it when the sun went down and we could all sit together to enjoy a meal and reminisce about the day. The month went by much too fast, and I still feel as though it all happened a short time ago.

I now find myself graduated from film school and working to continue my pursuit of a career of filmmaking. I knew from a young age that I wanted to get into filmmaking—acting just so happened to be my first opportunity at it. I'm grateful for all the years of experience I gained from stage acting with direction from Amanda and the many teachers I had in school, all leading to my chance to be in my first feature film. Whether I'm acting or behind the camera, I find all aspects of production so enjoyable. I want to extend my gratitude to the cast and crew of *The Only Game in Town* for giving me such a wonderful first-time experience on a movie production. I hope you all continue to do great work in this industry. I can promise you that I will too.

I called everyone together in the common room of one of the houses. I wanted to thank everyone for staying the course and getting us to this point.

Yes, we had lost many on the way. Yes, the shoot was being completed in this fifteen-day block, the last chance for the film before summer ended and we lost all our cast to the wider world.

I told them that right at the outset, Josephine had said that I was going to be run ragged this year—producing the film, launching a film festival, and as she rightly predicted, directing the film. I found myself saying over and over: "My wife was right!" (And when the film wrapped two weeks later, the youngsters got me a T-shirt that said: "My wife was right!")

It was a long speech because of course I do like to talk. Yet as the sun went down and the summer looked so bright and full of promise, I wish I could have done a Nelson speech: "Engage the enemy more closely." I always liked that one, it means "get stuck in" or "get your retaliation in first" or "kick them where it hurts"—all the things I wish I'd been able to do along the way. But when you're making a film, you have to be diplomatic and avoid confrontation, even when confrontation is thrust in front of you.

I also wish I could have called upon some Winston Churchill–style oration, pledging to fight them on the location shots, fight them on the close-ups, and never surrender. To be honest, I was tired, and the thought of going into battle for two solid weeks and more hadn't yet sunk in. But I think as speeches go, it did the trick.

I'm a home bird. I have found, in our home just outside River John, a piece of heaven. It's full of green trees and birds and peace and quiet. The prospect of leaving it for two weeks was not something I welcomed. I also knew that if I stayed with everyone else during the shoot I would never give my mind the rest it would need to stay sharp and focused. For the sake of a twenty-minute journey home each night I was happy to leave the young cast and crew to party on after a day's shooting. I had lived the project on a daily basis for almost two years. I would need my own bed.

Going into War

I harnessed the feeling of being the underdogs and fed that to the cast and crew to get them fired up and full of energy to get the job done. It helps to build a team. I really did feel under siege myself, but I tend to internalize conflicts such that I carry the stress in me and don't let it show.

I started to find inspiration to keep up the fight everywhere I looked. Take That's song and video for the "The Flood" was particularly apt. Splendidly rousing. (Whoever makes the film of this book needs to get that track in.)

We made a funny team. The youngsters were excited and eager, ready to rush headlong into this big adventure. Their parents and all the adults involved were angry and fired up with anti-establishment fervour. Somehow, we made it work, we found as many people willing to help us as we found wanting to make life hard for us. We utilized crowd-funding and called in all the favours we could.

The locals along the North Shore were fantastic, individuals and business owners who went the extra mile to help keep us on track. Homeowners like Rob Assels and Lesley Longhorn who gave up their house for a day—a very long day—to be part of the film. The fact they had just taken delivery of a batch of adorable puppies gave the cast and crew the chance to cuddle and coo between takes.

You see, some people were happy to help, in whatever way they could. All films need an element of local co-operation and goodwill. We found in our supporters along the North Shore what amounted to a resistance movement, people prepared to dodge bullets and feed the desperate troops while the baddies hunted them down.

The local press, chiefly the *Pictou Advocate* and *New Glasgow News*, found that having a full-length feature film being produced entirely within their communities was a great story that could provide some twists and turns and a little glamour for their publications. They have been an immense source of support for us, and despite the fact that I'm not always in the mood for an interview, they deserve to get whatever story they want when they want it.

More than one journalist thought the idea of being an extra in the film was a good angle for a story. And on more than one occasion I turned around from one arduous scene or another to be confronted by a smiling reporter wanting me to say a few words for the press.

I am not the best photo subject at the best of times, but with my eyes red from stress, sleepless nights, and the wild hair of a director "in the zone," I somehow managed to refrain from stating brusquely "no comment" or "how did this journalist get on set? Isn't this a closed set?"

Instead, I learned that the best people the press should be talking to were the stars: Jesse Hemmings (Cormack), Jessie Craig (Odette), and David Mortimer (Alastair). Jake Chisholm was also far better at PR and social media than I was, and he took on the task of press liaison with great energy.

In the darkest times of this film, during the chaos of early summer 2015, or the carnage and stress of the hurriedly rescheduled period of intense shooting in July and August, or the long, slow agony of stalled post-production (more on this in the next chapter), there has always emerged a new set of champions to our cause.

Being our champions didn't require them to bear arms for us. So desperate was I for support (or vindication) that any words of encouragement were enough to stir the emotions and give me the courage to go "over the top" one more time. So many phone calls and emails of support came out of the blue. I felt like a drowning man who was continuously being thrown a lifeline.

When he heard that the CCRSB was making life difficult for us, and then the possibility that the provincial film tax credit might not being available for us, MLA Tim Houston let it be known he would give his support. (I haven't yet needed to keep him to this, but I am sure I will once the paperwork is filed with the Department of Finance.)

I exhibit a character trait that will likely be my downfall. I'm stubborn. I always have been. At age four, on holiday in Mablethorpe and angry that my two older sisters were able to go horseback riding without me, I positioned myself in front of the horses, blocking the exit from the stable yard like some pale imitation of Emily Wilding Davison, the suffragette who was killed by the King's horse at the Epsom Derby in 1913.

Stubborn is as stubborn does. It's a trait connected to not taking no for an answer, but it's actually more complex than that. It's about digging heels in, being dogged in the face of opposition. It's about being slapped and going back for more.

My dad was stubborn when he continued to push my brother around in a wheelchair long into his eighties, despite angina and hip and knee replacements, and against everyone's better advice.

So when you tell me I can't make a film, or I can't make it here, or I can't make it with these people, then I'm hardly going to take any notice of you. And every smile or thumbs up I received along the way was seen by me as admiring acknowledgements of my hero status. Such is the nature of the stubborn, that we stubbornly kid ourselves that the fight isn't futile, that we're doing it for a greater cause.

Here, now, two years later, I am prepared to admit that the film was made because I was too stubborn to let it go. I only needed the indication that I was fighting for others "less fortunate" or "more deserving," and I could justify marching everyone to the brink of destruction.

So there you go. All of the people who offered support and encouragement, it's your fault we skirted with disaster.

Or without you, I wouldn't have had the belief that it wasn't futile.

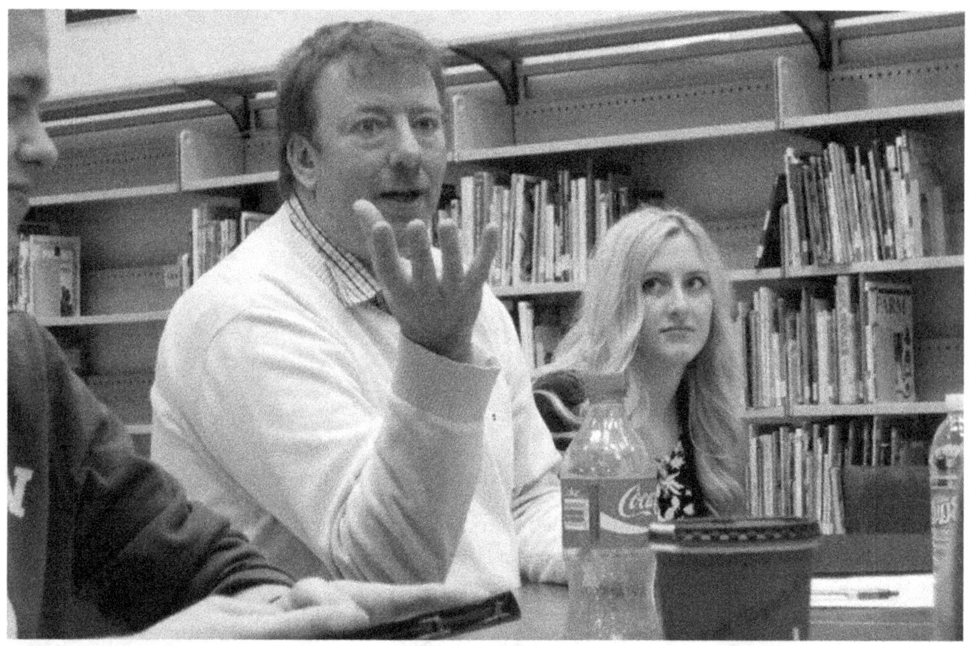

Stuart Cresswell and production manager Janelle White at a script reading. (Credit: Fateh Ahmed)

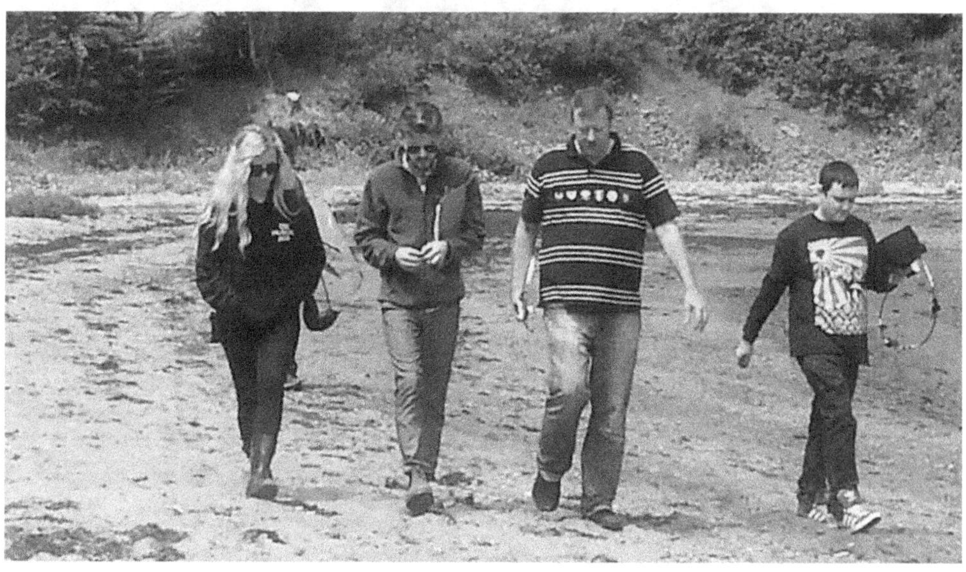

Stuart Cresswell the director, second from right, discusses the plans for a shoot on the beach at Seafoam with 1st AD Jake Chisholm, production manager Janelle White, and camera operator Liam Petite. (Credit: Gina Barrett White)

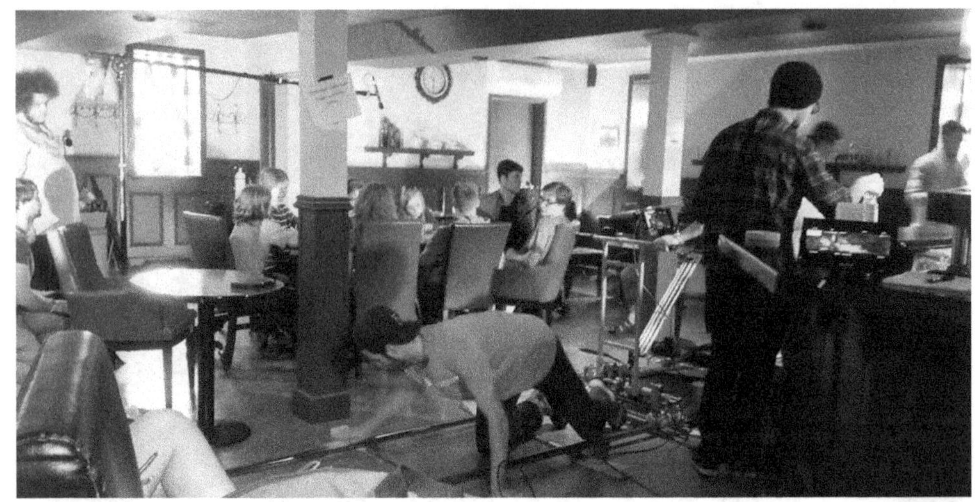

Cast and crew preparing to shoot the Slater club scene in the Sinclair Room, Tatamagouche. (Credit: Jeanette Gormley)

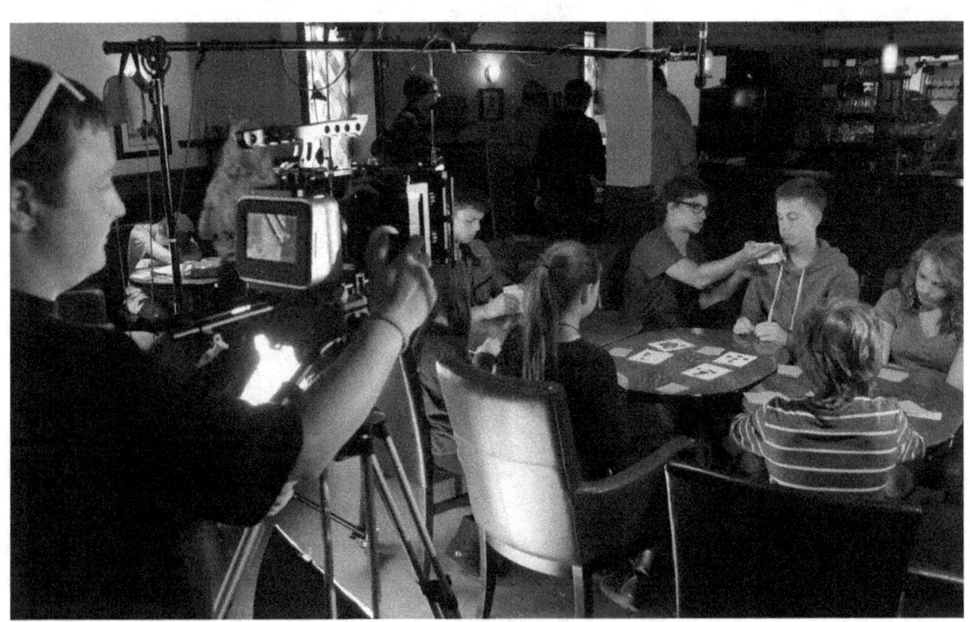

Shooting in Slater's club. (Credit: Fateh Ahmed)

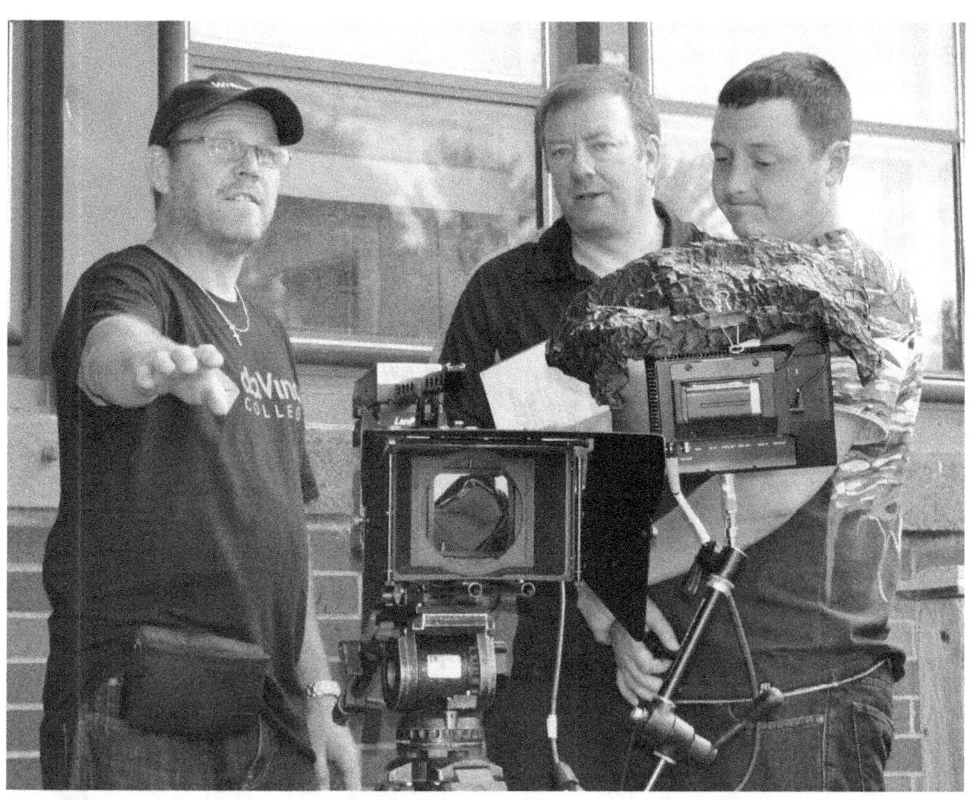

Ashley King, director of photography, Stuart Cresswell, and Liam Petite, camera operator. (Credit: Carol Dunn)

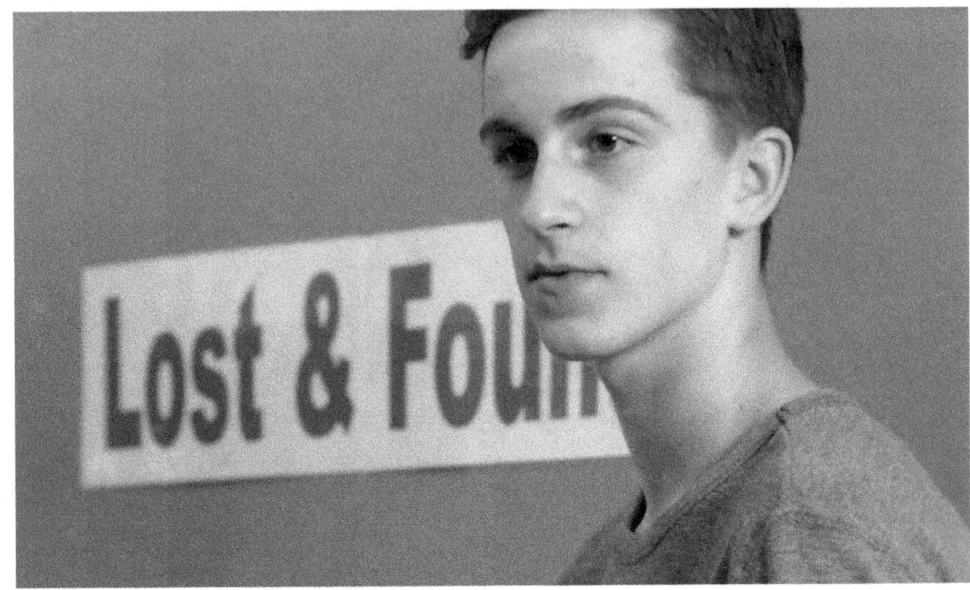

Jesse Hemmings, who starred as Cormack Vertue, is shown during an the early part of the shoot in 2014. (Credit: *TOGIT*)

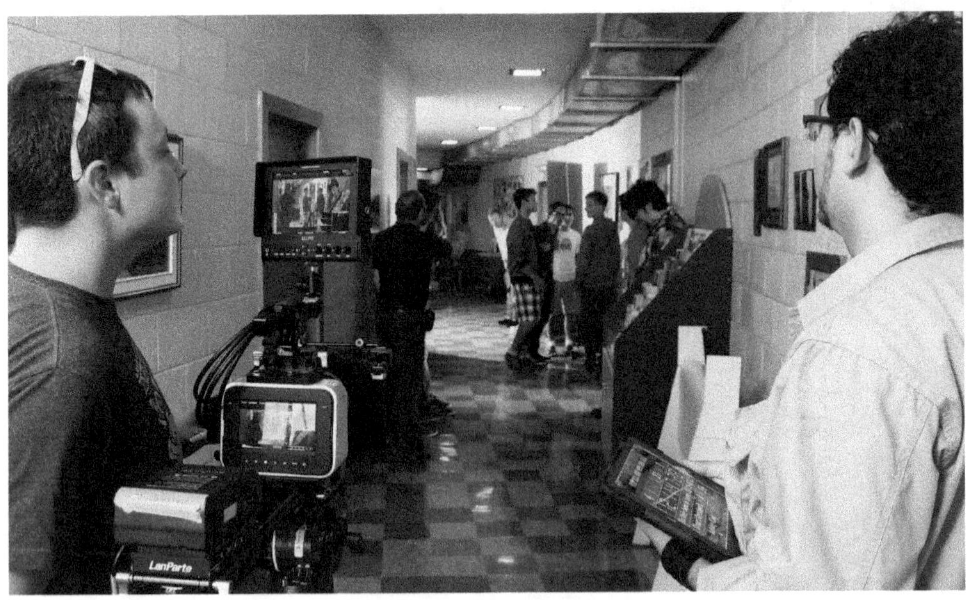

Shooting a scene at the Tatamagouche Centre. (Credit: *TOGIT*)

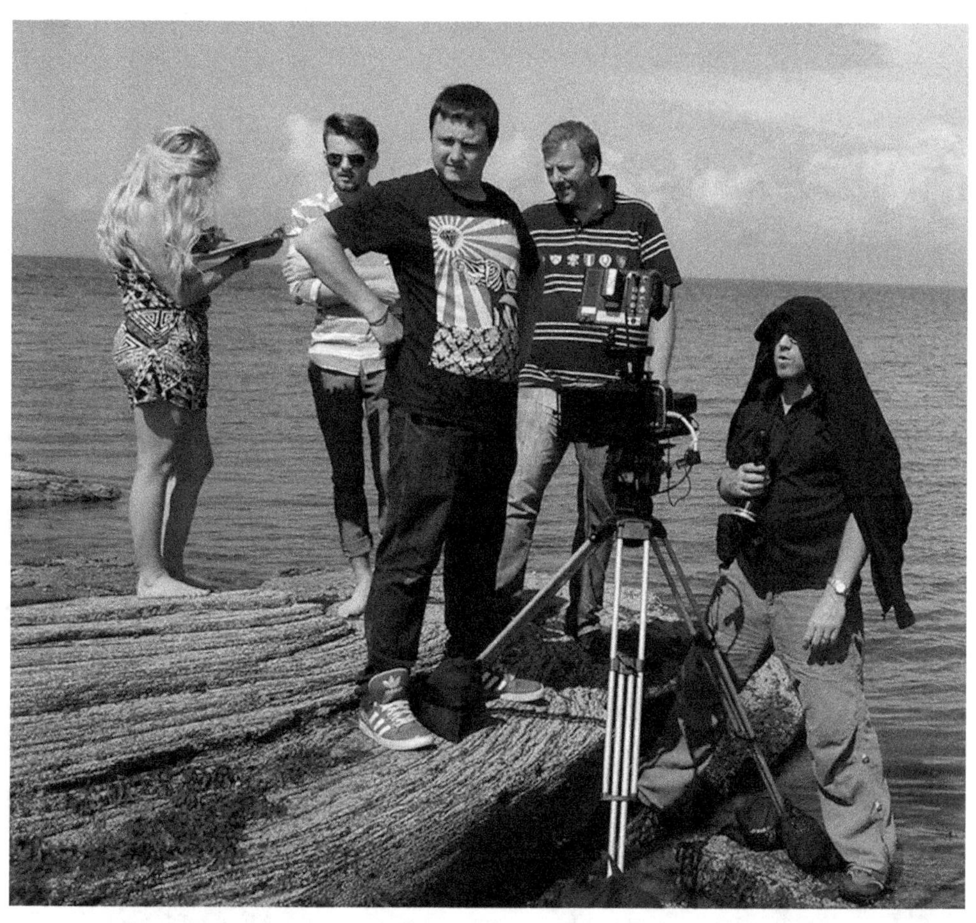

Left to right: Janelle White, production manager, Jake Chisholm, first assistant director, Liam Petite, camera assistant, Stuart Cresswell, director, and Ashley King, director of photography. Location: Seafoam Beach. (Credit: Fateh Ahmed)

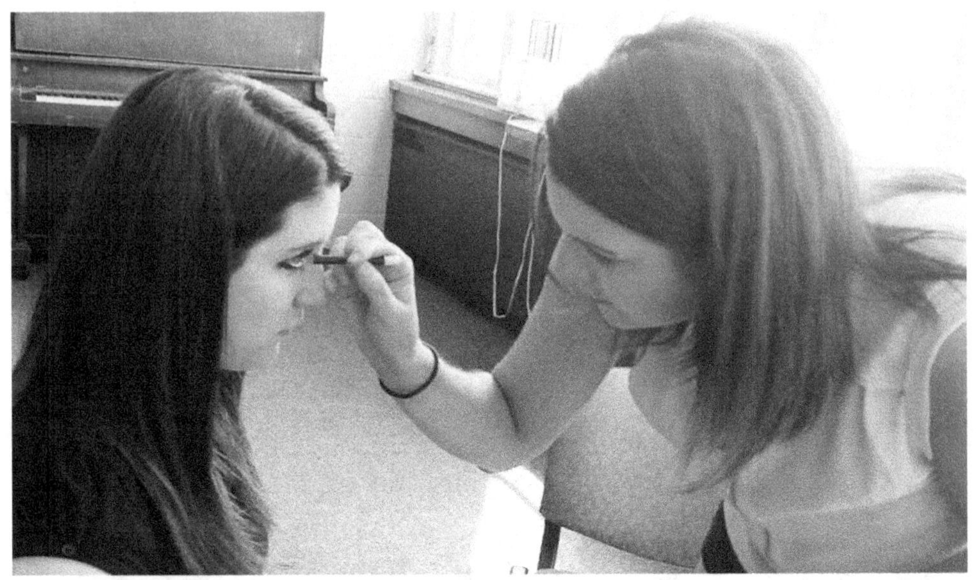

Colleen Patterson, makeup artist, goes to work on Tasha Woods (Christine). (Credit: April Staggs)

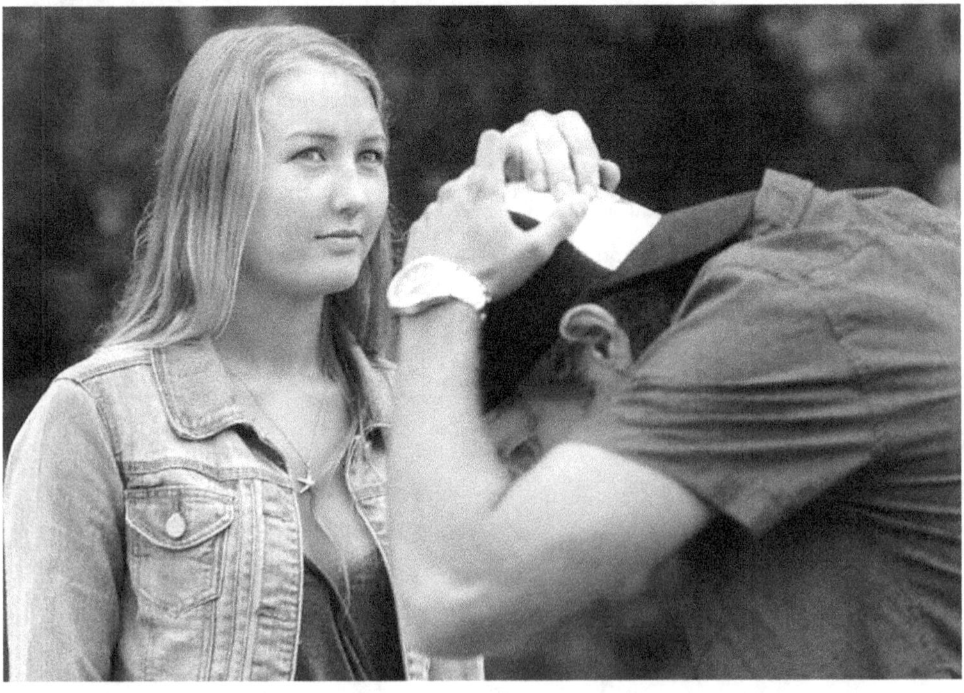

Jessie Craig (Odette) and Dave Mortimer (Alastair Ramsey) shoot a scene during a thunderstorm which made Dave a bit nervous. (Credit: Ashley King)

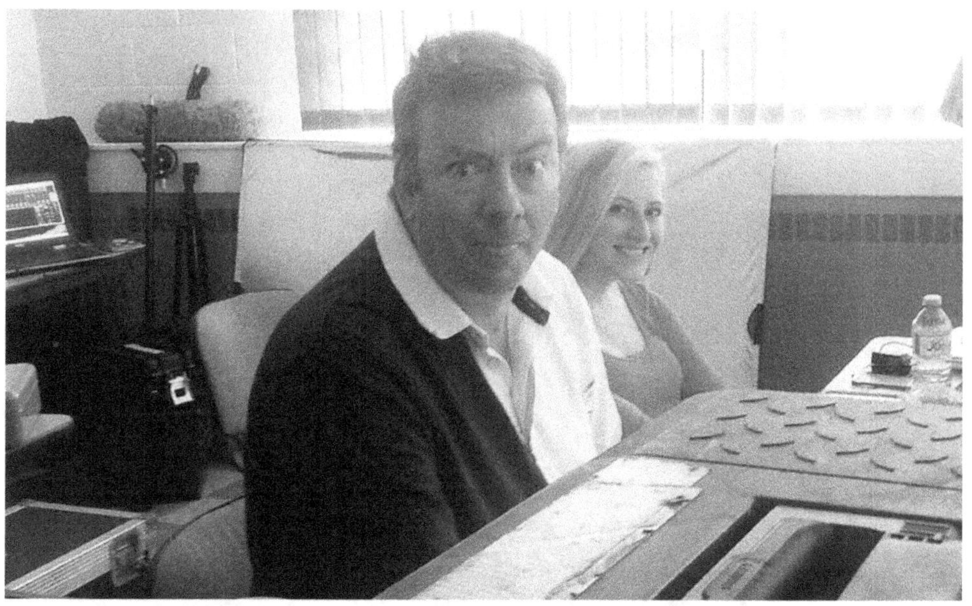

Stuart Cresswell and production manager Janelle White during the frantic final day of filming. (Credit: Gina Barrett White)

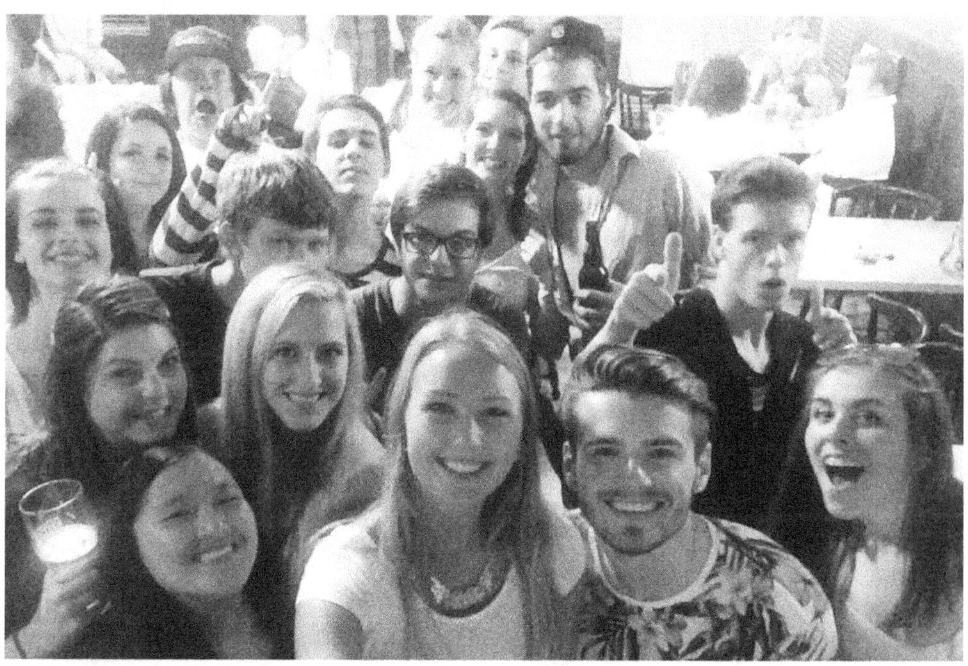

Many of the cast and crew during the wrap party at Big Al's in Tatamagouche. (Credit: Jessie Craig)

Jesse Hemmings Jessie Craig David Mortimer

with Aiden Jamieson Aldo Orsi Josh Fifield

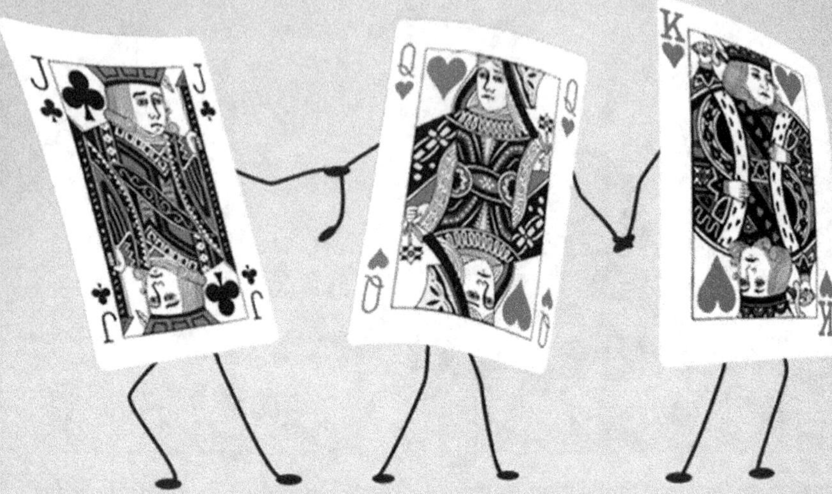

THE ONLY GAME IN TOWN

An autistic teenager, forever in trouble at school, displays a rare talent for the card game solitaire

An original comedy written and produced by Stuart Cresswell

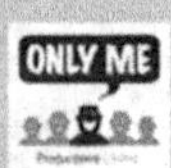

Only Me Productions & Simple Films

www.onlygameintownfilm.com

Movie poster.

PART THREE

THE DIRECTOR'S EPIC

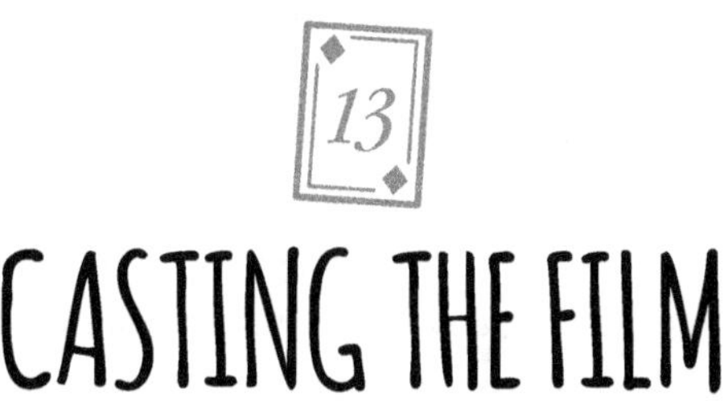

CASTING THE FILM

It wasn't supposed to be my story, the director bit. I wanted someone else to direct, I was desperate for someone else to direct. My long-suffering wife, Josephine, commented in 2014 that I was taking on too much.

"No!" I said, having a stab at the meaning of the word. "It's going to be fine! The writing is done, I'm only producing, and most of that work will be done by early summer. Cory will direct!"

"You will end up doing it all."

My wife was right. I know this. She's always right. I'm just a chap who thinks he lives in a sitcom with people watching his every move, a bit like *The Truman Show*. Only I'm funnier, and when I deliver my lines I can even hear the audience laughing.

I live to be funny. It's my thing. I used to have handsome and funny as my thing, but looks are temporary, now it's just funny. I can hear readers now, laughing at the cheeky, affable little chap that I am.

I was directing a comedy, but here I was, barely prepared and struggling through some bitter fighting and turmoil in my role as producer. How in the world could I separate the two roles and retain some of the humour I would need to make this film work?

And all the while I'm asking: How different would this film be, the story of the film, if Cory had been able to direct? What would he have written in this chapter?

Casting and Crewing

With this film there was no distinction between the role of producer (me), who hires the crew (including the director), and the director (eventually me), who chooses the cast. Under normal circumstances, actually under my intended plan, the two roles would have been separated, but this film has never had much regard for plans.

"If you have no one in your film, all you have is sprockets!" said Dov Simens. That was true twenty years ago when I attended his course, hosted by Raindance. It's more true today. There is a level of expectation in film that there is a "name" in the cast, whose own brand the audiences buy into, which makes them watch it at the cinema or on Netflix. Remember that nowadays services such as Netflix allow you to search for films by actor.

To produce a $5 million feature with nobody famous in it would be financial suicide; in fact, I doubt the financing package would ever be complete in that situation. At the ultra-low end of the budget scale, it's not such a factor. But still, once the film has been made you will want people to find it and watch it.

Having John Dunsworth in the film would definitely have given us a stab at promoting the film in Canada. However, I had always seen the film as strong enough to stand on its own, launching a score of new careers instead of cashing in on existing ones.

There was one particular test I gave the young actors during workshops. We had the usual exercises, such as preparing your own breakfast, during which the actors would imagine themselves in their kitchen making their favourite breakfast. It's a handy exercise as you watch for concentration skills, along with the consistency of their actions. I explained that for breakfast, I invariably had toast and Marmite.

"What's Marmite?" they and their parents would ask.

"Well it's essentially the bits of gunk leftover after the beer-making process, scraped out of the fermentation tanks and put into jars."

I went on to explain that it is extremely healthy and good for you (though you aren't allowed to talk of it that way) and can boost Vitamin B12 levels for people that are lacking such things. Well several of the mothers felt the need to give it a try. I even suggested that all the cast try some Marmite, just to see.

There was method in the madness. Marmite has a slogan: "Love it or hate it." I was looking for a main character, Cormack, who didn't seem to fit with the rest of his peers. Always just a little different. One way to demonstrate this would be to have him eat Marmite for breakfast.

At the next workshop I was inundated with jars of Marmite reduced by one thin spread, just enough for a slice of toast. No one could stand the stuff. But Jesse Hemmings seemed to enjoy it. He was our Cormack!

Jesse Hemmings, "Cormack Vertue"

It was the best three weeks of my life. I can't really say which part was my favourite, but one of the most enjoyable parts was getting to know the people working on the film, and I'm still in touch with friends I made on the set. *The Only Game in Town* was a great learning experience for me, and it definitely helped me decide that this is what I want to do. Having someone like Stuart directing helped a lot because he made it easy to understand what he was looking for.

One of the most challenging things during filming was when we had to shoot this scene where I was eating a piece of toast covered in Marmite. We kept shooting the scene over and over again in order to get multiple takes, so I had to keep slamming the Marmite into me.

I remember so many times over the three weeks we would just stop filming for a bit because we were all laughing too hard over something somebody had done or said. I'm grateful to have had the opportunity to discover what it's like to work on a film, but what's more valuable to me are the connections I made with the people I worked with. I hope that when the film is viewed, the audience will be able to share in what we felt, and experience that same connection.

Indeed, Jesse Hemmings was a surprise. He came to later workshops, just when I was worried that I might never find a Cormack. He had the ability to give us a boy on the Asperger's scale, and more importantly he took direction well.

During the workshop phase of development, and having seen almost one hundred young people in that time, it was clear that certain young people had an edge on the others. I find it not at all surprising that the young people who secured the lead roles were all serious about building careers in the industry. Some had already done performance work to a high standard in theatre or music. It was no accident that over the course of twelve months, our own young leads made their parts their own.

I only later found out that Jesse is an award-winning vocalist. He turned up with his best friend, Aldo Orsi. Aldo was also experienced on stage with music and acting. The two of them had that playing style that spoke of old friends. If they choose to, they could be Ant and Dec, the English duo who are all round entertainers, OBEs, and possibly TV's hottest pair of presenters. Or better still, if ever the planets align, I would like to revive the Bob Hope and Bing Crosby *Road to…* style of films with Aldo and Jesse. As the workshops came to an end in autumn 2014, it was clear that these two would be cast as Cormack and Joe. I was halfway to my four key roles.

Aldo Orsi, "Joe"

For me, *The Only Game in Town*, as both a production and an experience, was unforgettable. I honestly didn't know what I was getting into! But as the abstract idea of "being in a movie" turned concrete, being on set and in front of a camera became something I thoroughly enjoyed. And working with such an energetic crew bolstered the experience. I got to work with my best friends, on a project that will stay with me forever. And there are not enough thanks I can give for it all. *TOGIT* may be my first venture into film, but I hope it won't be my last.

Josh Fifield was a different kind of good. There was a sensitivity in his playing, a more low-key understated performance, and at first I bounced him around. I couldn't decide if he was Cormack or one of his friends. I just knew he could do what was necessary. As we approached the end of 2014 and began to get some scenes under our belt, the interplay between him and Jesse and Aldo really worked. He was perfect for the role of Rob.

The role of Chris was the hardest to fill. An outsider with brains. The part had been read by some good talents, but they played him too well. Chris should not be well-spoken, his intellect is constantly undermined by his delivery. Aiden Jamieson came on board very late. He wasn't perfect right off the bat, but we shot a few scenes with him as Chris just to see how it might work. Aiden would grow into the part over the coming months.

"You might be able to write this, but you sure as hell can't say it!" Harrison Ford's outburst to George Lucas on the set of *Star Wars* is well-known. There are times in a script when technical stuff needs to be said. Poor Aiden! How many lines of his were talking of this formula or that hypothesis? The fact that he stumbled his way through them is just about right for his character. Imagine having to say this as a chat up line to the girl of your dreams!

CHRIS
Tammy?

(Swooning)
I know you said I'm too young for you, but I'd like to point out that Évariste Galois was a teenager when he invented a new branch of mathematics, group theory, to prove that the quintic, which as we all know is an equation with the term x5, is not solvable by any formula.

So the four main boys were chosen—or as I prefer to say, the characters chose their actors. The main love interest in the film is Odette. There was no shortage of talented young actresses who could have brought something special to the part.

Odette is based on a girl from my own bumbling attempts at wooing the girlfriend of an older and more attractive boy. She is the unattainable, the epitome of the hazardous quest, the siren's call to all lonely preteens, luring them to their doom on the rocks of first love.

Reading my war story to my school friends early in the mornings, I had learned the art of purple prose. My heart was ready to fall in love, and there were many girls of my own age to fall in love with, and I did at some point with most of them. But Odette was aloof, mature, powerful. She was two years older than I was and carried herself as many teenage girls in the mid-seventies did—ready to take on the world on at least equal terms to their male counterparts. She had attracted my attention, and very soon, as often happens with me, it developed into an obsession. So I wrote her a love letter.

One morning while playing Hot Rice—a fast-paced playground game played with a hard ball—the huge and attractive Alastair Ramsey walked up to me. Everyone knew Alastair Ramsey. A sporting god with film-star looks. To be approached by him, especially as someone so much his junior, was an honour.

"Are you Stuart Cresswell?" he asked.

"Oh yes, yes I am!" How great was this?

"Did you write a love letter to Odette?"

Seemed like a strange question to ask me. I thought he might be inviting me to play football with the big lads. "Yes! Yes I did!"

The punch in the stomach was the hardest thing I've ever been hit with. It came out of the blue; a similar punch killed Houdini. The air left my body and I struggled with staying upright. I wasn't the sort to get into fights at school. I would employ all sorts of humour as evading tactics, and where possible, run away. But let's be clear. This punch hurt!

"Odette's my girlfriend! Leave her alone!" I think at that point, Alastair (and our audience made up of my football and war story friends) expected me to buckle and hit the ground in tears. The truth is that I was too shocked to do anything. My mind raced, but I'm sure all I could think was, *Thank heaven he hit me in the stomach! At least my face is still all right!* I was as conscious of my good looks then as I am now.

Alastair seemed to stand looking at me for ages. It was an uncomfortable moment for both of us. He wanted to know why I wasn't crying, and I wanted to tell him I admired him so much for the goal he scored the other week.

Eventually, it became clear to everyone that there would be no more drama, and Alastair shrugged his huge shoulders and walked away. I swallowed my pride and my breakfast for the second time, and pretended that this sort of thing happened every day.

Whenever I saw Odette after that, she and her friends would snigger—and I doubt my suspicions that she was laughing at my ridiculous attempts at a romantic letter were unfounded. The romance quickly faded.

I was keen to pay tribute to all that by incorporating it into my script.

When Cormack eventually delivers the love letter to Odette, he feels ten feet tall. Within seconds, as Odette and her friend giggle at his clumsy purple prose, he feels as though he has been stabbed through the heart. It's funny, isn't it? We can survive the physical pain of a massive punch to the gut, but love can rip the soul from your body.

The parts of Odette and Alastair, which are far from being bit roles and pay homage to the great people I was at school with, had to be portrayed with care and respect. Alastair was never written as a mere school bully, because he wasn't, and Odette was that balance of pre-girl-power girl-power and casual indifference to silly small boys.

Jessie Craig attended most of the workshops right from the start. She was eager, had the right temperament for acting, and the mix of good looks and mischief required to play Odette. I only found out later that she was desperate to make a life out of acting. I imagine she'd had to contend with many sideways glances and raised eyebrows. She was a young girl from Seafoam, having attended River John Elementary School (before it was closed down), and I know she would have been told many times to think about a proper job and a real future. No one ever achieves fame and fortune in Seafoam, River John, Shepshed, or Coalville, or in fact in most of rural Leicestershire and even more rural Nova Scotia. But she was focused on acting as a career, and it showed.

Odette's boyfriend, Alastair Ramsey, needed to be so good-looking he would melt the screen. (It's the sort of role that, obviously, in my day, I would have been cast in, though Alastair Ramsey falling off his chair for comedy effect would have lost some of the edge and prowling menace.)

When we talk of commitment to the profession and taking a chance on your own future, I can't speak highly enough of David Mortimer. Yes, he's good looking; it turns out he had done (and still does) some modelling. But he was driving from Glace Bay, Cape Breton—easily a four-hour drive—to get to the workshops.

I liked David. From the start he was pleasant, polite, and natural. The camera loved him, and there was no one else we saw that could give the part of Alastair Ramsey the right mix of elements.

There was also something about him that reminded me of my cousin Neil. For many years, Neil and I were pretty close. We had adventures and despite our young ages—I think I was about nine at the time, and he about eleven—we thought nothing of hopping a train and travelling for three hours to the seaside, having an ice cream, and heading home again. All of this without telling any adults where we were going.

As we grew older we saw each other less and less, and soon it was just weddings and funerals. The last time I saw him was at my dad's funeral. Neil had been battling his own cancer at the time, but he looked well. He died within the year at the age of fifty. So when I met David and something about him reminded me of Neil, it was obvious I would want him around.

I tried to explain the "art of casting" to a class several years back. For film and television, more than stage acting, it's about the actor's relationship to the camera. It's a look. The way they fit with other characters on screen. Talent is important, yes, and I saw better young actors than David during the workshops, but none would have been convincing as Alastair, and none had that mysterious, magical connection with the camera that brings the audience closer to the character.

My young leads were a great bunch, and I can't help feeling that the fact the truly talented and those with determination ended up being cast in the main roles vindicates the approach we took with the workshops. With forty-plus speaking parts and most of them young people, the supporting cast also needed to be found, and the workshops helped me to find them all. Sadly, despite my pledge that anyone attending the workshops would be on screen at some point, many of them lost interest once the main roles had gone. Which is a shame, because they would have had fun and possibly had a tasty part anyway.

We had one of those moments in filmmaking that turn the script on its head. The part of Slater, the devious card-game operator, had started out as the main villain, most likely to be played by someone comparable to the brooding menace of Andrew Halliday's MacDonald. (Andrew was excellent by the way. The camera loved him, and he's another with a great career ahead of him.)

Slater should be even more of a threat to our heroes. Think Jabba the Hutt. We auditioned several young actors—bigger, older people, all more than adequate to play the part. But Slater's gang looked increasingly as if it would be made up of actors in the younger age range, eleven to fourteen. This meant that an older Slater just wasn't going to work.

When I wrote Slater in the outline, I deliberately kept the name simply as Slater—no gender was ever implied—but I was painfully aware that I needed more strong female roles. Eventually, during the later stages of scripting, Slater "identified" as female, but certainly not younger than Cormack and his friends.

Elyssa Alguire tried out for the part of Slater and gave to the role that bored yet self-assured slyness that gave her the right amount of menace. Elyssa had proven herself in workshops despite her young age (thirteen), but with her in the role, it meant that Slater's gang of card hustlers and vagabonds hiding out in her uncle's abandoned club could all be on the young side and we could use the younger actors for Slater's gang without it looking odd.

This changed the dynamic of the scene involving our heroes but it really works. The most frightening people a teenage boy has to deal with are those who aren't yet teens. You can't hit them, even in self-defense; they are "untouchable." When we shot the scene of the boys being frisked by Slater's gang, I demanded that the take run on for several minutes. It needed to be excruciating for everyone and then descend into slapstick. I loved Slater's entire gang.

Through the chopping and changing schedules, we lost Brian Holmes, who was to play Alex Crowley, and I had not been able to get John Dunsworth for Principal Joyce. They were among the key adult roles that we had to find quickly.

I thought about Colleen MacIsaac, a talented actress I'd worked with on my film *Broken*, but I always considered her too young-looking for one of the mother roles. She sent me a photo of herself looking haggard and world-worn. She got the part of Odette's mother. One of the most nerve-tingling scenes in the entire film is Colleen and Jessie having a heated kitchen argument. The entire cast and crew on set that day felt moved.

The other mother part—that of Cormack's mother, Cathy—was a shoo-in for Amanda Gillis, who ran the youth theatre in New Glasgow and who had shot a couple of scenes during 2014. The dates and schedules got screwed up so many times, and by accident her name didn't get shifted to a new set of schedules. I had called on help from folks in the industry to suggest people I could work with—all non-union of course. Our casting helper in Halifax, not seeing a name against the role of Cormack's mother, found another actress and committed her to it.

I was caught between a rock and a hard place; I was going to let people down whichever way I chose. In the end, I reasoned that if I was asking for someone's help and advice to cast parts, then I should take it, but that didn't make it any easier for me. I had to break the news to Amanda that the part had gone elsewhere. I would have been angry in her position, so I can understand why she was. It was a strange spot for us to find ourselves in, and even though there were mitigating circumstances I didn't, and still don't, feel good about it.

The end result was that we had Fiona Kirkpatrick Parsons joining us as Cormack's mother, Cathy. Fiona was certainly experienced and talented and brought great sensibility to the role.

Fiona Kirkpatrick Parsons, "Cathy Vertue"

It all began with a tweet from @TOGITFilm on July 10, 2015: "I think you may be the one Kevin Kincaid suggested for a movie part shooting north shore July/August." That's definitely not a tweet one sees every day.

I didn't quite know what to make of it, but Kevin Kincaid had cast me in some local commercials and I was pretty flattered that he suggested me. I was a bit wary, but I tweeted back that I would email and, moments later, I received, "Fingers crossed your schedule works." I honestly wondered if someone had made a mistake or was pulling a prank.

After an email (with some of the script) and a phone call, I was informed that I had the part. A principal role. In an actual movie. I was gobsmacked and beyond excited. I'd been doing some stage work for about three years, but I had always, always wanted to be in a film. This was the first and only time I'd been cast in anything without an audition, never mind a feature film.

I really fell in love with my character, Cathy, Cormack Vertue's devoted mother. She has a huge heart and, like any mom, she loves her child more than anything. As a mom myself, I absolutely related to her protectiveness of Cormack. Cathy had split with her son's father while she was pregnant and was determined to raise her boy on her own. She tries so hard to reach her son emotionally, only to be greeted with very little emotion in return; yet Cathy remains generally optimistic, soldiering on, undaunted by Cormack's inability to respond to her on an emotional level. A challenge for any parent, never mind one who is facing it all on her own. I love her strength and her pluck.

I had an amazing time on set and was constantly inspired by all the terrific actors (young and more "seasoned") in this film, including Jesse Hemmings, who plays Cormack, and the fabulous Craig Gunn, who plays Crowley. I'm forever grateful for all the lovely friendships I made during the shoot and especially grateful to Stuart for casting me. We had such a collaborative and fun atmosphere during this film, creating memories that I will treasure all my life.

Card cheat brings disgrace to town

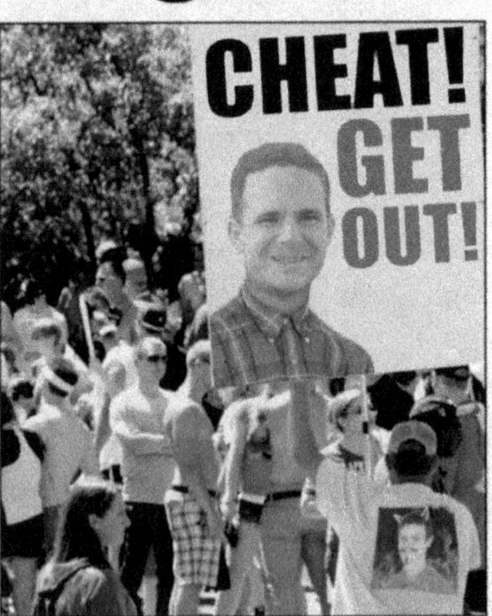

Our small town is hanging it's head in shame today as it is revealed that the local solitaire phenomenon Alex Crowley is nothing more than a cheat.

Alex was revealed as a cheat in an inquiry into betting scandals surrounding the formerly sedate and sober world of solitaire. Alex rose to fame in 1996 when he astounded crowds with his ability to complete every single game of solitaire in the Canadian National Championships. Jaques De Monde, the reigning champion for over ten years committed suicide last year after his humbling defeat. People are calling for the statue of Alex, erected in the town square in 2001, to be pulled down and replaced with a memorial to Jaques or a shrubbery.

PHOTO CREDIT: S CRESSWELL

A fake newspaper clipping showing Craig Gunn as a young Crowley. In the film, Crowley keeps press clippings of his success (and his failures, apparently!) in a memory box.

Alongside her was Craig Gunn, now the main adult character of Alex Crowley. I had seen him in a couple of short films, and he certainly had a presence on camera. Craig was able to blend the scheming menace of a bitter and tormented solitaire coach with the subtle humour of the slightly absurd take on the sports movie genre. He was also a great support for the young cast and led by example at every opportunity.

We auditioned tirelessly for Principal Ambrose Joyce. It's the monologue, you see. That one speech, a page and a bit of script. I had in my head precisely how it should be delivered. Someone suggested I do it. I was hurt. Joyce was late fifties; I was early-mid fifties.

In one audition, the actor had a problem with his dentures. On every syllable there was a clicking sound that echoed around the room. He seemed oblivious to it. I offered him a glass of water.

"No thank *click* you, I'm *click* good."

I had visions of the key speech being the biggest casting disaster since John Wayne played Genghis Khan. Maybe I could do the part.

I asked my friend and North Shore neighbour, author Gary Blackwood, if he could suggest anyone, having done a bit of theatre and film himself. He had already been signed on to play the contest judge in the solitaire tournament scenes.

Gary suggested Rick Shaver. Rick auditioned and while he wasn't exactly what I was looking for, he was certainly what I found. Which is another aspect of casting to bear in mind. He brought something different to the role, but it was consistent and believable.

Rick Shaver, "Principal Joyce"

I've always loved movies, theatre, and performing, but when the time came to make those life and career decisions we all must, I chose to ignore those loves and chase the pedestrian and practical instead. A few years ago, mostly by accident, I returned to acting things out in front of people I didn't know, thanks to local community theatre and a couple of local amateur films that were, and still are, a delight to do. *TOGIT*, I saw, was at another level altogether.

When I arrived at *TOGIT*'s location and took a look at the set and the activity around it, my first reaction was, "Wow, this movie set looks like a set you'd see in a movie about making a movie!" I was excited to be a part of it, and much of that excitement was because there were so many people energetically doing what they clearly loved, and in particular, so many young people actively pursuing their passion.

Being involved in *TOGIT* afforded me the rare opportunity to witness a world that might have been mine had I made different decisions back in the day. It was, if you like, a bit of "in your face" shoulda/coulda/woulda, both thrilling and poignant.

With that notion rattling around in my head, I have to say that it was a great thing to witness that many people, at that particular stage in their lives, doing what they obviously loved, and clearly determined that the road taken would be the one they wanted. I hope they hold that thought for a long time.

And I can't believe that I got paid to do something I like doing that much. You say there's an entire industry built around this model? Who knew?

Such was the scheduling mess we found ourselves in that we struggled to cast one of the minor adult roles—at all! At one point or another we'd had several names down for the part of Slater's dad, a one-scene part with a few lines of important dialogue near the end of the film.

As we assembled at the Tata Centre for the final block of filming I auditioned yet another actor for the part. He was happy to help us out and ready to shoot the scene in a few days' time. On the morning of the shoot for that scene, I received an email from him giving his excuses and wishing us all the best and hope it didn't cause a problem…

Well of course not! Why would it?

I was too preoccupied with the turmoil of our last day's shoot to do anything right away, but the scene was fast approaching. Passing the "green room"—the room where the huge number of extras were assembled for the day's filming—I noticed Shawn Kowalski. Shawn had been to a couple of the workshops the previous summer. I had offered him the part of Chris. I'd heard nothing back from him and moved on to cast Aiden. I spoke to him, asked why he'd not responded, and there was some talk of ignoring emails for a while. I shrugged. Young people—they are either connected to the Internet as if it is life support or they cut it off altogether.

I asked him if he would like to have a speaking part. He looked at me with a great deal of apprehension.

"Here's the script!" I said, scribbling some changes on the paper. "You are now Slater's big brother. Your uncle owns the club she's been using on the sly."

The look of apprehension intensified.

"Thanks, Shawn! And don't worry, you have half an hour before you're needed on set!"

The only other role to give me a similar casting headache was Magda Goebbels. I had seen so many talented actresses, but none really getting close to the look and fake German accent that had implanted themselves in my head. I was dissatisfied with the shots we'd done early on, the stand-alone flashback sequence with Magda. We finally reshot it in May 2017. Fateh Ahmed was a great sport to allow us to decorate his apartment with Nazi pictures and memorabilia; I was very nervous about accepting his generous offer. The actress who finally played Magda Goebbels, and got her spot on with all the comic timing I knew she possessed, was Josephine. "My wife was right" for the part.

Josephine Cresswell, "Magda Goebbels," Production Accountant, and Producer's Secretary

When my husband, Stuart, asked me to be involved with the making of the film *The Only Game in Town* as 1st AD, I declined, as the film was being shot mainly over weekends. And then when the schedule changed to a summer block, I had already decided that I wanted the summer off.

Two years and some months later he asked if I would play the part of a comic Magda Goebbels, as this scene needed to be reshot. Although I had done some acting in my youth, I was at first a little worried about the fact that I didn't think I would be able to do a German accent. I needed time to watch a couple of episodes of *'Allo, 'Allo!*, a British comedy show from the 1980s that was about the Second World War. There was a female German character in it, and I wanted to listen to her so I could practise. I never actually got around to watching any of the show and time was soon upon us to do the filming, which would be done one morning in [associate producer] Fateh Ahmed's kitchen. I had found a suitable dress from the second-hand store and showed up on the morning of the shoot and was transformed into Magda by Colleen, the makeup artist.

Once the camera started to roll I found that I did actually feel like I was the comedic Magda. I soon got into character, and the German accent just came to me automatically. I absolutely loved it and had a whale of a time. So thank you, Stuart, for allowing me to perform again!

Casting forty plus speaking parts, including recasting and, in one instance, thrusting one of the extras into the limelight with a scene and dialogue of his own, was a lengthy and involved process that lasted from February 2014 right up to reshooting Hitler's bunker in May 2017.

If we were shooting again tomorrow, I wouldn't change a single thing.

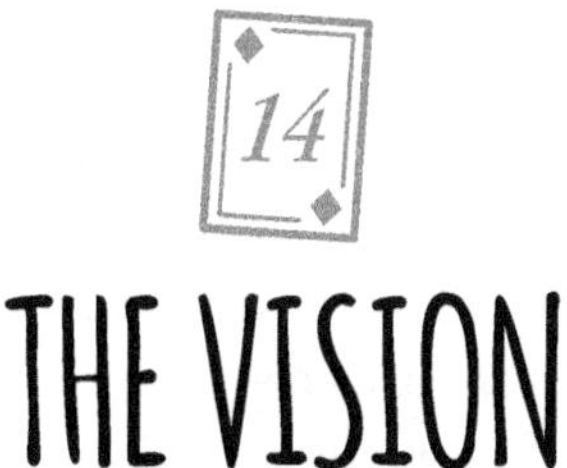

THE VISION

I had to stay true to my vision for the film. My lack of prep could be offset by my total knowledge of the script (I had written it), the characters (I had lived with them for a decade), and the actors (I had already worked with many of the young people for about a year).

So, what was the essence of this film? Why did I want to make it? (There you go!) I started with a very simple idea, the desire to make people laugh. To have them entertained and to feel a little bit better than they did before they saw the film. That is the purpose.

Humour, though, is very subjective. I know for a fact my sense of humour isn't everyone's. It is a concern for me that the people who seem at odds with my style could well be most of those employed to fund feature films in Canada!

And yet, I spent fourteen years directing theatre, mostly comedy, much of it with young people. I know I can make people laugh. I have done so.

The first thing a director needs is confidence in his script. Under normal circumstances a director won't sign on to a project without being handed a tasty script that he (or she) feels he can live with. Like it or not I was the director, and this was the script we were using. Although in truth I wasn't being deluded about my script. It had been through the tough process of analysis by a top consultant, done well at overseas contests, and made John Dunsworth's brain explode—in a good way.

So the film is a comedy, and there should be no shying away from that. Yet it becomes more than that, more than a sequence of cheap laughs. It becomes about a set of characters that you love, that you have seen grow and come to life with the skill of the actors. I owe it to them—characters and actors—to do right by them. To be honest to them and to let the world see them and fall in love with them.

Setting up for Comedy

After Cory pulled out in May 2015 and I had convinced myself that I would be director, I sat with Ashley King, my trusted DoP, and we planned the style of the film from that point on. It was obvious to both of us that some scenes would have to be reshot. If I was going to direct now I had to really make it my film. I wanted the film to be natural, to have a sort of relaxed, shot-on-35mm feel to it like *Gregory's Girl* and with a steady, mounted camera style that allowed the young actors to play out scenes in comfort. We needed to make the camera operations, the camera itself, invisible to the actors. For most this was their first time in front of a camera, and we needed to make the experience less stressful and more relaxing for them.

In the making of this film I tried to ensure we would have the camera on the person who was talking, only cutting for reaction a) if it was necessary and b) if the actor was giving a reaction (which would only happen if the character needed to react). Filling the screen with someone's face for three seconds when all they are doing is listening to someone with a blank look on their face (Cormack aside) will not engage the audience.

Our film is a comedy. It centres on four boys and their interplay. For me, the best scenes were the ones where we had a static camera and just allowed the four boys to develop a scene and go wherever it took them. To me, the longer the camera stayed on Rob, Joe, Chris, and Cormack, the better our chances of having a great film.

Yes, yes. I know that you will now tell me that we need dynamic shots in films, but this film is about relationships and comedy, and to me the audience needs to be invited in, not excluded. They need to warm to the characters, they need to see the conversations unfold and the characters express themselves.

And I'm not saying that I didn't want different camera angles. When you shoot a scene you always use several camera positions, which draw the audience's attention to different characters or points of interest—what we call scene "coverage." This is also vital to having places to cut to and from during the edit. The plan was that all of this coverage would be done in the simplest, quickest way and be "invisible" to the young actors. The way to do that is to put the camera on legs (a tripod) and cover the scene by moving the tripod and camera to the required positions. What I didn't want was tracking shots, jib shots, crane shots, hand-held shots. Things that took a long time to get right and would interfere with the young—and often inexperienced—actors and their delivery of the scenes.

Our schedule was tight. We had to shoot seven or eight pages of script a day, sometimes more. It would be hard, but it's a conversational story, largely told through dialogue. We're not talking action scenes. We agreed to put the camera on legs and shoot quickly.

I love Ashley to bits. We've done a lot together. We first connected in Halifax at the Atlantic Film Festival in 2008—two British ex-pats making a go of it in Nova Scotia. He knows his stuff about cinematography. The shots from summer 2015 look stunning. But he was going through some personal stuff at the time and didn't really give me the facts about it, perhaps because he thought I had enough to worry about. Instead, he gave me new things to worry about.

Ashley is a perfectionist. Somewhere along the way he saw *The Only Game in Town* as his chance to make a real mark in his trade. Our crew was also light, in personnel numbers and in experience. Jake Chisholm was 1st AD (First Assistant Director, the link between cast, crew, and director, the person responsible for ensuring those involved in the scene are ready and the production sticks to schedule), his first such role. He did a grand job behind the scenes and was nice to everyone. But what I really needed was my usual 1st AD, Josephine, who had been through the process before and knew how to crack the whip. Had we been able to keep to the original schedule (whatever that was!), Josephine might have been persuaded to do the job, but now we were shooting in a block right in the middle of summer; she wanted no part of it.

Janelle White, as production manager, was another first-timer. She was meticulous and treated the production money as if it were her own; she kept spending on sundries to a minimum and helped put the schedule back in place. Yet still, because of her youth, she felt unable to push those on set with more seniority than her. There was little she could do during production, though, as costs escalated due to delays and weather, but she has since told me she wishes she had felt able to take control of more aspects of the shoot to ensure budgets were adhered to. I still think Janelle did a great job nonetheless, and she followed her experience on the film with two years of study in the Film Arts course at the Nova Scotia Community College.

Janelle White, production manager

In the making of *The Only Game in Town*, I had the honour of exploring the role of production manager. Fresh out of high school and on the road to film school I couldn't have asked for a better opportunity! I was very grateful to have had the experience and memories to cherish and take with me to film school. Now graduated from my film program I look back at the time I had on set of this film and smile. I worked with people who were motivated and full of fun and loving energy. I learned a great deal of what it means to be part of a team. I got to become a leader, and I'll forever be grateful for getting to experience that.

When I look back, amongst the stressful and hectic film work on our plate, we had a lot of fun! We got to spend most of the shoot at the Tatamagouche Centre where we felt very welcome. Getting to make this film on the North Shore of Nova Scotia where I spent a lot of my childhood was special as well. Being very close to home and actually spending a day shooting in my home was extremely cool! We basically became a family. I didn't really know anyone coming into this production, but we all clicked and became very close.

I look forward to seeing the final product and how all of our hard work came together. I know it's going to be a success!

The end result for me was that while I was away being director and getting the best out of the actors, no one was keeping tabs on Ashley, who ignored the shooting plan and spent hours with his crew setting up elaborate tracking shots and crane shots, which all look great, mind, but badly affected the blocking for the scenes and therefore the performances. But most importantly, it continually pushed us for time.

We would turn up at a location and wait for hours while all the natural light was blacked out to be replaced by enough lights to film the final scene of *Close Encounters of the Third Kind*. Again, everything looks great, but it wasn't what was ordered nor planned and budgeted for. I would arrive on set in the morning to find that Ashley had got the crew to start work at seven; they would be halfway through setting up an elaborate shot that wasn't called for. I was faced with getting the crew to spend another two hours dismantling the gear and setting up the correct shot, or leaving them to complete their set-up for an hour.

This happened every day. Every day. Instead of finishing at six o'clock as planned, we were running to nine o'clock. People began to tire. Costs mounted. Nothing changed. I took him to one side, showed him the shot list and how quickly we had to work. Nothing changed. I was struggling to get the performances I wanted from the cast. They would be on set, ready to begin the scene, and we would all then have to wait another thirty minutes while the camera was adjusted or the lights reset.

I contemplated my options. I had none, of course. I was fixed on the schedule, which was our last chance; we couldn't go over the number of days because the Tata Centre had other bookings. And who could replace Ashley at this stage?

I was confused as to why Ashley seemed intent on ignoring everything I said. I have no doubt as a cinematographer he has the obsessive desire for perfection that makes him good at what he does. Buddhists tell us that our greatest strengths are also our greatest weakness. I recognize that in me too. I have the drive to push on when all others would stop, but that can be—and may be in the case of this film—the cause of my own destruction. For Ashley, his obsession to get the perfect shot each time outweighed in his head the need to get *every* shot.

That was no good to me. A collection of stunning shots does not a film make. But having a cohesive story was secondary to Ashley's own goals for the film.

On the final day of the shoot, for the big tournament scene that was actually the finale of the film, with fifty or so extras and just about everyone in the cast in attendance, I came in to a set that included a neatly laid track that the camera would be mounted on; everything would effectively be shot in one direction. This meant it would be nigh impossible to get different camera angles on the many characters we had and would severely limit coverage.

We played out the first shots and I sat and observed through the monitor. My heart sank. It was the hottest day of the year. We couldn't have the air conditioning on because of the noise it made, and we couldn't open windows because of noise from outside. I had more than a hundred people turned up for their big day on film.

Yet what I saw on the monitor was nowhere close to the vision I had for the scene. There, alone with my thoughts and the image on the monitor, I actually said to myself, "It's ruined!"

By this time we were already running late—a mountain of shots to do, a story to unfold, so much important dialogue to capture, and we had been here for two hours and just completed the set-up of track and lights.

If I called an end to the shoot now and sent everyone home, could we ever get everything back in place again? No chance! Still, my lips began to form the words, "Okay everybody, let's call it a day!"

Directing Style

This wasn't the first time I'd directed. It wasn't the first film I'd directed. Over the years I have developed a style that might not be everyone's cup of tea, but it works. In both theatre and film, my goal is to the get the best out of the actor for each scene. The difference in film is the way you use the camera to focus the attention of the audience and sometimes to even tell a story in itself.

When working with actors, especially on a script that I have written, I find it important to allow them to find their own way to deliver the scene. This is where it becomes a collaboration, when the actor brings his or her experiences and view of the character into the scene. Only if there is something vital in tone or delivery do I make a statement of preference. More often we'll try the lines in a number of ways and find the way that works for both character and story development.

The longer I have to work with the actors, the better the performance, one would hope. I try not to over-tinker. We'll rehearse while the camera crew are setting up, and if the set-up is pretty elaborate or the space is tight, I'll work with the actors in a different room so we can use the time wisely.

So often, rehearsal time was cut short by the crew calling "ready." But then we spent more time waiting on set as things clearly weren't ready. This was a mark of a crew and director not in unison. There were two different films being shot. I now knew exactly why Cory left the project because he felt his prep time wouldn't be there. I could feel it myself. That lack of cohesion, of a shared direction, a unity of purpose. Another month of solid prep would have ironed these things out, but I didn't have that month.

My friendly, low-key style of directing was being undone by an oppressive and often chaotic set-up. That was all my responsibility at the end of the day. It was down to circumstances during pre-production and even once we'd begun shooting, but at the end of the day everyone felt the pressure and dealt with it differently.

Our young crew worked so hard: Steve Greenwood, Dalton Richards, Georgie Milburn, Evan Burgess, Mike Smith, Liam Petite, John Holmes, Alejandro Quintanilla. The irony is that they really shouldn't have needed to if we'd stuck to the planned style.

Another crew member that deserves a great mention is Ron MacNutt. A North Shore stalwart of all things audio, Ron came on board and provided a mountain of stability and professionalism, and the youngsters loved him.

I also want to give a nod to our fantastic makeup artist, Colleen Patterson. Colleen was by necessity on set every day. She has a great range of special effects makeup that would blow your mind, and I'm happy to say we made some use of her talents with our film—from the red raw cheeks on Joe's face when the soccer ball hits him, to the nasty looking bruised and cut nose on Cormack after the vineyard fight, to making Colleen MacIsaac appear haggard, tear-streaked, and world worn, to turning Josephine into Magda Goebbels. Colleen deserves the highest praise for her talent and attitude.

I was conscious of the need to keep the young cast in the right frame of mind for comedy. Instilling a sense of fun while at the same time getting the job done was a balancing act I'd always managed in my days of theatre.

I like the idea of on-camera pranks. When we first introduced Joe (Aldo Orsi) on set in his solitaire "kit," I wanted to capture the moment Craig Gunn (playing Alex Crowley) first sees him. I took great care to position Aldo so his solitaire kit was hidden from Craig and took the unusual step of shooting Craig's close-up first to get the reaction. I expected Craig to succumb to hysteria, but he's such a good actor he didn't flinch until we cut the take. Still, everyone else on set was able to shriek in delight at Aldo's costume. As for the rest of you, you'll have to wait for the big screen reveal.

I turned the tables on Aldo soon after. When Natasha (superbly played by Breanna Roy) was supposed to squirt water on his face to inspire him to greater solitaire accomplishments, I told her to pour the entire bottle of water over him. Which she did.

Sadly, such comic breaks were few and far between as we struggled to balance the tightening schedule with the need to keep everyone relaxed.

Breanna Roy, "Natasha"

I had been in a few musicals before, but working on *TOGIT* was my first time acting on camera and I found it really enjoyable! The stress of getting it bang on the first time isn't there like it is in musicals and plays, so it was a lot of fun. The cast was super talented and everyone in the crew really brought their best to set every day. All in all filming *TOGIT* was a great experience for me and Tatamagouche is a beautiful place to film.

Playing Natasha was great because I had a lot of wiggle room with her character, so I could just do something weird and have fun with it and it would still fit. I'm really happy I had the chance to be included.

AT THE MERCY OF THE ELEMENTS

You already get the picture. Here is a low-budget film with big ambitions, beset by ongoing conflicts with three major bureaucratic bodies. We were also prisoners of my own past and my absolute determination to not let another film grind to a halt once production started.

Possibly all of that ambition too was part of the problem. It came as a huge surprise to most of the cast that they were actually getting paid for working on the film. I'm thinking most expected it to be one of those "everyone gives up the next ten weekends to make the film" type of thing. Which is normally allied to a vague promise of sharing some non-existent profits, because how can a film made in such a way get big enough to sell and generate profits?

I've been in such films. I've made such projects. I wasn't at that stage in my career anymore. *The Only Game in Town* had to look and feel and behave like any other professionally produced film.

DAVID MORTIMER, "ALASTAIR RAMSEY"

The first time I heard of *The Only Game in Town* was when my dad showed me an article in the paper for auditions/workshops being held about 4.5 hours away from my house, and what seemed crazy at the time seemed equally as much worth going to.

Growing up in the small town of Glace Bay, Nova Scotia, gave me the "small town, big dream," wannabe Mr. Hollywood at a very early age, so when I saw the opportunity to be in this movie, I thought right away that this was my ticket to fame. My dad and I drove around 9 hours every time there was a workshop being run by Stuart, the director and writer. I wanted to make sure that I locked down my role in the lead cast. I was also in my second year of university at Cape Breton University taking a Bachelor of Engineering Technology in Environmental Science so my days were long, but none of that mattered because I wanted to be a part of the project even more than I wanted to stay in bed in the morning, which is really saying something.

Although this project wasn't a promised flight to LA or a summer blockbuster that we all dream about starring in, it was a chance to do what I love and be surrounded by people that were as passionate about their dream as I was.

When we filmed in 2015, I dropped everything to get there, and it was a dream come true. I was living on a film set, doing what I loved six days a week, *and* I got paid for it! The cast and crew all got up together every morning, ate together, lived together; we shared a lot of coffee and laughs at 6:30 in the morning in beautiful Tatamagouche, Nova Scotia.

I felt like I was in Hollywood. I woke up with the sun with excitement to go work out, always running lines with my co-stars, sitting through hair and makeup, doing interviews for the local news and papers, being called to set, jumping in front of a camera, then running off set to eat, sleep, and do it all over again the next day. We couldn't have asked for a better team to make this movie, and I am so grateful that I was able to be a part of it for that short period of time.

Being a part of this film revealed to me how badly I wanted to be an actor and make this experience my life's work. I have the cast and crew to thank for making *The Only Game in Town* such an unforgettable time of my life.

If anybody doubts the value of film and television production on a region's economy, check out the money spent by our meagre production in the rural communities of North Shore Nova Scotia. For a short period of time there was a boost to the local economy of around $250,000. It made a difference. Wages were paid to local cast and crew who would spend that money in the future close to home.

The Tata Centre is in a great spot, right on the water and away from the main town. Whatever money we had spent there was worth it—the Centre provided us with home, office, and shooting locations.

There was only one issue with the Tata Centre that they couldn't resolve for us. During the days we were staying there and scheduled to film, there was also an annual peace gathering hosted by local Mi'kmaw groups. There would be a fire of peace kept lit throughout the event, and people were expecting to be able to meditate and engage in friendly discussion. Sometimes there would be chanting and ritual, even drumming.

When filming dialogue scenes, there is a need for general quiet during takes. It was clear that, where possible, we should try to keep the two sets of Tata Centre users apart, to allow each to do what they needed to do without upset.

We adjusted the schedule again, looking at where we needed to shoot indoors to see if it coincided with the peace group's indoor sessions. On the whole, we did okay. Everyone did their own thing, right up to the call that camera was ready, at which point we'd ask the peace group to be quiet for a few minutes while we did our takes. Sometimes they were in the middle of something and we had to wait. Sometimes we forgot to tell them they could go back to being a "not quiet peace group," and they remained unnecessarily silent for hours. Other times, they were not silent.

So picture the scene. The story largely takes place in a school (well actually, an "education centre," given the immense age range of the students), where every time we set up a scene in the corridor, or the office, or the playground, the sound of drumming and chanting could be heard in the background.

Ron MacNutt's eyes would widen and he'd fiddle with the levels on the boom until eventually he would signal "cut." The schedule slipped while we waited for a lull in the drumming and chanting. Sometimes we would call an early lunch. Sometimes we shuffled scenes and moved off-site. Sometimes there was no other option but to ride it out. But they were a peace group, and apart from the drumming and chanting sessions they were the ideal co-tenants of the set.

We did have one other issue. To this day I don't know if it was a misunderstanding or what, but members of the peace group apparently overheard someone, part of our team, make a derogatory remark. They couldn't be sure who said it, as it happened during a busy and hectic meal break, and the alleged comment seemed so out of character of any of the youngsters on set. I apologized profusely. All I could do was speak to the entire cast and crew as one. I could tell by their perplexed faces that they felt hurt by the accusation, but we'll never know who said what or why, and thankfully no lasting damage was done.

As the shoot progressed, another set of tenants also moved in to the Tata Centre. These were an international group of writers who had booked the stay for peace and quiet as a writing retreat.

Once again, the potential for conflict was there from the start. Around thirty young people, still buzzing from a day's heavy filming, would return to their accommodations and feel the need to let their hair down and unwind. As you can imagine, they weren't doing this quietly so as not to disturb anyone.

An angry writer confronted me. "We have come here for peace and quiet! We have to be quiet when you demand it for your filming, but when I asked your crew to be quiet last night, they gave me abuse!"

I apologized again. I apologized a lot for things that happened. I apologized for the accidental damage to one of the Tata Centre offices during the shoot. I apologized for the state of the building and the empty water bottles, or the mountains of half-eaten pizzas in the accommodations.

I apologized when the crew blocked off access roads to a restaurant while we set up an elaborate crane shot (which wasn't on the shot list). You can't help but admire the exuberance of youth. Asking them to politely ask drivers to wait for a few minutes while we shot a take very quickly became a raised hand to stop all traffic for a long period of time.

When the restaurant owner marched over to me, fuming, I apologized and then asked him if he could run the wrap party for about sixty people. He seemed okay after that.

So the schedule, now carefully rearranged so that our paths would cross as little as possible with the peace group or the writers' retreat, had been adapted, and all should have been smooth sailing.

Except that in summer in Nova Scotia, there can often be heavy rainstorms.

We could now add to our list of opponents to our film the great weatherman in the sky. It really was uncanny how every time we needed to shoot outside, the weather changed and the rain poured.

We needed to shoot a few scenes during a soccer practice. The Tatamagouche High School was perfect; the soccer pitch was right there in front of the building. When use of the school fell through, I had to hunt around for local clubs that could help us.

Now soccer isn't huge in Nova Scotia. It falls a long way behind ice hockey, baseball, and even rugby. And in fact it suffers from that oddity of naming that occurs in North America. The game is clearly football—it's played with the feet—but the game of football in Canada refers to the game where the ball is kicked once every twenty minutes or so. And that's not football's only problem here.

Played by girls, soccer is a decent game, but the boys are used to the style of play found in hockey, rugby, and American football, namely everyone runs around really fast and bashes into their opponents as much as possible. The sad fact is that for lack of anyone else, soccer has been coached to young players by well-meaning parents whose only experience of sports was of course hockey and American football. Consequently an understanding of the technical nature of the game is abandoned and replaced with a focus on the physical side.

Our little scenes of soccer playing are vignettes of that reality. That girls play soccer here very well, and boys just want to have fun.

The fact is that we had to travel from Tatamagouche to Antigonish, about 130 kilometres away, to find a soccer club that had sufficient numbers of boys and girls to stage a coaching session that our cast could be part of. (Thanks so much to the Antigonish Celtics!)

On that first day of a shoot that held so much fun and laughter, the sun shone outside the Tata Centre as we filmed indoors. When the time came to leave for Antigonish, a huge storm hit and torrential rain poured. We checked forecasts; our entire region was being hit. We drove for two hours in frightening conditions and arrived at McDonalds in Antigonish with the rain still pouring and the roads almost flooded. We even called our soccer club contact and to see if there was an indoor venue we could use. I knew, however, that would have been a disaster; I have recorded in such places before and the sound echoes so much it would have been nigh impossible in a short space of time to get it right. As it turns out, there wasn't an indoor space available anyway.

We checked the radar imagery of the storm, which indicated the rain would stop in an hour. We stayed in McDonalds; everyone had food and sat and watched the torrential rain, wondering if it would ever stop. Putting the club and all the extras back on for another night was nigh impossible, as was asking us to find time in our schedule to travel here again. It had to be tonight.

Just as the radar predicted, the rain stopped and we drove to the location. The pitch was sodden, with huge puddles of standing water in the goal area—which was perfect! We rushed through the shot list, battling now the changing, decreasing light at the end of the day. We had some fun with the visual comedy. I think these are some of my favourite scenes in the film.

It's a simple thing and works really well because of the timing of the edit, but one of the laugh-out-loud shots is when Cormack follows Odette's mischievous advice and kicks the coach's only soccer ball out of the park. When Jesse Hemmings did this in the middle of the football (sorry, soccer) pitch in Antigonish as the light faded, I yelled out with delight.

By the time the sun went down we had got everything we needed. Tired, hungry, and facing a two-hour journey, we dined out at a local pizza place before setting off for home.

The weather continued to mess with us throughout the whole shoot. When Jessie Craig and David Mortimer filmed their break-up scene overlooking the gorgeous Tatamagouche Bay, the rain began to fall and we sheltered the camera and the two actors under umbrellas between takes. As the skies grew progressively darker, the challenge was to make the different takes have the same look about them. Jessie's hair got wetter, and while we all stood there, Ron holding his boom-mic up like a lightning rod, rolls of thunder filled his headphones. Lightning crashed and we hurriedly finished the scene, with the final words of the break-up coinciding with a huge crash of thunder. We decided that would have to do.

Another scene that was to take place outside was the confrontation between Alastair Ramsey and Cormack, when Ramsey thumps Cormack in the stomach. As this is based on a real scene out of my life (see above), it was to happen outside. When the time came to shoot the scene, the weather changed and it poured. I'm talking monsoon.

We had few options. The peace group had use of the Tata Centre interior. We decided to use one of our accommodation houses that had the look of a school corridor. We had one place we could stick the camera, so that's where it went. The blocking worked fine as we played the scene through, and in fact I am really happy with the way this scene worked out. Part of me thinks it's because the camera didn't move and the actors were able to do their thing.

Filmmakers have an underlying need to be in control of everything. Unknowns are bad, half-knowns are worse. A day in pre-production saves three in production, or something like that. (I'm guessing if that was true, then if you did enough pre-production you would finish your film without going into production.) Still, the point is, and it needs to be made for those of you using this book as a road map to making your own film: things will happen that are beyond your control. If you have a bigger budget and the extra capacity of rain days built in, or some kind of insurance against disasters, then you have a chance of getting through things. But bigger films than ours have come crashing down. Far better to be adaptable. Not all adversity has to kill you. We had to adapt and think quickly in order to keep the film moving forward, never wasting a day but always, every day, having to do the extra hours.

During our tussle with the school board, I had seriously considered the option of using a school hall or other large building and building our sets inside that, but it wouldn't have saved us anything on the exterior shots. We were still at the mercy of the elements.

Sometimes though, we struck lucky. Jessie Craig and David Mortimer played out a scene in River John, overlooking the river at its most beautiful spot. As the light faded and we rushed through the scene, behind Jessie and her big film-star eyes was a huge moon. Had we been on schedule that day, we would have been too early to see it and not got one of the nicest shots in the film.

Jessie Craig, "Odette"

The summer that I filmed *The Only Game in Town* was hands-down one of the best summers of my life. I made so many wonderful friends and memories! What an awesome experience for my very first feature film!

I can remember going to all of the audition workshops, hoping and praying that I would get even a small role, so you could imagine the pure excitement when I found out that I had been given the female lead role, Odette.

We filmed the first scenes in December of 2014. I had wanted to be an actress since birth, but being around all of the lights and camera equipment really made me realize that I wanted to make a career out of acting. That whole winter I was counting down the days until the next scenes. I had scenes in May, and then finally we got the news that everything was being completed in July.

During filming, I learned so much about the film world, which was a huge help for when I started to study acting at the Toronto Film School. I loved my character, Odette. I feel as though I could totally relate to her, which made portraying her that much easier. She was such a fun character to play. I had a balance between some hilarious comedic scenes and some emotional and challenging ones as well. As an actress, I love a challenge, and *The Only Game in Town* gave me just that.

My favourite scene in the whole movie was shot at the beach behind my house on the most beautiful day, which was an added bonus. That beach is my favourite spot on earth, and that scene just made it even more special. All in all, the experience of playing Odette in *The Only Game in Town* was one of the best experiences I have had in my life so far, and one I certainly will not forget!

We shot at around thirty different locations along the North Shore, more if you count the places we shot just for their aesthetic beauty as B-roll. Each location had its challenges: too much light, not enough light, difficult to access, noisy, cramped, open to the public. The weather was just another hurdle we had to clamber over.

We arrived later than expected at Jost Vineyards in Malagash, the setting for a very dramatic scene with our four boys. The sun was setting, and the crew began setting up the crane for a stunning shot that looked down the lines of vines toward the winery below and the blue water of the bay in the distance. This was actually one crane shot I had asked for.

I love the winery. I worked there for a couple of summers when we first came to Nova Scotia; it was a good way to meet people, feel I had some worth, and learn something new. I had always thought a scene at the vineyard would be good. It would surprise people outside of Nova Scotia who would not associate this part of the world with winemaking. I wanted to have things throughout the film that would surprise audiences like that.

(For one of our crowd-funding campaigns, we asked Jost Winery to label some wine with our film poster but slightly altered—the word *Game* crossed out and *Wine* inserted above it. The Only Wine in Town proved to be our most popular perk.)

So, the winery shoot. The crane took a while to set up, during which time the sun was setting faster and the light was changing by the minute. But that wasn't the only problem.

I don't know if you've ever been to a winery, but at certain times of year they are not the tranquil places you might imagine them to be. Grapes are very attractive to birds, deer, bears, raccoons, as well as people. To leave more grapes for the people, vineyards employ a range of devices that scare the wildlife off, from flying kites that look like eagles, to loud recorded gunshots, sirens, white noise, and so on. Filming during such times would have been impossible.

Instead, we filmed at a time when the birds weren't being kept at bay. As such, a murder of crows had settled in for the night very close to our scene.

I like crows. They are very intelligent. We have a family of them that use our garden, mostly in winter, and we help them with food. I had a pet crow when I was a youngster in Shepshed. We found him on the front lawn as a wounded baby and nursed him back to life. He was always hungry so we called him Scrounger. At night, he slept for his own safety in a cage my dad made on a raised platform on the outside of the shed. Our cat Oliver would try to open the cage, and between the two of them, every morning Scrounger would manage to get out and fly up to the windowsill of my dad's bedroom. Dad would often be there sleeping, desperately trying to recover from one shift pattern or another at the factory.

Scrounger would squawk and tap on the window until someone went down and fed him. We tried to release him into "the wild," but he found his way home before we got back ourselves. So we had to take him a long way from home and release him. I often wonder if he told his new crow family about me and how kind I was, and word spread through the crow world that I was a kind and caring person.

The murder of crows at the winery were vocalizing with growing intensity. The noise they made right through filming was deafening. Key dialogue was punctuated with angry exchanges from the crows, possibly upset that a large group of humans had set up some kind of bird-scaring contraption next to the vines they had selected for suppertime devastation. I have it on good authority their conversation went something like this:

"Oh look, what are they using to scare us away now?"

"Some kind of crane with an odd-shaped black thing on the end. Well that doesn't scare me!"

"That's just a decoy. The guy with the huge grey sausage on a stick is the real threat."

"Say! Isn't that Stuart Cresswell? Scrounger's friend from Shepshed?"

"All hail Stuart! All hail Stuart!"

"Stuart is here! Crow God Stuart is here, everyone! Let's show our appreciation and do the Crow God chant loudly for as long as he's here!"

(All together) "Oh Stuart! Oh Stuart! Befriender of the crows. He feeds us and he saves us, Stuart is very special to us," etc., for the next two hours.

So, back to the final day of filming and my mouth forming the words: "Let's call it a day!"

Of course I didn't actually end up saying the words. I had to think of how we could salvage the situation and ensure we got every piece of dialogue we needed to tell the story.

I had been put through the mill for sure. What started out in December 2014 as a well-prepared foray into film production with a beautifully simple project had found me by the start of August 2015 crawling on my hands and knees in utter shellshock at the battles and obstacles that had beset the production.

I watched as Ashley and the camera crew pushed the dolly along the line of track they had laid without my knowing. I looked at the order of the shots for the day. I called Ashley to one side.

"There's no way we're getting all of these shots today," I told him. He nodded in agreement. "If we stick to the shot list in that order, we're not going to get all the dialogue we need." Ashley nodded again. "We have to concentrate on getting lines recorded. We can swing back for reactions once we have that."

"Okay…." Ashley kind of understood. Well, he understood my reasoning, but he didn't understand my method. But he soon would.

We did what no filmmaker ever does, what I told you earlier in the book never happens—a thing that will forever sit as a black mark against my directing career.

We shot the last six minutes of the film exactly in the order they will appear in the film. I had decided that the only advantage to the great railroad Ashley and his team of navvies had built was that the camera could be moved from one face to another during the final tournament scene very quickly. The blocking (where the actors stand and move in relation to each other and the camera) would be painfully wrong, and the coverage nigh impossible to achieve, but I was out of options.

In telling you this, you must understand how bad I feel now. But at the time, for anyone who ever thought I was a pleasant and easygoing person, it would have been a considerable shock.

I am ashamed to say I delighted in it. Watching the camera and grip team pushing the camera and dolly up and down the track in the airtight, heat-sealed, studio-light–heated, overcrowded room, with sweat pouring from them as they moved from one actor delivering a line to the next actor and so on, felt like payback.

At one point, with the camera at one end of the track having just filmed an actor delivering his line, I then instructed the camera to be pushed to the other end for the next line, and then come back to the original spot and shoot the next line in the script. Ashley stopped and scratched his head. He was just about to question the tactics when I barked: "Come on! Come on! We have to keep rushing through this or we'll never get it done."

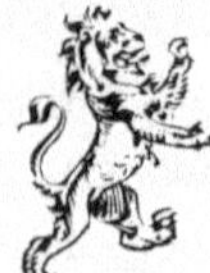

MIDLOTHIAN CHRONICLE

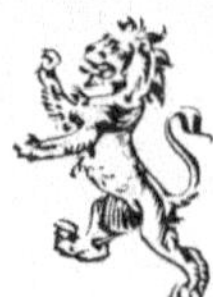

Friday 23rd July 2017 75c **Midlothian's answer to The Chronicles of Narnia**

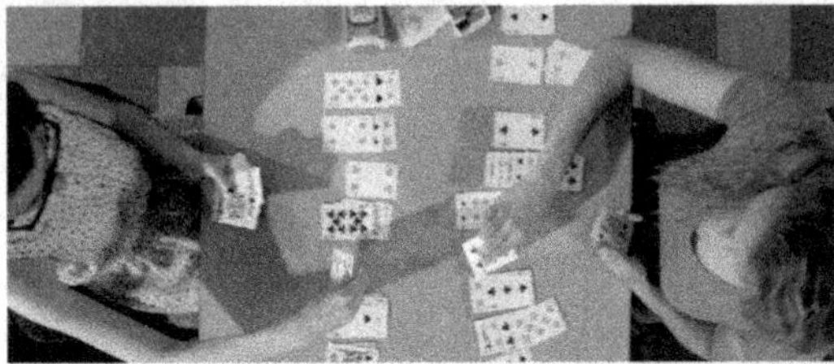

Huge Crowd Expected in a Hot Cramped Room for the Final

By Betty Swollocks

The biggest event in Midlothian Competitive Solitaire history is set to take place in one of the smallest rooms in the school, thanks to some poor planning by school officials.

"We were taken by surprise at the number of people wanting to watch the final," said a school official. "We honestly didn't think anyone would want to watch this stuff, but we're so proud of our players. If they win the final, we will certainly be looking to build a state of the art solitaire arena."

NOVA SCOTIA IS ON THE FIDDLE

By Armani El-Bow

Many have called the giant fiddle at Port Sydney on Cape Breton Island a waste of tax payers money, a joke, an eyesore and an embarrassment, but it attracts lots of visitors all year round. The Giant Fiddle, or to give it it's full name, Fidheal Mhor A'Ceilidh, is at the centre of one of the best celtic folk music festivals in the world. Celtic musicians from all over the world descended on Port Sydney to celebrate their rich celtic heritage and indulge each other with a few ditties at the Maritime Fiddle Festival.

This is what most people think the Giant Fiddle represents, however the artist, Cyril Hearn, had a hidden motive for his design. "It was meant as a cheeky dig at the tax laws set up to benefit the rich and powerful at the expense of others. The sheer size of it represents the scale of the fraud." It was reported that Mr Hearn was depressed that the subtle meaning of his anti-social art statement was completely lost on people.

"I could spend all day just fiddling..."

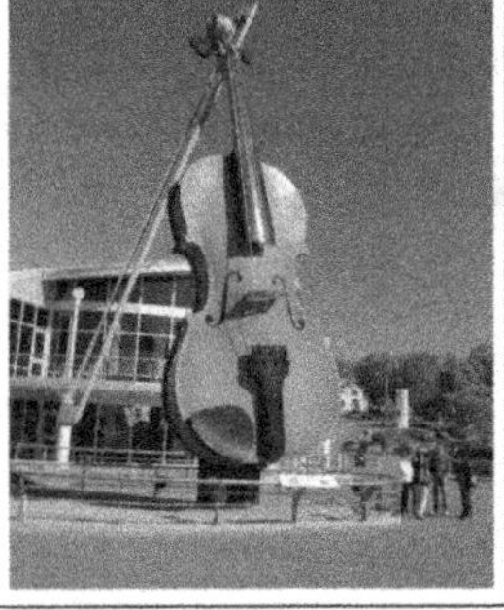

WE WILL NEVER PRINT FAKE NEWS!

By Betty Swollocks

The Midlothian Chronicle is proud to announce our pledge to you, the people of Midlothian, that we will never knowingly print what President Trump refers to as Fake News*. We have the lowest number of defamation cases and libel suits made against us than any other newspaper in the region called Midlothian Chronicle. Our track record in these cases is also one of the best in the business, due mainly to our excellent legal team and also our connections within the judiciary system. Several of our competitors have lost very public and very costly court cases in recent years, including the infamous 'Celine Dion ate my hamster' libel case. Midlothian Chronicle would never publish anything so malicious about our national heroine, unless we think it will really boost our sales and won't get us in too much trouble. In short, we are the newspaper you can rely on not to not let you down. We will always strive to bring you the news our puppet masters want you to hear in order to further their plots for world domination.

*We reserve the right to print actual news that is factually accurate despite being labelled as fake news by Trump because he doesn't agree with it.

TOP CANADIAN GYMNASTS COMPLAIN ABOUT LEOTARDS
COMPLAINTS ABOUT NEW TEAM LEOTARDS MADE FROM SEAL FUR
PAGE 5

SENIOR POLITICIANS ARE ONLY IN IT FOR MONEY
SURVEY POLL SHOWS HOW MUCH TOP POLITICIANS EARN
PAGE 12

POLAR BEARS GETTING FAT AND LAZY ON OUR TRASH
UNNATURAL DIET MAKES POLAR BEARS FAT AND LAZY
PAGE 19

REFUGEES HELP MAKE CANADA GREAT AGAIN
SYRIAN REFUGEES TO BRING BOOST TO CANADIAN ECONOMY
PAGES 23-25

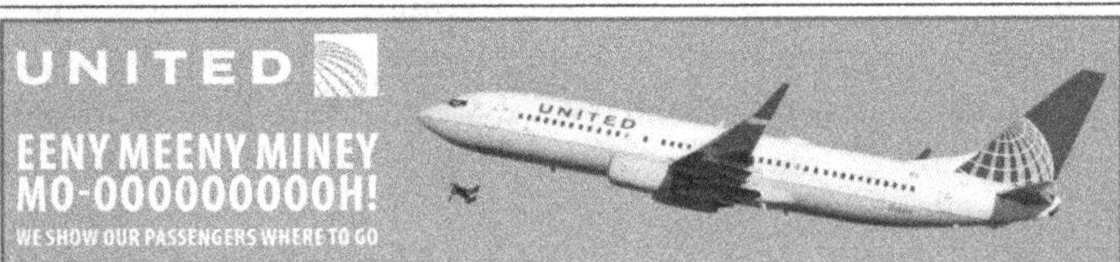

A newspaper story written after the final tournament scene was filmed. The scene fell short of the goal of a huge sporting finale, so this story attempts to explain it away, saying the school had miscalculated the level of interest in the event and only provided a small, cramped room.

Jake Chisholm, 1st AD, was running in and out with new extras as the scenes unfolded, cramming more and more people into the room where the final tournament of the film was taking place. The camera and crew ran up and down the track and the actors delivered their lines as if we had suddenly begun filming a performance of a stage play.

When we got to eight o'clock and the last shots of Cormack's triumph were in the camera, there was tangible relief—and I have to say amazement—that we had actually done it. I embraced Ashley, and somewhere in the sweat and tears was the knowledge that we couldn't have got the film to this stage without each other.

We staggered to the wrap party as if we had just completed the 250 kilometre Gobi Marathon. The restaurant was barely open (nowhere likes to stay open beyond nine o'clock in northern Nova Scotia, not even if there are fifty people turning up), and the youngsters and their parents who had helped us along the way had that feeling of being part of something bigger than themselves.

I remembered my days in theatre many years ago. I always hated the sense of loss that follows the final performance, when that intense period of shared creative endeavour is over and you realize that you won't be seeing the people who had become your family in recent months tomorrow or the next day. It was one of the reasons I wanted to move from theatre to film.

Here, now, in Big Al's in Tatamagouche, I was having those feelings again.

THE DIRECTOR SIGNS OFF

So that's kind of it for The Director's Epic, the bit that's exclusively the director's story. I think we just about survived the roller coaster of production. I would have preferred more shoot days, more time, more money. Still, against all the odds, at a time when the industry had retreated into a corner to lick its wounds, our little film eventually got all of the scenes in the can (or on the hard drive, as it now happens).

Of course a director remains involved in the edit and post-production, but I would also be back to wearing the producer's hat then too.

Ashley King, cinematographer

Like many of those involved, this was my first experience of working on a feature film shoot. Shit scared and excited all at once. Witnessing the journey of the young crew from the days of the early shoots in 2014, through to the mad rush of final weeks of principal photography and to the wrap, it was incredible. Watching confidence grow, egos evaporate, and teamwork build. The talent really did rise to the top. When you consider the budget for production, I thought it was an amazing feat the production team pulled off.

I made many new friends along the way, and the best thing of all was the amazing community spirit that was shown by the Nova

Scotian people who allowed us into their houses to film the scenes. Memories I will hold dear for the rest of my life.

I still wonder what the chapter would have been like if Cory had written it. But then of course, if Cory had been able to stay on as director, it would mean all the tax credit disaster and change to schedules and so on would never have happened, which would mean the film didn't really have any extraordinary battles and there would be no need for a book.

NOVEMBER 21ST 1998

FIVE ARRESTS MADE IN SOLITAIRE FIXING SCANDAL

CROWLEY FORMER KING OF SOLITAIRE ARRESTED AFTER SPECIAL INQURY

Report by Nick Themall

Day five of the inquiry into the sensational solitaire fixing scandal has ended dramatically with the arrest of five people.

Alex Crowley along with Chris Dyer, Matt Marriott, David Hames and Nigel Fellows were arrested as the inquiry came to a close and the chair gave their findings ,and recommendations on how to proceed. The five were all suspected of involvement in a solitaire fixing scandal where large bets were placed at various locations throughout Canada. It is alleged that Alex was an unwitting participant at first, but soon came to realise there was more money to be made from the gambling than from the prize money. There have been calls to increase the prize money in the sport of solitaire to avoid such contamination, but officials are reluctant to speculate if this will help the future of the sport or damage it.

The four men and one women arrested will be questioned at the Halifax police station, where the main investigation will take place. A control room has already been set up and operating throughout the trial, collecting eveidence, testiomnes and will come into full swing now the allegations have been made official.

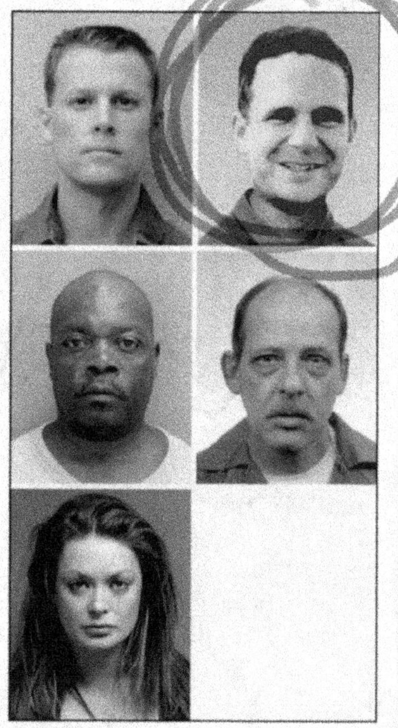

The "solitaire scandal" ends dramatically in the film, as reported in this fake newspaper story with headshots.

The film, however, would have been very different, I'm sure. I can't imagine this film being done with loads of prep time and everything slotting in where and when it should. Cory would have had a different way of looking at the script and the scenes, and that is exactly what I as the writer and producer wanted from having him on-board. What insights could he have brought to the film? How would he have tackled that quintessential British humour?

We'll never know. And I for one will forever feel that something was lost. Despite the thrill of directing my own first scripted feature, I would still have preferred it to be someone else.

Jake Chisholm, First Assistant Director, and "Calgary Coach"

Three weeks seemed to go by like a year, yet at the same time it felt like a weekend getaway on an island just off the coast of Ireland, population fifty. The cast and crew quickly bonded over the span of three weeks on the gentle land of Tatamagouche.

I was the First Assistant Director and acted in a small part toward the end of the film. Our days were always filled with a touch of stress, a lot of laughs, and hot lights. The days would usually start around 7:00 A.M., and we would be on set until early evening or sometimes until 11:00 P.M. Nobody minded the long days since it was such an adrenaline rush to watch and be a part of something big. We were very blessed in the sense that the entire cast and crew got along well, and we had mostly decent weather, which in Nova Scotia, can be very worrisome.

The last day of filming was very bittersweet for the cast and crew. For me, the last day was the hardest to deal with. As the minutes ticked by, we all would casually look at each other and think, we have to say "bye for now" at some point today. It was a phrase no one wanted to say or think about, but eventually it became our reality. Though we hugged and parted ways, the day was so much fun. We had a zillion extras on set, which I had to manage and then keep everyone decently cool because we were inside a very hot building with very hot lights. We all handled the heat and "bye for now"s; we closed the set and packed our belongings. The end of filming had come, but the post-production was just about to kick into high gear.

PART FOUR

POST-PRODUCTION

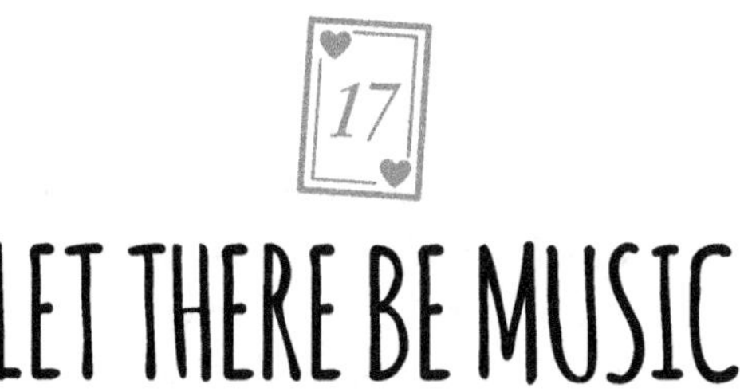

17 LET THERE BE MUSIC

There must be a point in everyone's life, if only for the briefest time, that they imagine themselves as a rock star. Hasn't everyone been in a band at some stage in their lives? Haven't we all performed in front of our bedroom mirror with a hairbrush microphone?

I was a small boy during the first wave of swinging Britain during the sixties, with two older sisters into The Beatles and The Rolling Stones. Growing up, music played a huge part in my life, and I loved many different styles. I remember being invited to my friend's house across the road so he could play me the latest record he'd bought; it was 1973, so I was ten. The song was the Max Bygraves's version of "Deck of Cards," and it had obviously impressed my friend because of its soldier story. Not to be outdone I ran back home and returned with my favourite record of the time, Tchaikovsky's "1812 Overture." I can still remember my friend and his mum politely listening to the whole thing with blank looks on their faces.

I loved music, but I wasn't very musical. One of my sisters, Julia, played violin to a high standard, but apart from a spell playing cello and double bass in the school orchestra, I was too busy playing football to learn an instrument.

Later in the seventies, when I was about fifteen or sixteen, music really began to speak to me. I loved the energy of British punk rock and the rebellious lyrics struck a chord (hmmm…). I went mad for music and found punk and post-punk new wave styles to be powerful antidotes for the darkness of home life at the time.

When bands like U2 first arrived and synth-rock bands such as Orchestral Manoeuvres in the Dark and Ultravox, I found myself inspired by songs and themes to create stories and scripts and poetry. The emptiness of human lives in failed industrial settings as depicted by Joy Division and early New Order or The Jam seemed to match my own existence at the time. Having had one stint as a bass player in a very poor band, I took out my first ever loan and purchased a Roland synthesizer. For a while I worked for a pittance in a recording studio in Leicester—which in those days was a very long bus journey—until I overstayed my welcome. I joined a band but they played seventies rock—Thin Lizzy, Boston, that sort of thing. I needed music to help me through the teenage anger and experiences of a shattered home life; Thin Lizzy and Boston and the like were not going to do it for me. I couldn't play the damn synthesizer anyway, so essentially my stab at stardom through music would never materialize.

I continued to seek out great music though, and even to this day I enjoy finding new songs and artists that offer something of value.

In 2005, I studied Music Business and Management though the National Open College and passed as "exemplar." When I asked the tutor what that meant, he told me my coursework was to be used as the standard for the following years, which is kind of humbling. As part of the course, I managed a couple of bands and artists and enjoyed being able to provide a platform for those who took the time to learn their instruments and help them further their careers.

The music I had always wanted as the soundtrack to *The Only Game in Town* played an integral part in the creative vision and the marketing strategy. As I write this section, we are approaching the point in post-production where the music is being added.

Most low-budget filmmakers overlook music until the end. In fact, by and large, a film is made and then a music supervisor will be engaged and they will purchase bits of music tracks that kind of fit the mood and, most importantly, the budget.

As a result, it seems that all too often low-budget films end up with an unrecognizable tune played by thrashing guitars, or a job lot of tracks by the producer's sister's boyfriend's band. I do remember being advised very early on to "do the music yourself." The thought of subjecting film audiences to me making some noise with some instruments filled me with dread.

You most certainly get what you pay for. And I know full well that musicians get really angry when some up-their-own-backside filmmaker contacts them and explains how much they love their music and it would be perfect in the film, but, having paid for everything else, they have no money. It speaks of undervaluing the skills of the musical artist. It ignores the costs that have been incurred by the musician and the record label, as if somehow they are less important than the costs incurred to make the film.

I need you to understand that right from the start, even as producer I was determined to feature a specific list of songs. They formed the creative feeling behind every scene I wrote.

I was very attached creatively to this film, and the music was just another lens through which I saw Midlothian and its setting and the characters. It can be quite overwhelming for a director to come onto a project and find such "interference" in the creative process coming from a producer. I hope Cory didn't feel that way, but I can understand if he did.

As we work on the film and in some cases add the particular tracks I want, we can see that they appear as if written for the film. The songs could be released as a soundtrack album. I'd love that.

I want you to imagine a film where we watch people playing the card game solitaire. No matter how we shoot it, it's still boring. There is no way to dress it up and make it an exciting spectator sport. Until you add the music. When we cut one of the tournament scenes and then add the music track "Hard to Beat" by English rock band Hard-Fi, everything changes. There is excitement, drama, tension, and pace. Using this music is going to be vital in bringing the film to life.

Underpinning all of this work and ambition for the music was the experience and talent of Colin Vearncombe. This is an excerpt from an email Colin sent just after we had begun filming at the end of 2014 and he'd read the latest script.

> *Spent the last 36 hrs in bed with a... nasty bug... headache, muscles aching like I was beaten with a stick, and a hideous plague cough! Which of course gave me some time for reading (hooray).... Very much enjoyed* TOGIT; *I can* see *it... it leaps from the page. Well done and I shall of course be pledging.... For me it reads like a Bill Forsyth film in Canada... and can take any bittersweet music as counterpoint or engine, but you may have a different concept.*
>
> The Only Game in Town *is of course a gift of a song title, and I'd certainly give it a go if you were looking for a song to kind of encapsulate*

the feeling of the movie, i.e., bespoke... Tell me exactly what you'd want from it and me. Just a thought....

Thank you anyway...you made me smile and indeed laugh out loud a couple of times on a day that didn't promise such things.

Best,

CV

Colin was going to do the title theme, and I'm sure with his name attached, the other artists whose music we wanted would have been only too pleased to be included in the film. You'll find out later on why this never happened, but I hope you understand that right from the start, the music was set to play a key part in *The Only Game in Town*, and my creative vision for the film was deeply connected to the music and the people in charge of creating it or deciding which music to "buy in."

There would also be bits of incidental music to fill in the gaps. Right at the very start of planning the film, I met with Bonnie and Spencer Morgan, who, through their company, Cicada Music, would source the music I wanted, create a soundtrack CD, and write other bits of music. Their fee and the music costs formed the basis for the application to Telefilm for completion funding.

My advice for any upcoming directors would be this: do not leave music to be an afterthought for your film. When you are visualizing each scene, consider it with music; it helps to set the mood of the piece. There will be enough places in your film that require a bit of music because the sound recording was bad, or there was no atmosphere track, or there is some weird bit of editing that you can't avoid. Don't think that such an emergency, Band-Aid, coverall type of music and approach will suffice for the music for the rest of your film. Take it seriously.

For me, the music is key to attracting a wider audience to the film when it's released. All that's required is that we have enough cash in the project to pay for it. As the production costs had mounted during the crazy scheduling and production period, we were going to need that completion funding from Telefilm.

The First Cut and Beyond

The first cut, as they say, is the deepest. It's certainly a brutal cut. Add up the hours of filming we'd done, the number of takes, the different angles to get the coverage. In the old days of film editing, this is where entire scenes or characters would "end up on the cutting-room floor." First cut should be a loose edit where only the best takes make it through. It's the full story, but with too many paragraphs.

The first two stages of the edit, logging and first assembly, had not suggested any serious issues. In the days of digital filmmaking, a new role has been created, that of data wrangler. This person removes the full data disk from the camera and transfers the clips to at least two robust hard drives. Any problems such as data corruption can be spotted here and hopefully can be rectified before the production moves on to another scene. The metadata of the clips can also be entered here, with information about the clips or takes that can help later on.

Ashley worked long into the night after each day's shooting so we could view the rushes (or "dailies," that day's footage), and I don't recall any data issues in our very hectic schedule.

We used three 250 Gbyte solid-state drives in the Black Magic Production Camera—a very nice rig by the way, with a set of six prime cinema lenses. We ended up with around 10 TB for the entire film.

First assembly was the next stage, and when we finished, our editor delivered a long and rambling at 2 hours 45 minutes of feature film. Our film was expected to be around at 100 minutes in length. First assemblies are going to be long, for sure, they are very loose versions of the story, but they should have all the scenes. Even at 165 minutes there were whole scenes not included in the cut.

Telefilm, who, if you recall, had found out about the film through some press releases, suggested there would be funding available to help us through post-production. All we had to do was give them a rough cut. The money was quickly running out. The extra hours shooting had added up, extra meals, extra costs. Our few minor investors had provided more money, but this was for marketing the film, not for post-production. The Telefilm money would allow us to buy all the music I had wanted from the start and allow us to use decent graphics and some effects to give the film a high-quality, polished feel.

We engaged an editor to get us through first assembly and rough cut quickly, so as to access the Telefilm funding. This was a huge mistake. We've been paying for it ever since.

The first assembly was very bad for me. It was the first time I'd seen what my film would be like in someone else's hands. It told me more about me and how I might have been if someone else had directed it, and I didn't like what I saw in myself.

I may be too hard on myself here. I know for a fact I'm not alone as a director with such thoughts. I met Hawaiian director Brian Kohne at a film festival and he told me that he couldn't stand the editor's job on his film *Get a Job*. So much so, that he sacked him and completed the edit himself.

Struggling to reign in my creative demon and ever mindful that there was a lot riding on the next stage, I wished I had had the balls to do the same. I got the feeling the editing was being done in a rush to suit the editor's own needs. I would have preferred us to have waited, just a little, until I could spend all the time necessary alongside him (or another editor). The film looked bad.

This was now the rough-cut stage. All the scenes are supposed to be in order and checked for continuity. There was no sense of comedic timing, the pace was lumbering. To shave off the surplus time, the editor had actually omitted several key scenes and still only managed to bring the film to a desperately long and plodding 130 minutes.

That was it. That was all the money gone, and the film was its own fat cousin. The editor departed, leaving us with a film that we had to use to encourage more investment and obtain some Telefilm money to put right what had been done. Still, I consoled myself with the knowledge that Telefilm wasn't expecting a finished film, and they had indicated they wanted to help.

By the time the film was ready for Telefilm, the contact we had there who had been so interested in *The Only Game in Town* had retired. I swear, my timing in the film industry is terrible. The replacement was not such a big fan of the film and asked me to apply for the funding, which came as a surprise but probably shouldn't have.

I showed the film to Craig Cameron, the executive producer, and he tried to be as kind as possible. We submitted it to the Atlantic Film Festival, hoping that by the time September 2016 arrived, we'd have received the Telefilm money and been able to complete the film to the standard we wanted.

So we found ourselves at the start of 2016 in a hiatus as we waited for news of funding from Telefilm to help us complete the film with all the trappings and bells and whistles that we wanted at the start. The film needed saving, and Telefilm was the only one that could do it. Any involvement from them would have encouraged small investors—yes, I was still courting them, aware of the need to reduce some of the interim debt financing—to support us.

I didn't know just how long we would have to wait for an answer.

A Tragic Loss

On Sunday, January 10, 2016, on his way to Cork Airport, Colin Vearncombe was involved in a car crash and suffered serious head injuries. He was in a stable but critical condition, and as word spread through his network of friends and supporters, everything else seemed to hang in the air, as if all the world was holding its breath, waiting.

Colin never regained consciousness. Despite the best attempts to save him, the trauma to his brain was too severe. On January 26, 2016, just as I was about to step into a meeting, I got the news that he had passed away.

None of this of course affected me as much as it did his family and close friends in the town of Schull, Ireland. It's difficult though, not to personalize it, because for me, Colin was an inspiration and a source of great encouragement in my writing and filmmaking career. I remember sending him the outline for *The Only Game in Town* way back when it was *Patience is Vertue*. He had always been a part of the plan for the film.

With the film at a standstill, I found myself slipping into a dark place. I couldn't see a way through. Since my own parents had died, I'd had no one that I really wanted to impress with my work, no one that I wanted to hear say "that'll do, Pig" or pat me on the back. No one other than Colin. His opinion really mattered to me.

I still miss the long drawn-out email conversations about nothing in particular, but I miss his words of wisdom and encouragement and his guidance even more.

For a while, the film had little attraction for me. I felt that of all the obstacles we'd faced, the loss of Colin's friendship surpassed them all. My mood changed and I considered making the entire film a tribute to Colin and his music. I wanted all the music to be his. It would change the entire mood of the film. I had to be talked out of it.

The Doldrums of Post-Production

The months slipped by and still no word from Telefilm. I had to move on to other projects. I thought it wise to contact Nova Scotia Business Inc. and make sure they were prepared for our forthcoming application under the "old" system of tax credits, which required a completed film at time of submission, so it would still be a little way off. But the Telefilm money was coming—

I wasn't prepared to countenance the possibility that we would be refused. So I sat and waited patiently. (It is a virtue, after all....)

My conversation with NSBI proved there were still battles, roadblocks, and wars to be won. Despite the Nova Scotia government's own ruling that productions "started prior to July 1, 2015, were under the old system of tax credit"—a situation that *TOGIT* was clearly in—I discovered through initial discussions with NSBI and the Nova Scotia Department of Finance that they do not expect to allow us to claim money that was part of the original finance plan in 2014. That despite *TOGIT* starting well before the July 1 deadline, and despite the fact that had the government *not* changed the tax credit rules and caused everyone's schedules to explode overnight. If not for that, we would not have lost our director, our locations, and our investors and would have been able to shoot most of the film before July 1 anyway. They were still happy to make an arbitrary decision in our case and go against their own publicly announced rules.

That is a battle for the future. Somewhere down the line, arguments will still need to be made. There may be a longer-term impact on the financial position of the film as a result, but here is a good time to revisit that position, as countless different permutations of the structure of the film's financing have been playing out over two years.

1. The budget was $250,000.
2. The finance plan was originally made up of Nova Scotia tax credits (~$80,000), private equity (~$80,000), and sales to Canadian TV/distribution (~$80,000).
3. Apart from a small amount of equity—around $25,000, the result of several stages of crowd-funding through Indiegogo—we ended up debt financing the whole film, with the plan to recoup when sales and bigger private equity came in.
4. When the film industry was thrown into insecurity by the government in 2015, any large equity funds that had been promised melted away.
5. The plan was still to bring in equity once the film was completed, as that would offer a great degree of certainty for any investors.
6. The promise of Telefilm completion money still hung in the balance, and NSBI now cast doubt on any tax credits being applied. We were left with the option to find equity partners to come in on the project once completed, and to make sales to Canadian TV as soon as possible after the film is finished.

How many of you would take a chance and commit that sort of money to a film project under those circumstances? The film, and I can say this now that we are almost at the end of post-production, is a great-looking film with superb performances. We *will* get good sales from it, and even without tax credits I remain convinced that we will recoup. If no other investors come in, then we'll not have to share our money with anyone else!

Still, it makes scary reading. Each step along the way, something has happened to knock the plan sideways. In fact, we've been knocked so far sideways we'll soon be back on the original track.

Making a film always carries some sort of risk; as the producer, you are the one carrying the risk. You have to weigh up the level of financial risk, the potential return, and the belief in that particular project.

That said, if I had known what lay ahead before we started shooting, I'm not sure I would have proceeded. Thankfully, I was busy on other projects through the first part of 2016, and we had decided to embark on a series of renovations and improvements to the property in River John that houses office space for Simple Films (and Only Me Productions).

In March 2016, our son Oliver and his wife, Sarah, introduced us to our first grandchild, Henry. I found myself thinking in terms of retiring, properly, and spending long summer days with my grandson and long winter evenings writing a novel. I even pictured the winter months being spent in Italy and not Nova Scotia with its frozen sea.

Henry's arrival made me aware that I was now at that stage in my life, the grandparent stage, and life would begin to slow down, and yet, at the same time, I felt a renewed drive to power on and play the long game, put things in place for a future that was no longer mine.

It's a strange mix of feelings, and I'm sure that all new grandparents go through the same conundrum. And that too touched a nerve in me. Just a few days after Henry was born, Colin Vearncombe's son had what would have been Colin's first grandchild.

I am constantly reminded how fortunate I am to see this new development in our family. There is a lot to be thankful for, and even though the trials and tribulations of filmmaking can sometimes drag the spirits down, I am surrounded by great people and, here in River John, a strong sense of community. It also helps that no matter how vexing the day's work has been, when the work day is over, the beaches are just five minutes away. Summer indeed belongs to Nova Scotia, Canada's Atlantic playground.

The year 2016 marked a special point in our family's journey. It was ten years since we'd been born in Nova Scotia. We had arrived stumbling and blind, anxious, and homesick, before becoming aware that we were lucky enough to have found a people so welcoming and warm that we could take comfort, even when so far from all those we loved.

In those ten years there were many personal achievements for all of us, but the arrival of Henry signalled the start of a new chapter for the Cresswell family in Canada. It became really important for me to celebrate all we had achieved, and I gave myself the task of securing a family break for all of us. We could only manage a weekend away at the Digby Pines resort in August as we were all so busy, but all the same, it felt good.

I had plenty to keep myself busy through spring and summer. On the back of a really successful Sunrise Film Festival in 2015, with filmmakers and audiences coming from all over the world, I had decided to run another one later in 2016. It helped. Whenever I had an empty moment I would wonder just how long it could take Telefilm to follow through on their earlier positive reaction and give us the money to complete the film.

I am not known for my patience. It is not one of my virtues, and I despise inactivity. The entire year of 2016 was effectively a washout for *TOGIT*. Waiting on the news from Telefilm and the emotional hammer-blow of losing Colin Vearncombe meant that it felt like a long way back to the film for me. I had become so good at putting it to the back of my mind that to an outsider it must have looked like I'd lost interest. I would get nudges from the cast and their parents: "Is the film finished yet?" Jessie Craig more than most seemed desperate for the film to come out.

The investors and lenders began to niggle and make demands, rightly so, but I struggled to find a way back into redoing the edit on the little money I had left. My options were limited.

Fateh Ahmed, who had been instrumental in helping with camera rental and providing crew during the making of the film and had also been producing the behind-the-scenes footage that could one day be made into a decent documentary, asked if he could compose some music for the film. He's also a talented musician.

On hearing that the film was stalled, he offered to help in any way, and as the investors were keen to see how the music would fit with the film, Fateh and I began to pick apart the current edit and slowly piece together the film in order to play around with some of his original compositions and to see where the music I had always wanted would work best.

I have been constantly asked by the eager cast, and others, why it has taken so long to complete the film. It's true that a producer's worst nightmare (yes, even worse than aborting a film that is just about to start!) is to have a film stall in post-production. It smacks of all sorts of things, most of which don't look good on a producer's CV. This book is about honesty and trying to tell it like it was. So here goes.

The monumental task of getting the film to production sapped every last bit of energy from me. It sapped all my finances too, but mostly it was energy. I had nothing left to give after fighting battles at every turn, and when Telefilm offered to give us some money to finish it off, I was happy to accept it.

In light of that, I left the rough cut in the hands of an editor who had a narrow window of opportunity to complete it, and when it landed on my desk, I had a difficult call to make. Telefilm was giving us money to complete the film, right? So what we could give them obviously could not be the finished piece. But how unfinished did it need to be?

I hate the thought of this. Most people must feel the same. Would a car manufacturer send out a car unfinished to see if you want to buy it? I felt that unease that most people would feel sending out something before it was ready. I know from speaking to Telefilm that applications for completion funding are rarely submitted. I can see why.

Anyway, what Telefilm had from us was an unfinished, rambling, first cut with little to suggest the high production values we had applied during the shoot. While I went off to work on other projects and waited for the go-ahead from Telefilm that would allow us to finish the film, I found myself drifting away from it. Looking back I may have been hiding, refusing to face up to what the lack of news from Telefilm must mean. Surely, if the news was good they would have told me much sooner, right? I have lived under the sword of Damocles at different points in my life, and I learned not to look up.

So I kept my head down and even resisted the urge to call Telefilm for an answer.

There was of course another reason for my inaction. I don't want to labour the point, but the sad loss of Colin Vearncombe really took the wind out of my sails. It's ironic, but he was just the person who would have been able to lift me out of a malaise caused by the death of another close friend. That year, 2016, was a lost year for the film, and really it's because I had no appetite for a fight anymore. I had lost the will to wade through the scenes while all I could hear in the background were Colin's songs.

At one point in 2017, for no reason other than I thought it would be a nice idea—perhaps some promotional use might come out of it, or we could release a charity single for Asperger's causes—Jesse Hemmings (Cormack) stepped into the recording studio to record a version of Colin Vearncombe's song "This is Life."

This is what you waited for,
No rehearsals, no more stalling,
This is life.
Have it tattooed on the inside
Of your pink and sleepy eyelids:
This is life.
This is life.

Absence makes the heart grow fonder,
Grow more foolish than we can ever guess.
You feel your nerve ends slowly coiling
And you hope the answer's "no," the answer's "yes."

The words of that song had played in my head throughout the period Colin was in his coma. I couldn't shake the image of him as such from my mind. I had written a film script in the mid-nineties with a final scene in which a father sat in tears in a hospital room as his son lay in a coma. "This is Life" was the song that would accompany the scene. Colin never particularly liked the script.

While I and thousands of his fans around the world waited for news, hoping that the answer would be "no," that it would not be the end of a wonderful life, my nerve ends certainly coiled. We were both looking forward to becoming granddads for the first time, as it happened within a few weeks of one another. I was looking forward to swapping stories with him and maybe one day taking my grandchildren to southwest Ireland to meet his.

This is life.

Jesse has a great voice. He's won many awards for singing. He did a great version of the song, and I hope one day we get to use it somewhere. *The Only Game in Town* seems the logical place, but much would depend on our financial position and the ability to pay publisher fees.

When Telefilm finally decided not to fund completion of the film I was shaken back into the real world. If they weren't going to fund the film's completion, how were we going to do it?

Walking back to happiness

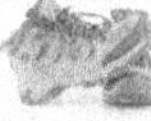

Page 22

Why politicians always tell lies

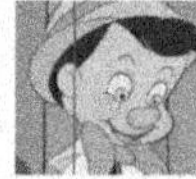

Page 42

$1
Friday 23rd
July 2017

Midlothian Gazelle

The newspaper of choice for those with questionable choice

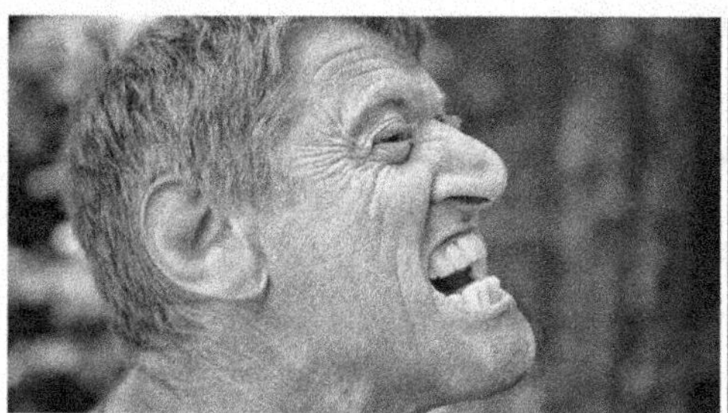

Whole world on brink of collapse due to a global biscuit shortage

Gary Baldi

As if the state of world politics and economics wasn't bleak enough, having to deal with healthcare shortages and benefits cuts, we now have to endure a shortage of biscuits. Poor grain harvests, partly due to global warming, have led to depleted resources available for the manufacture of biscuits.

This setback follows on from the chocolate shortage after cocoa crops failed for several successive years. This led to manufacturers reducing the amount of chocolate on their biscuits initially in order to conserve their reserves until manufacturers were eventually forced to concede defeat and stop producing chocolate biscuits altogether. With this new grain shortage, biscuit manufacturing business empires are crumbling.

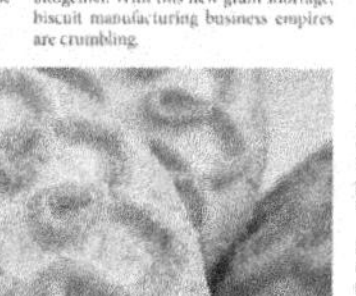

"I don't want to live in a world without gingernuts"

The knock-on effect in world politics has been catastrophic, with diplomats and world leaders turning their noses up at gluten free biscuits and rice cakes. It seems strange that World War III could be caused by a shortage of jammy dodgers. There has been a spate of suicides where people left notes declaring "I don't want to live in a World without gingernuts."

Hopefully the global climate will improve and we will see better harvests in the coming years before a world leader loses his cool and slams his hand down on the nuclear button in frustration at the lack of jaffa cakes.

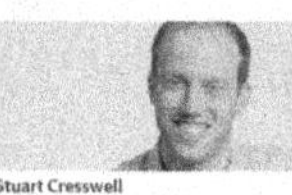

Stuart Cresswell

Solitaire is addictive says a new report released by The World Health Organisation. The rise in teenagers playing with themselves is worrying according to spokesperson Hans Solo. He claims that the trend is unhealthy and can lead to a deterioration in ocular health and even blindness. The question on most people's lips, is why solitaire? With all the advances in computer graphics and next gen consoles, why do teenagers choose to spend their spare time fumbling around with a pack of cards in their bedrooms. Perhaps it could be that computer games have reached saturation point and no longer offer the thrills they once did, where the nature of playing cards offers a tactile experience. Some extreme Christian groups are worried that it is connected to devil worship due to the chequered history of playing cards and their association with tarot cards. Time will tell I suppose, but one thing I know is that we will never stop teenagers playing with themselves in their bedrooms.

Cormack Vertue - The rising star of Solitaire

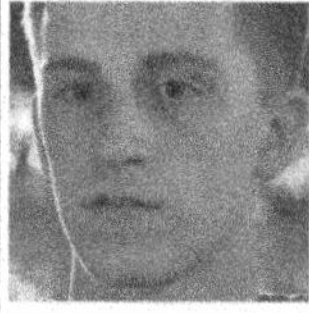

Giordani Bruno

Good players come and go in competitive solitaire. The tension can be too much for many players, and careers are pitifully short. But Midlothian Education Centre's Cormack Vertue could be the first superstar of the sport.

"He needs to keep his focus. Keep putting the hard work in. But he stands on the verge of greatness." High praise indeed from none other than Ashton Pinkerton, who has trained more solitaire champions than anyone else since the great Ellwood Dandersley between 1932 and 1939.

"Vertue plays 'old school' style. And he's a natural. Until now, he's had no professional coaching, but he's learning under Alex Crowley...everything he needs to do be a winner." continued Pinkerton quite slyly.

Towers of London (Ontario) to face Midlothian in a Solitaire Contest

Giordani Bruno

Deaf, Dumb and Blind Tommy is likely to be the major threat to Midlothian in tonight's Solitaire encounter. Tommy is one of the most decorated players - he never leaves a contest without a trophy and his exploits are legendary.

Coach Crowley of Midlothian is both impressed by Tommy's stats and rightly worried about his team's chances. "I've seen him play. He stands like a statue, becomes part of the deck of cards, feeling all the suits, Always playing clean. He plays by intuition, The scoreboard's counters fall. That deaf dumb and blind kid, Sure plays a mean game of solitaire!" "How do you think he does it?" Asked our reporter.

"I don't know what makes him so good." replied Crowley, at which point a lawyer for Roger Daltrey entered the room and ended the interview.

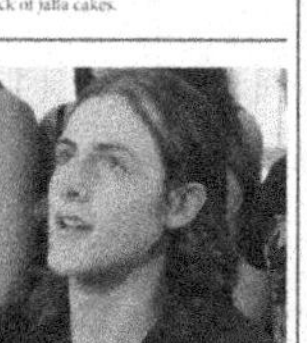

IN OUR WEEKEND SUPPLEMENT ON SUNDAY

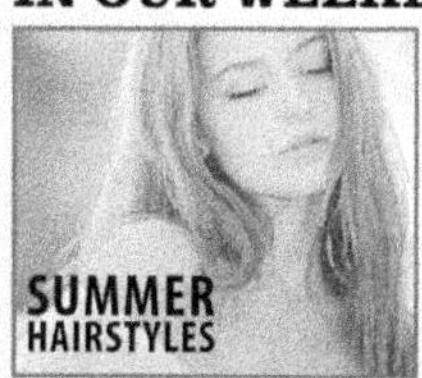

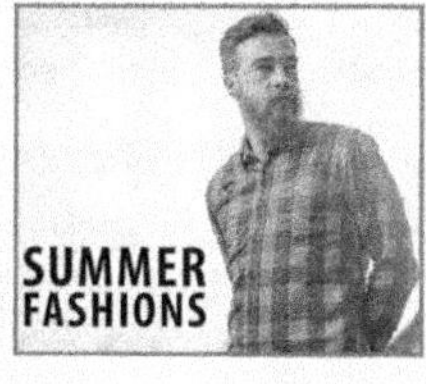

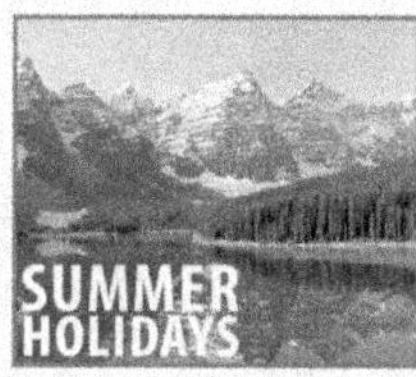

This fake newspaper has two solitaire-related articles. The first is about Cormack and his prowess. The second prepares viewers for the scene involving the tournament with deaf, dumb, and blind "solitaire wizard" Tommy.

Telefilm gave some thin reasons for not supporting it. They didn't like the fact that Cormack was a "passive" hero. I questioned that. There are many great films with a passive hero: *The Man Who Wasn't There* to name but one recent film, and of course *Being There*, both films showing a hero who never sets about his own resolution.

The Only Game in Town, however, had a hero who was far from passive. Cormack's powers of putting cards in order extends, as we find, to putting people in order. He says it in the script, we see it in the film.

Or do we?

I revisited the rough cut I sent to Telefilm all those months earlier. Sure enough, the key scene that makes this clear had been omitted from the rough cut. I was devastated. The rough cut we had used to convince Canada's major funding agency to help us out was bereft of many important scenes and funny moments.

It was nobody's fault but my own. It matters not I was exhausted. As the director and producer I should have been fully on the ball with this. I am not the type of person to rant and rave; I've seen directors who do and it's counterproductive. I do believe that if you are paying someone to do a job, and you hired them because you thought they could do it, you should let them do their job. Clearly there needs to be guidance and suggestions, but we're not doing brain surgery, and no one will die if someone makes a little mistake.

I am happy to be called too soft or a pushover. But that's not true either. If there is something crucial or I must have a particular shot or line delivered in a certain way, then I can dig in my heels. Yet here, as we stumbled through the opening harrowing months of 2016, I had clearly dropped the ball.

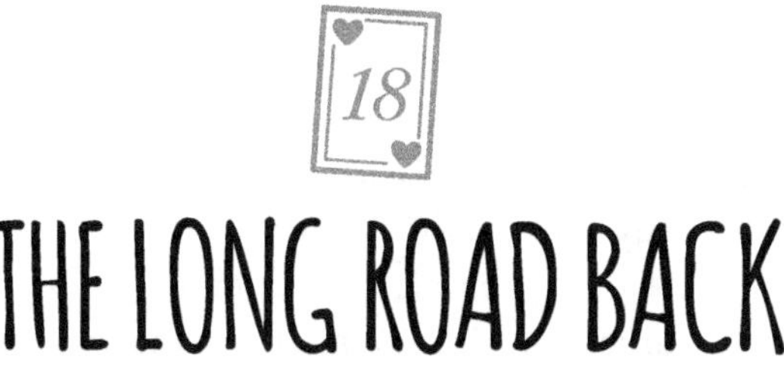

18 THE LONG ROAD BACK

It was Fateh Ahmed who threw me a lifeline. I'm not sure at what point he must have wondered about the film, but he called me late in 2016 and offered to work with me until the film was done.

It seemed like a plan, and I was grateful. My options were limited and it was time to get my head out of the sand.

We both anticipated that the film would be complete early in 2017. That filled me with new hope, and on that basis I threw any money I had into getting the film finished, in the knowledge that I would be selling the film soon enough.

We were over-optimistic.

Throughout 2017, we spent days battling issues caused by different edit systems. This was a real pain. More than that, it came as a surprise. Video editing systems have come a long way, and the workflow now contains a plethora of plug-ins and add-ons for effects and post-production tasks, so the assumption would be that a file generated by one edit system would be accessible to another system running the same software. Our film file had been virtually "locked" into one particularly obscure version of the software, which meant a long period of conversion so that we could make the changes to the film that we needed.

It got worse. We made the decision to use, where possible, the rough cut where it worked, only changing the scenes that were absolutely necessary—in effect, to save time. We thought it made sense. As we moved through spring 2017, we realized we'd made a mistake but pressed on, believing the end to be just around the corner; it was certainly still a quicker option than starting the whole thing from scratch.

Only now we know different. Every change we needed to make caused a huge headache. Imagine needing to trim a few frames off the end of one clip that has edited (spliced) to another clip. Depending on how the transition had been done in the rough cut, we would have to find the clip we wanted to change, trim it to the point we needed, and then find the clip that the editor had used, which wasn't always easy. We struggled to find the three seconds of clip here and there that we needed in the mountain of 4K files of scenes and takes. Another ultra-high-definition (HD) standard for film and TV, 4K is twice the size of standard HD, which uses 1080 lines of vertical resolution; consequently, 4K makes for stunning images. It produces huge amounts of data too, and our entire film needed a 10 TB drive for storage.

I was brought up on photography. Film type, not digital. When I was seven, my uncle Ray gave me a camera. When I was twelve he gave me an 8mm movie camera. I learned very quickly to frame up a shot at speed. More importantly, I learned not to waste my shots. Film is expensive to buy, you can't reuse it. It's expensive to process. It's slow to edit. I still have the film splicing gear I used to use. I loved it. It was all very tactile, all accurate and certain. You didn't make a decision to cut and splice lightly, there was no undo button.

I'm not the only person to say this, but the film industry changed when video first appeared, and now that we're digital it's even worse.

I have just completed a shoot for BBC and CBC amid conversations around the way filmmakers have become lazy or even simply bad as a result of never having to use film in the process. I'll explain.

With film, every roll of the camera uses a physical stock, which has to be paid for. Each reel has to be processed. Even if half of it is trash, you still have to pay the lab. Viewing the processed film ("rushes") and creating an edit list takes time. Colour correction is another laboratory process, and so on.

Filmmakers today, especially those whose experience is that of a self-shooter—a one-man band roaming around making documentaries that they themselves will edit—think nothing of filling up racks of hard drives with footage that they can sort through later.

The much-loved phrase "We can sort it in post!" is by and large a huge myth. Yes, software and plug-ins exist that can do so much, but it still takes time. The minute the self-shooter, the DoP, or the camera person is removed from the edit workflow—as is the case in most productions—the volume of data the editor must wade through creates a mammoth task. Leaving things to be "sorted in post" is an abdication of responsibility.

For *TOGIT*, we were lucky enough to have as our DoP Ashley King, who, despite my anxiety over the extended set-ups, ensured that at least with the lighting of each scene we would be saved the burden of too much time correcting during post-production.

The downfall was that with cameras rolling before we were really ready to go, every take was easily three or four times the length it needed to be. Having shot on 4K, these files were huge and created issues in storage and computer processing speeds and render times. It also meant that as we searched for a particular take to replace the existing one in the original edit, Fateh and I had to troll through vast amounts of footage before finding the one we wanted.

At a time when the Nova Scotia industry in general has taken such a hammering, it's clear to me that we can only truly get things back on track by turning out a new generation of top industry people. I have no doubt that the existing courses are good at turning out those new filmmakers who can grab a camera and, with the luxury of time, craft a story in their own way. My feeling, though, is that we need to make sure students adopt the mindset of *film*makers and strive to waste nothing and leave nothing to be corrected, even by themselves, in later parts of the production.

All I know is that throughout 2017, every spare day Fateh and I had was spent prizing apart the original plodding edit and putting back the comedy timing, the focus on main characters, and the key scenes that had somehow gone missing.

The re-edit was a challenge such as I had never undertaken. We worked slowly, script at our side, painstakingly pulling out clips and frames that added nothing to the story, and locating and inserting key scenes and lines of dialogue that had been cut by the previous editor simply to make the duration of the film work.

It reminds me of an exercise I had to do in physics at school. I wasn't that good at electronics and stuff; I found it too hard to concentrate surrounded by so many things I could include in the sitcom perpetually running in my head. The teacher wanted us to make an electromagnet. We had a board with two V-shaped prongs coming off it, and we had to wrap copper wire around a piece of iron and slot it into the prongs, then run a charge through the wire.

I was elected leader of our group of budding Oppenheimers and entertained everyone by wrapping the wire around the iron. The only problem was that I had wrapped too much wire around it, and it wouldn't fit in the support prongs. I am nothing if not utilitarian, so I borrowed Phil Stothard's six-inch knife. (Yes, he had a knife at school; yes, we all did; yes, we used to play with them in the playground. No one got hurt, murdered, or even stabbed. In fact, one day, a crazed knife-wielding maniac got into the school and could have killed several children and staff, but as we were all armed with our own knives, we took him out and prevented a massacre. Okay, that last bit didn't really happen, but it's been several pages since I wrote something controversial, so I thought I'd throw it in.)

So, using Phil's knife I simply sliced off the excess copper wire on the sides of the electromagnet and hey presto!, the magnet fit snugly into the prongs.

"Sir!" all six of us called out after several attempts at switching on the power had failed to make the electromagnet do whatever it was supposed to do. "Sir! Ours isn't working!"

Bless Mr. Rodgers, a very frail man, totally unsuited to teaching teenagers. He skipped over to our table in his soft, brown shoes. He studied the set up for a moment, then said, "Well, it's not likely to work! Some idiot has shaved the wires off!"

My point is, and the anecdote is relevant, our editor, in an attempt to get the film down to a more realistic duration, had shaved off all the bits that made the film work.

Fateh and I were editing whenever we could, but it was all we could do to find a couple of days a week. When other work commitments dictated, we were forced to leave it for a few weeks and then return to it. Whenever it felt as though we were near the end, a scene gave us a new problem and we lost more time.

I continued to find plenty of other work to occupy my mind, which was great, but there were still too many nights when I would wake in the small hours and remember the precarious position I was in financially. Such things take their toll. My parents taught me one thing: when confronted with an extremely stressful situation, bury your head in the sand and hope it goes away. They looked after Andrew long after they should have, well after the point beyond which the situation became dangerous—two frail, old people manhandling a 260-pound invalid up and down stairs. They taught me well. For the most part, I have ignored the situation the film has been in since the end of 2015. I'm surprised the stress hasn't found me yelling and ranting and raving, but I have lain awake with the cold sweat of fear down my back. And I have stood alone at the bottom of the garden and prayed to the river, or the stars, or the eagle, or my dad's ashes on the riverbank.

I have ceased being angry. It's true to say there is no one to direct my anger at right now, but being passive and resigned to my fate is not a role that sits well with me.

I try to reason it all through, imagine that when the time comes our case will be in the hands of someone with common sense. Why didn't we just wait like everyone else and get some of the new fund later on? It would have made sense. We could have kept Cory Bowles. But we had already been told that we were not eligible for the new fund because we had already started production.

So I toss and turn once more with the thoughts and imagined conversations playing out in my head, which always end in the same way: with the film sapping every last cent out of me and consigning me to a lifetime of debt and drudgery.

The trickle of damp fear runs down my back as I realize that all of this was set in motion in 1996 when I walked away from *In the Air at Whitby*. Every step forward that I have taken since has really been a step deeper into the hole I've been digging for myself.

And then, in the darkest hour just before dawn, when I'm struggling to see a way through the mess, I remember the film. I remember the countless young people who not only shared the journey but made the film part of their own. I am happy that I have been able to give so many an experience of a lifetime and a step on their own paths to a career in film and television. That's why I made the film. And the film will be my salvation.

I have to believe it will all come good. I must have faith in what has been created. It's a great film and people will pay to see it. And I am correct: the film has to be right and perfect, and I cannot again allow it to be seen by anyone else unless it is in the condition I want it to be in. I cannot afford another Telefilm situation.

I just wish I knew with some certainty when it will be finished.

I am indebted to Fateh Ahmed, who somehow has managed to keep plodding away on the project, empathic to my need to get this film right.

FATEH AHMED, ASSOCIATE PRODUCER AND EDITOR

As department head of the film program at daVinci College, I considered *The Only Game in Town* a very good opportunity for my graduating students, a film that would provide them with lots of experience in the real world. My initial role in the film was as associate producer, facilitating the supply of gear and equipment through the college as well as having our students be part of the crew. I also made sure that the students were being dealt with and treated in a decent manner while all their needs were being addressed.

When we arrived for the final two-week shoot in Tatamagouche, I was pleased to find that we each—actors and crew members—had our own room and everything was properly set up for us. The production phase was stressful for the most part and wasn't necessarily fluid due to increased stress over the tight schedule.

Things went quiet for some time, then I interviewed Stuart about his experiences with the film for my own documentary *Without Consultation*, which tells the story of the negative impacts on the industry in Nova Scotia resulting from the tax credit change and how the film environment in Nova Scotia was fairly poor and underperforming; the Liberal government's decision to slash the film tax credit had serious implications for the development of the post-production process for *The Only Game in Town*. In *Without Consultation,* Stuart speaks clearly about the challenges he faced in order to complete the funding process for the film, given that the funding and the even the film office no longer existed! Around the interview we spoke about the music for the film, and I offered my help in any way to get the film completed. About eight months after production ended, Stuart asked if I would be interested in being involved with the post-production and editing.

There were other factors that were involved in the film not being funded for post-production. The main one was that the first cut that was made did not truly address the director's vision and didn't speak well to the story. It took us roughly a year to get the film into shape. We kept a tight schedule throughout that year for post-production. Slowly but surely the story started to make sense, and we could see the film coming to life. At this point, we've reached a picture lock, yet audio post-production, music, and colour correction are all aspects that need to be addressed and completed.

And I need to go see a counsellor.

During 2017, as my workload piled up with new projects for CBC and BBC and a short film about the ship *Hector*, the painstakingly slow process of getting the film to match the script and come back to life began to take its toll on me.

You will know by now that I find it hard to walk away from something, but in my head I was chastising myself for being so stubborn and pushing ahead with the film when all reason argued against it. This was my fault. It's my fault we're here trying to glue together fragments of a Ming vase that we had tipped over and smashed to smithereens on the floor.

In all reality, though, the point of no return had been crossed in December 2014, when the first scenes were put in, or during spring of 2015, as we began to flesh out more of the story. By the time summer 2015 had arrived, we had spent too much money and gone too far to pull it back. Reassurances from the government about the security of part of our financing plan only served to further commit resources to the project. Whether or not those reassurances, like so many others offered by McNeil's Liberal government, turn out to be unfounded, the simple fact remains that the film was produced to be sold and screened around the world and to make money. Regardless of government input, the film still must, and shall, do just that.

I want to get the excitement back with *TOGIT*. I want to see the joy on the faces of those involved, and I want to see the reaction of people who know nothing about the film. I want to see if they get my sense of humour. If they do, then I have three more scripts ready to complete. I've just heard that Phil Nodding, my former mentor at the East Midlands Screen Commission and an award-winning writer in his own right, wants to work on a project with me. *The Only Game in Town* shall be a stepping stone to new ventures for me. Getting it completed and out there in the big wide world is a vital part of that process.

A Great Actor and Friend

It's October 17, 2017, and I have just heard that John Dunsworth, one of the all-time good guys in the industry in Nova Scotia, died yesterday. John loved this project, he wanted to be in it and we wanted him to be in it. Being around John for that short time during 2015 and bouncing ideas off him—and getting some bounced at me too—was a great privilege.

It was an honour to hear him speak so highly to others about our film. As many have said in recent months, he was a generous man, and many of those working in Nova Scotia today have great stories to tell about him. For me, someone who felt like a perpetual outsider, having John in common with the rest of the industry here is a small consolation for never having had the chance to work with him.

Only a few months back, I asked him if he would write a piece for this book; he responded within a few hours.

He was a great actor and a friend to many. He will be sorely missed.

The Completion

The film has trundled along through a painful period of re-editing. There have been countless times that Fateh and I looked at each other and remarked that it would have been easier to start from scratch than to pick apart the film from the state it was in. Still, we make a decision and have to press on as best we can.

We missed a year of approaching festivals and screenings and potential sales, and the patience of investors and financiers has worn precariously thin. I can say now that despite my outward air of casual confidence and my declaration that everything will turn out fine, I have been made aware that the end of the road is approaching fast. The film now has deadlines beyond my control and beyond my power to be certain we can meet them. The film will either be complete, or it will grind unceremoniously to a halt, never to start again and drag me into a place I still can't admit is a real possibility.

Even now, here in spring 2018, if I were to think for a moment about how it could all still go wrong, I'm sure my sweats would begin again. I am not stupid, and I have worried and still do worry that this was too big a risk even for me.

There is room for celebration. The film has finished. We are about to submit our application for the government tax credit. We have a list of festivals around the world we are targeting and will begin submitting soon. We hope to have a screening in Nova Scotia—a press and cast/crew screening probably in Pictou, then maybe one in Halifax. And if we can be part of the Atlantic Film Festival that would be great.

I still hope that I have not taken one chance too many and that my risk-taking and devil-may-care attitude hasn't been the ruin of us. I often stray on the side of "if you build it they will come." That's hardly a business plan in an era where credit is hard to come by. Does it help if I am convinced we're on to a winner with this film?

There is a mantra that Josephine and I live by. It steered us through our journey to Canada. It sits in pride of place on the fridge door as a reminder every time we go for milk.

> *"You cannot live sheltered forever without being exposed and at the same time be a spiritual adventurer. Be audacious. Be crazy in your own way, with that madness in the eyes of man that is wisdom in the eyes of God. Take risks, search and search again, search everywhere, in every way, do not let a single*

opportunity or chance that life offers pass you by, and do not be petty and mean, trying to drive a hard bargain." —Arnaud Desjardins

I'll say it again: I believe in our film. I believe in the young people who will become stars as a result. I believe in the older professionals who brought so much to every aspect of it. I believe in the judgment of others who saw in the pages of the script some pleasant comedy and some kind of quality. Andrew Ellard, Colin Vearncombe, Cory Bowles, John Dunsworth. Better judges than me when it comes to all things creative.

It still makes me laugh, which must be a good sign, as I've spent the last three years listening to the same gags and comic dialogue over and over. And although at some moments, after a long day in the edit suite at the end of tiring week, I have been my own worst critic and despaired at some aspect of the film, I have also found myself laughing out loud because this scene or another really works.

I believe that audiences are ready for a movie that makes them smile, makes them feel good, allows them to remember their own younger years. And I believe that right now the world needs to have a group of characters they can fall in love with.

First love.

So why did I want to make this movie? I'll get all musical again and quote a line from a song by Prefab Sprout, another track that I suggest gets used when someone makes a film of this book: "Nightingales."

What is that we do makes us what we are?
If we sing are we nightingales? Shine, are we stars?

I made this film because that's what I do. I have tried *not* to make films or TV shows or write scripts. I have sometimes been forced not to. But in truth, I have to. I must. It's what I can do, and I'm not the world's best, far from it, but for me this job is The Only Game in Town.

THE CAST AND CREW

The Young Stars

Cormack Vertue	JESSE HEMMINGS
Joe	ALDO ORSI
Rob	JOSH FIFIELD
Chris	AIDEN JAMIESON
Alastair Ramsey	DAVID MORTIMER
Odette	JESSIE CRAIG
Natasha	BREANNA ROY
Donna	VERONICA TRENHOLM

The Adults

Alex Crowley	CRAIG GUNN
Cathy	FIONA KIRKPATRICK PARSONS
Principal Ambrose Joyce	RICK SHAVER
Pinkerton	MICHAEL BARTON
Odette's Mother	COLLEEN MACISAAC
Gran	ELIZABETH SPENCE
Magda Goebbels	JOSEPHINE CRESSWELL
Calgary Coach	JAKE CHISHOLM
Calgary Coach 2	ROB BARRETT
Secretary	APRIL MACDONALD
The Judge	GARY BLACKWOOD
Soccer Coach 1	CHARLEY CRESSWELL
Soccer Coach 2	DREW BOUDREAU
Uncle	STUART CRESSWELL

The Youngsters

MacDonald	ANDREW HALLIDAY
Emma	CARLEIGH HALLIDAY
Slater	ELYSSA ALGUIRE
Sonya	DEANNA MANN
Christine	TASHA WOODS
Steffie	SAFFRON KEEBLE
Hudson	MEAGHAN GORMLEY
Gary	NIK WOODS
Robinson	DAN SMITH
Lizzie	KIONA OSOWSKI
Tammy	KASEY DEVRIES
Tommy	GREG WHITE
Slater's brother	SHAWN KOWALSKI
The Twins	CASSIDY AND MATAYA SANGSTER
Alastair's henchmen	COLLIN HILL, LIAM PETITE, MIKE SMITH
MacDonald's gang	STEVE GREENWOOD, JOHN HOLMES, EAMON MCCARRON
Goebbels children (off-screen)	HENRY CRESSWELL

The Crew

Writer, Producer, Director	STUART CRESSWELL
Executive Producer	CRAIG CAMERON
Associate Producer	FATEH AHMED
Associate Producer	SARAH CRESSWELL
Script Consultant	ANDREW ELLARD
Director of Photography	ASHLEY KING
Sound Recordist	RON MACNUTT
1st Assistant Director	JAKE CHISHOLM
Production Manager	JANELLE WHITE
Producer's Secretary and Production Accountant	JOSEPHINE CRESSWELL
Production Assistant	EAMON MACCARRON
Camera Operator	LIAM PETITE
Camera Assistant	ALEJANDRO QUINTANILLO

2nd Camera Assistant	KIRILL POLSTAINEN
Gaffer	COLLIN HILL
Key Grip	STEVE GREENWOOD
2nd Grip	JOHN HOLMES
3rd Grip	MIKE SMITH
Best Boy	GEORGIE MILBURN
Electrician	EVAN BURGESS
Electrician	DALTON CHASE
Key Makeup	COLLEEN PATTERSON
Casting	KEVIN KINCAID
Casting Director	GARY BLACKWOOD
Fixer	BRIAN HOLMES
Production Trainee	GRACI YOUNG
Art Department	CHRIS DYER, SARAH CRESSWELL
Graphics	CONRAD MCEWAN
Editor	FATEH AHMED
Offline Editor	ASHLEY KING
Craft Services	APRIL MACDONALD
Wardrobe	GINA WHITE
Composer	FATEH AHMED
Music Supervisors	CHARLEY CRESSWELL, STEVE FERN, BONNIE AND SPENCER MORGAN
Legal Services, MacLean & MacDonald	IAN MACLEAN

With thanks to:

Cory Bowles, Phil Marriott, Chris Leach, Chris Dyer, John Dunsworth, Graham Linehan, Carl and Donna Sparkes, Katja Burtis, Shannon Bouchie, NOBL, Lesley Longhorn and Rob Assels, Big Al's, The Train Station Inn, Ann Latimer and Eugenio Orsi, Antigonish Celtics Soccer Club, daVinci College

This film is dedicated to Colin Vearncombe, 1962–2016

ACKNOWLEDGEMENTS

This book would not be here were it not for the great team at Nimbus. Terrilee, Whitney, and Elaine, who felt there was a story here that needed to be told. Especially, Marianne, who skillfully edited and coaxed out of me not just a better telling of the story, but the story that I really wanted to tell.

Which is strange, because I must be the only writer who didn't want to write the book that's about to be published. Having to write it meant that the film itself had a drama of its own. I would have preferred it to be made without the fuss.

I need to thank all the cast and crew for being patient with the film and for writing about their own experiences. Careers and stardom are beckoning for some of my key young cast, and I'm immensely proud that our film found them and gave them a chance to shine and the confidence to pursue their own dreams.

I was reminded recently that I grew tired of giving individual directions to my four main actors—Jesse Hemmings, Aldo Orsi, Josh Fifield, and Aiden Jamieson—who were invariably on set together. In the end I just got their attention by shouting "Four!" "Four! Sit on that log and swat some imaginary bugs!" or "Four! Play solitaire and talk about entropy in a coastal vineyard at sunset." Yes, we made good use of north Nova Scotia's stunning locations.

I'm especially grateful to John Dunsworth, who supported us at the start and was happy to write his thoughts for the film because he knew how much it meant to me. That's caring, that's giving. I can still remember the keen eye and sharp wit when he was "talking up" the film to anyone who would listen.

I need to thank Paul Oliver for being so quick with the facts about my school days when I couldn't remember. I knew he would. And the team from those early days at Ideal World TV: Mark Thatcher, Paul Lavers, Debbie Flint, Gary Ashburn, Shaun Ryan, Ellis Ward, Victoria Showers, Stewart Curtis, Thea Balich, Tijen Omer—such great people from whom I learned so much. The same can be said for Phil Nodding; I hope we get to work together on *The Only Sitc-Com in Town* very soon! A big shout out too to all the people at Raindance and the great work done by Elliot Grove and his team on behalf of all indie film makers.

Like all writers, I have had to take a journey of self-discovery when writing this book. It has been painful at times, to realize that events set in motion two decades ago trapped me and forced me on a path that was more difficult than it should have been. Josephine, my wife, tried to tell me, but I wouldn't listen. And I should have, because she is always right. Thank you, Josephine.

Thank you, Shepshed. Thank you, River John.

Thank you, reader.

For updates on *The Only Game in Town*,
visit www.onlygameintownfilm.com

www.ingramcontent.com/pod-product-compliance
Lightning Source LLC
LaVergne TN
LVHW010614100826
845148LV00014B/2972

* 9 7 8 1 7 7 1 0 8 6 3 7 0 *